Issues Before the 45th General Assembly of the United Nations

The United Nations Association of the United States of America is a national organization dedicated to strengthening the U.N. system and to enhancing U.S. participation in international institutions. UNA-USA carries out its action agenda through a unique combination of public outreach, policy analysis, and international dialogue.

Through a nationwide network of chapters, divisions, and affiliated organizations, UNA-USA reaches a broad cross-section of the American public. The Association provides information and educational services on the work of the U.N. and on other global issues for students, scholars, Congress, and the media; and each year it coordinates the observance of U.N. Day (October 24) in hundreds of communities across the nation.

UNA-USA conducts policy analysis and international dialogue through the Multilateral Project, a grass-roots national study program; the Economic Policy Council, America's premier business and labor forum; and a series of Parallel Studies programs with the Soviet Union, China, and Japan.

Issues Before the 45th General Assembly of the United Nations

An annual publication of the United Nations Association of the United States of America

John Tessitore and Susan Woolfson,
Editors

Lexington Books
D.C. Heath and Company/Lexington, Massachusetts/Toronto

Published simultaneously in Canada
Printed in the United States of America
International Standard Series Number: 0193–8096
International Standard Book Number: 0–669–24813–4
Library of Congress Catalog Card Number: 82–640811

The paper used in this publication meets the minimum requirements of American National Standard for Information Sciences—Permanence of Paper for Printed Library Materials, ANSI Z39.48-1984. ∞™

Year and number of this printing:
91 92 10 9 8 7 6 5 4 3 2 1

Contents

Contributors

José E. Alvarez (Legal Issues chapter), on leave from the George Washington University National Law Center, where he is a Professor of Law, has been examining issues relating to law and U.S. policy toward the United Nations under fellowships provided by the Council on Foreign Relations and the Carnegie Endowment for International Peace.

Libby Bassett (Environment section) is a consultant writer-editor on environment, development, and population for, among others, the United Nations Environment Programme, the Global Forum of Spiritual and Parliamentary Leaders on Human Survival, the Women's Foreign Policy Council, and UNA-USA.

Sylvia Bolivar (Other Social Issues: The Status of Women), a UNA Communications intern, is a recent graduate of Smith College, where she majored in government.

Margaret M. Broderick (Other Social Issues: Youth) has been interning at UNA-USA while pursuing a liberal arts degree at Brooklyn College.

Frederick Z. Brown (Indochina section) is a Senior Associate at the Indochina Institute of George Mason University, Fairfax, Virginia.

Serge J. Bushman (Drug Abuse, Production, and Trafficking section), an intern in UNA's Communications Department, is completing his studies at Columbia College, with a concentration in history.

Robert M. Dickson (Other Social Issues: Crime) served as a UNA Communications intern while completing a master's degree in International Affairs at Columbia University.

Felice Gaer (Human Rights section) has been Executive Director of the International League for Human Rights since 1982.

Lee A. Kimball (Law of the Sea and Antarctica sections) is a Senior Associate with the World Resources Institute in Washington, D.C., and until May 1990 served as Executive Director of the Council on Ocean Law.

Craig Lasher (Population section) is a Legislative Assistant and Policy Analyst at the Population Crisis Committee, a private nonprofit organization that works to expand the availability of voluntary family planning services worldwide.

Frederick K. Lister (Finance and Administration chapter), author of *Decision-Making Strategies for International Organizations,* served the United Nations in a variety of capacities during his 34 years as an international civil servant.

Martin M. McLaughlin (Food and Agriculture section) is a consultant on food and development policy.

W. Ofuatey-Kodjoe (Africa section), Professor of Political Science at Queens College and at the City University of New York (CUNY) Graduate Center, directs the CUNY Seminar on Contemporary Africa and the fellowship program of the university's Ralph Bunche Institute.

Edmund Piasecki (The Information Issue section) is Research Associate for UNA's Policy Studies program.

Sterrett Pope (The Middle East and the Persian Gulf section) writes regularly on the Middle East for *World Press Review* and *The Inter-Dependent*, among other publications.

Benjamin N. Schiff (Arms Control and Disarmament chapter), author of *International Nuclear Technology Transfer: Dilemmas of Dissemination and Control,* is Associate Professor of Government at Oberlin College.

Ethan Schwartz (Making and Keeping the Peace, Central America, Afghanistan, Cyprus, Other Colonial and Sovereignty Issues, and Refugees sections) is U.N. correspondent of *The Washington Post.*

John Tessitore (Coeditor) is Director of Communications of UNA-USA.

Katarzyna Wandycz (Health section; Other Social Issues: Aging, the Disabled, the Homeless), a reporter at *Forbes* magazine, has served as production manager for the BBC office at the United Nations.

Susan Woolfson (Coeditor) is Managing Editor of Communications at UNA-USA.

Preface

Anyone harboring doubts about the old maxim that life begins at forty has only to look at the United Nations to dispel them.

Five years ago, when the United Nations celebrated its fortieth birthday, more than sixty heads of state were among the thousands of diplomats and dignitaries who observed the world body's coming of age—an occasion marked by scores of General Assembly addresses, countless dinners and receptions, and so many motorcades that New York's traffic conditions deteriorated from the normally abysmal to a Dante-esque vision of automotive hell.

It seems fair to say that those who participated in that celebration viewed it principally as one of those milestones that, for political and other reasons, ought to be observed with a degree of ceremony. Probably few, if any, of those men and women from around the world entertained the notion that in just five years the international organization they had come to salute would change in important and dramatic ways. Nor is it likely they imagined that a place of tense and often combative confrontation would become one of almost unprecedented cooperation and achievement.

In 1990, as the world organization marks is forty-fifth year and as the crowd of notables once again descends on Manhattan, there will, no doubt, be a good deal of reflection on the achievements of the last five years—of wars ended (Afghanistan, Persian Gulf, Western Sahara, Southwest Africa), of treaties signed (on the ozone layer, drift-net fishing, children's rights), of peace preserved (in Cyprus, the Golan Heights, Angola), of social and cultural advancement (international year of the homeless, of the child, of literacy), and of recognition won (Nobel Prize for Peace). There will be discussion of important U.N. structural reforms—in personnel, administration, and budget—and of the continuing issue of U.N. financing, with the large Soviet arrearages nearly paid off but the even larger U.S. arrearages continuing to grow, now well past the half-billion dollar mark.

But perhaps most of all, people will speak of the new spirit at the United Nations—a spirit manifested in the dramatic rapprochement of the two superpowers, without whose cooperation so much of the world organization's work would be impossible. In a pas de deux not previously seen at the world body, the United States and Soviet Union have demonstrated a willingness and an ability to make the United Nations work in the very manner its founders had envisioned. It is not altruism or new-found religion that has led them to this point but the recognition that global problems can be addressed best—at times, can be addressed only—in a global way. Here the United Nations has shown itself to be indispensable.

As this book makes clear, the scope of U.N. activities is growing. In 1989–1990, for example, the world body for the first time in its history oversaw an election process in a sovereign nation—Nicaragua. At the same time, it provided the largest transition team ever to oversee the peaceful movement from colony to new state—Namibia. And U.N. involvement is growing in a political dispute of almost unrivaled complexity over the future of a beleaguered Asian country—Cambodia. Concurrently member states are asking the United Nations to assume a leadership role in a myriad of social, economic, and humanitarian issues, from the war on AIDS to the war on drugs—so much so that many U.N. observers fear that the system is threatened by more demands than it can ever hope to meet.

Given the extraordinary changes in geopolitical affairs over the past few years and the concomitant changes that have occurred within the U.N. system, it would be folly to speculate too particularly about what the next five years will bring. But for all the uncertainties, what does seem certain is that as the United Nations approaches its first half-century, it is likely to play an increasing role in the relations among nations.

In preparing *Issues/45* we have, as in the past years, relied on the goodwill of a great many people, and we wish to use this space to acknowledge and thank each of them. First, to the talented contributors listed in the preceding pages, we extend our gratitude and congratulations for a job well done. Our schedule is a grueling one, coinciding with the academic spring semester and other pressing demands on an author's time. Nevertheless, these dedicated people accept the challenge of their assignments and do yeoman work in providing a manuscript at deadline.

Next, our thanks go to the men and women of the United Nations—too many to credit by name—who have given generously of their time and expertise throughout the preparation of this volume. Whether providing documents, advising authors, or reviewing early versions of the manuscript, their work is vital to the accuracy and comprehensiveness for which the *Issues* series is famous.

And finally it gives us great pleasure to acknowledge our cadre of editorial interns, whose volunteer project it has been to assist contributors and editors alike in the gathering of materials—even, in some instances, to work on the composition of certain sections. To this next generation of scholars and diplomats—Sylvia Bolivar, Margaret Broderick, Serge Bushman, EuRim Chun, Robert Dickson, Maureen O'Brien, and Amy Olener—we extend our deep gratitude and warmest wishes for the good years yet to come.

John Tessitore
Susan Woolfson

I
Dispute Settlement and Decolonization

1. Making and Keeping the Peace

The United Nations has had another banner year, and that is getting to be the norm, not the exception. In Central America and Namibia, decades-long efforts to bring peace have finally borne fruit. Nations are falling over one another to praise the world body and its diplomatic efforts. Most important, diplomats are turning to the United Nations with regularity as a candidate for taking on difficult tasks in proposed peacemaking plans.

The United Nations continues to be both the beneficiary and the catalyst for positive changes in the international climate. In many instances, U.N. peacemaking efforts have benefited enormously from the U.S.-Soviet rapprochement; the two superpowers have either directly or indirectly played a major role in guiding to the negotiating table most of those who have chosen to lay down their arms. The United Nations can ease the way, creating a vehicle for peace to be boarded the moment belligerents are ready; but it cannot force nations to choose the olive branch over the sword, and it can do little if the Security Council is divided.

Javier Pérez de Cuéllar has, throughout his nine years as Secretary-General, appeared keenly aware of the United Nations's powers and limitations. He has scrupulously guarded the world body's neutrality, refraining from taking an independent line on many issues. He works closely with the Security Council, as he did when the Namibian cease-fire almost broke down April 1, 1989, avoiding controversial pronouncements and proposals when these lack strong backing from powerful member states. He is the quintessential diplomat, a man who knows how to use his functions as an honest broker to nudge belligerent parties closer together, to find a path of common interest where none appears to lie.

This approach presents both opportunities and pitfalls—opportunities because it preserves the world body's usefulness as a diplomatic tool in a hostile world. It means the United Nations can rapidly step into the breach where the potential for a settlement exists but difficult functions must be carried out by a trustworthy partner. Carefully the Secretary-General can attempt to direct world discourse on a topic, guiding nations toward peace or speaking out on issues such as poverty and the environment.

But they are pitfalls because the world body may never blossom into the major advocate for justice and human rights its founders hoped for. On scores of human rights issues—Tibet, Tiananmen Square, the Baltic republics, oppression in powerful African, Arab, Asian, and industrialized countries—Pérez de Cuéllar has been extremely cautious or altogether silent. He scrupulously avoids comment on controversial topics, such as India's failure to hold elections in Kashmir or various despots' wholesale embezzlement of their nation's resources. Anything can be said in the General Assembly chamber, usually without public comment from U.N. officials. This quietism may be necessary to preserve the United Nations's diplomatic usefulness, but it disappoints those who hope for something more.

One can argue that this state of affairs is not really the United Nations's fault, for the world body can have only as much authority as its wealthy and powerful members accord it. Dag Hammarskjöld learned that lesson when he tried to assert U.N. authority in Africa over Soviet opposition. Now the United Nations has settled into an important role on some select issues but a marginal role in world affairs overall. The changes in Eastern Europe come to mind in that regard. With all the debate about the kind of security regime to create for a new Europe, with all the proposals floated for a strengthening of the North Atlantic Treaty Organization (NATO), the European Community, and the Conference on Security and Cooperation in Europe, there has been scarcely any mention of the world body. Certainly this reflects the decision of most industrialized nations, wise or unwise, not to develop a pancontinental, multilateral approach to global political conflict.

Nevertheless, the United Nations had a remarkable year. Two decades-old efforts to bring peace to troubled regions finally bore fruit. In Central America, 1990 saw the successful U.N. monitoring of a democratic election and turnover of government, a result that would scarcely have been conceivable one year ago. The same occurred in Namibia, where the world body monitored elections successfully in 1989, separated warring factions, oversaw the drafting of Namibia's democratic constitution, and finally brought the last colony in Africa to independence. Notably, these roles are no longer unusual for the world body. Cambodia, where all countries agree the United Nations must play a role similar to the one it played in Namibia, is a case in point. Nations seem increasingly willing to turn to the East River diplomats when a difficult problem needs solving. Yet it remains the case that conflicts can be solved only when all parties—belligerents and sponsors—are willing to negotiate. The Afghan civil war continues to simmer, Iran and Iraq remain at war, an end to Cyprus's division seems nowhere in sight.

In his 1989 speech to the General Assembly, U.S. President George Bush noted, "The war of words that has often echoed in this chamber is giving way to a new mood. We've seen a welcome shift—from polemics to peacekeeping." In 1989 the Soviet Union and the United States sponsored their first joint General Assembly resolution—a draft urging that the United Nations be strengthened. Whether concrete steps are taken remains to be seen.

2. The Middle East and the Persian Gulf

The Iran-Iraq War

After almost eight years of fighting, the Iran-Iraq War finally ground to a halt in August 1988, when Iran accepted the terms of United Nations **Security Council Resolution 598**, which mandated a cease-fire on the front to be followed by the withdrawal of both countries' troops to their borders and their exchange of prisoners of war. Four weeks later, in August 1988, the United Nations dispatched a 350-person peacekeeping force to the Persian Gulf to supervise the cease-fire, while the Secretary-General began negotiations with envoys from Iran and Iraq for the full implementation of Resolution 598 and a comprehensive solution to the conflict. Since September 1988, however, numerous rounds of face-to-face negotiations in New York and Geneva have made little further progress toward a comprehensive settlement. Both parties stubbornly pursue at the negotiating table political goals that have eluded them on the battlefield.

The war began in September 1980 when Iraq invaded Iran and asserted its determination to achieve full control over the Shatt-al-Arab and reverse the Algiers Accord of 1975, in which Iran and Iraq had agreed to joint sovereignty over the Shatt, a 120-mile waterway that joins the confluence of the Tigris and Euphrates rivers in Iraq to the Persian Gulf. The Shatt forms the border between Iran and Iraq for 60 miles at the head of the Gulf and is Iraq's only outlet to the sea. In late 1982, Iran drove Iraqi armies back to the border and began to press attacks into Iraq. Iraq sued for peace, repeatedly appealing to the Security Council and promising to abide by its several cease-fire resolutions, including Resolution 598, which the Council passed in August 1987.

Hoping to prevail on the front, Tehran refused to negotiate until the Iraqi government was overthrown and a successor regime agreed to pay massive war reparations. When at last Iran decided to accept 598 in July 1988, Baghdad responded by setting stiff negotiating conditions of its own. Although 598 made no mention of the Shatt-al-Arab, Baghdad now demanded Iran reopen the Shatt before negotiations could proceed. Iran has since refused to discuss the Shatt until Iraq reaffirms its support of the Algiers Accord. Although Secretary-General Pérez de Cuéllar successfully negotiated the cease-fire in August 1988 and has since kept the two parties talking, little progress has been achieved beyond supervising the cease-fire and bolstering it with modest confidence-building measures on the front. The difficulty of the negotiations reflects the deep hatred engendered by eight years of devastating warfare, which has inflicted massive casualties on both sides, accounting for up to a million deaths and the injury and dislocation of many millions more, as well as economic losses estimated in excess of $100 billion.

Iran's decision to negotiate was the result of many factors: military, economic, and diplomatic. Tehran's most compelling motive was the sheer weight of attrition. Since 1982, Iran had launched five punishing winter offensives across the Iraqi border while directing intermittent probes and feints throughout the year. These campaigns produced only small territorial gains at the cost of hundreds of thousands of lives. In the course of the conflict, both sides raised massive armies. Iran at times claimed as many as 1.2 million men under arms, including Revolutionary Guards and other irregular forces, and Iraq may have put over a half-million men into the field. To meet Tehran's crushing advantage in manpower, Baghdad acquired a formidable arsenal of state-of-the-art Soviet and French weaponry, purchased in large part with $50 million to $90 million of renounceable loans from other Arab states in the Gulf. By contrast, Iran's armies remained ragged and underequipped; its high-tech U.S. weapons systems suffered from shoddy maintenance and chronic shortage of spare parts.

Lacking the military and logistic resources to break through on the battlefield, Iran pursued a strategy of attrition designed to exhaust Iraq's smaller economy and erode its weaker morale. But as the war dragged on year after year, Iran's economy proved the more vulnerable. Relying almost exclusively on oil exports for government revenues, Iran's war effort was severely taxed by the fall of oil prices in 1985 and Iraq's increasingly effective interdiction of Iranian tanker traffic in the Gulf.

At the start of the conflict, Iran was able to cut 80 percent of Iraq's oil exports by destroying Iraqi oil facilities on the Gulf and persuading its ally Syria to cut Iraq's principal pipeline to the Mediterranean. But between 1984 and 1988, Iraq gradually gained the upper hand in the oil war. Baghdad expanded oil exports by widening its shipments through Turkey, Saudi Arabia, and Jordan. At the same time, Iraq reduced Iran's exports by attacking Iran's oil terminals and shipping lanes.

Undeterred by a June 1984 Security Council resolution condemning attacks on commercial shipping in international waters, Iraq systematically began to interdict Iranian shipping in 1984 and successfully attacked Iran's principal Gulf oil terminal at Kharg Island in 1985. Iran retaliated against ships calling at Kuwait and Saudi Arabia, leading to the downing of an Iranian fighter by Saudi warplanes in June 1984. By late 1986 sustained Iraqi air strikes on Iranian tankers and oil facilities reduced Iranian oil exports at times to 700,000 barrels a day, against a 1985 average of 1.4 million barrels per day (mbd) [*The Economist*, 10/18/86].

Declining oil prices and exports cut Iran's oil revenues from $23 billion in 1983 to $6 billion in 1986, but the war alone cost Tehran at least $7 billion for the year [*South Syndication Service*, 11/28/86]. Iraq, on the other hand, continued to expand its oil exports, from a wartime low of 0.7 mbd in 1981 to over 2 mbd in early 1988 [*The Economist*, 1/30/88]. Falling prices cut Iraq's oil revenues in 1986 by half to $7 billion, but the completion of a new pipeline through Turkey the following year boosted oil exports to $12 million. By the end of 1987, Iraqi officials were boasting that nonoil revenues were paying for their country's war effort, thought to cost at least $5 billion to $6 billion annually [*Le Monde*, 12/16/87].

Throughout the eight-year war, the United Nations attempted to mediate through several channels. Between 1982 and 1988, Iraq repeatedly appealed to the Security Council to negotiate a cease-fire and agreed to abide by its resolutions. But until July 1988, Iran refused to cooperate with the Council, which it claimed brazenly favored Iraq. Iranian officials were especially bitter about the resolution the Council passed soon after Iraq's invasion in 1980, in which it called for a cease-fire in place while Iraqi troops were still on Iranian soil [S/17084]. Instead the Iranians tried to work through the office of the Secretary-General, whom they trusted as an impartial mediator, and it was to him that Iran turned when they chose to sue for peace.

Recurrent charges by both sides of chemical warfare, bombardment of civilian populations, and mistreatment of prisoners of war prompted visits to the front by various U.N. commissions and a tour of the Gulf by the Secretary-General in the spring of 1985. In June 1984 the United Nations placed military observers in Baghdad and Tehran to monitor civilian casualties in both countries. Between 1980 and 1988, U.N. mediation of the conflict produced short cease-fires and brief respites on some fronts but yielded no framework for peace negotiations.

In the summer of 1987, two new developments brought further pressure on Iran's revolutionary leadership to negotiate. In July 1987 the Security Council unanimously passed a new cease-fire resolution, which offered new concessions to the Iranians and implicitly threatened them with a Council-sanctioned arms boycott should they refuse to comply. Also in

July, the U.S. Navy began escorting through Gulf waters Kuwaiti-owned oil tankers that had been reregistered, or reflagged, as U.S. commercial vessels. This new policy increased U.S. military presence in the Gulf and marked a further U.S. tilt against Iran. Ostensibly intended to promote freedom of navigation in international waters, the reflagging effectively threw U.S. military support behind Iraq's interdiction of Iranian oil shipments, putting Iran's oil exports under further strain.

These new pressures, together with growing economic hardship and battle fatigue, apparently prompted Iran to forgo its sixth "final" winter offensive in early 1988. In April 1988, Iraq's recapture of the Fao peninsula at the head of the Gulf, as well as strategic marshlands on the marches of Basra—Iraq's first successful large-scale counteroffensives since 1981—indicated further erosion in Iranian morale, for years the key to its battle strength and strategy.

The genesis of Resolution 598 can be traced to mid-January 1987, when the Secretary-General publicly suggested that the Security Council undertake a new Gulf initiative and called a private meeting of its five permanent members for this purpose. This prompted an Anglo-American proposal for a new Security Council resolution that would threaten to embargo all arms shipments to any belligerent refusing to comply. In late July, after months of debate and negotiation, particularly among the Council's five permanent members, the Security Council voted unanimously for Resolution 598, which called for an immediate cease-fire in the Gulf "on land, at sea and in the air," deplored "the initiation" of the war, and advocated an inquiry into "responsibility for the conflict." The language condemning the war's "initiation" was a concession to Iran, first made in the Council's previous **cease-fire Resolution 582** of February 1986. The projected inquiry represented a new concession to Iran, although Resolution 598 made no mention of war reparations, alluding only to the need for international postwar reconstruction aid [S/Res/598].

As for the sanctions initially proposed by the United States and Britain, the Council committed itself only to "consider further steps to ensure compliance" of the mandatory cease-fire [ibid.]. France and China, both big vendors of weaponry to the belligerents, reportedly remained resistant to the idea of an arms embargo, and the Soviet Union would go along only if a U.N. joint naval force replaced the growing Western military flotilla in the Gulf.

Iraq accepted Resolution 598 within days and suspended its air attacks on Iranian shipping in the Gulf, allowing Iran to expand its oil exports during August, but Iran refused to accept or reject the resolution, offering vague and confused signals of conciliation instead. The Gulf remained calm for six weeks before Iraq resumed its attacks on Iranian tanker traffic at the end of August, reducing Iranian oil exports from 2.2 mbd in August to 1.3 mbd by early October [*The Economist*, 10/10/87].

When Secretary-General Pérez de Cuéllar visited Tehran and Baghdad in early September 1987, he learned that the Islamic republic could accept only an "undeclared cease-fire" until an international board of inquiry found Iraq responsible for starting the war [ibid., 9/26/87]. Weeks later, the Soviet Union blocked an Anglo-American proposal at the Security Council to impose an arms boycott on Iran. In October the Security Council drafted new negotiation guidelines for 598, allowing a cease-fire and an impartial inquiry into the war to begin simultaneously. But the Secretary-General could not bridge the bargaining positions of the two belligerents, who insisted on differently sequenced interpretations of 598.

The Secretary-General continued to monitor the war closely in the opening months of 1988, successfully bringing an end to the devastating "war of the cities" in March and twice inviting envoys from Iran and Iraq to New York for consultations [*The New York Times*, 5/25/88]. In early March, Iran reportedly told Pérez de Cuéllar that it was now prepared to accept Resolution 598 but not while the Security Council debated an arms boycott of Iran. The debate ended when the Soviet Union and China refused to support an Anglo-American draft resolution, but Iran delayed its official acceptance for another four months, distracted by Iranian parliamentary elections in April and May, as well as developments at the front [*The Middle East*, 12/88].

Responding to Iranian charges that Iraq had again used **chemical weapons**, this time against rebel Iraqi Kurds who had assisted the Iranian capture of Halabja, the Secretary-General sent an **investigative team** to the Gulf in April. A U.N. team had last visited Iran in April 1987. The 1988 team found that Iraq had again used mustard gas against Iranian troops. The U.N. Security Council took the occasion to reprise its past censures of Iraq's use of chemical weapons "in clear violation of the Geneva Protocol of 1925" [S/17191].

By the end of April, Iranian troops had captured Mehran and Halabja, two northern Iraqi border towns, but had lost Fao, Iraq's Gulf port, which Iran had taken in February 1986 at tremendous cost [*The Economist*, 4/26/88]. The debacle at Fao, followed by further Iraqi victories east of Basra, sparked a row between the leaders of Iran's regular army and the Revolutionary Guard, culminating in a televised confession of error by the Guard's commander in chief in June. In July, a full-scale Iraqi counterattack recaptured Mehran and Halabja and advanced to Dehloran, 30 miles inside Iran, which the Iraqis held for three days before pulling back to the border [*Middle East International*, 6/24/88, 7/22/88].

In late July, in a letter to Pérez de Cuéllar, Iran declared its desire to negotiate an immediate cease-fire on the basis of Resolution 598. Two days later, Ayatollah Khomeini took public responsibility for the historic reversal: "Taking this decision was more deadly than taking poison," he confessed with acid candor. "I submitted myself to God's will and drank this drink for His satisfaction." The same day Iraq announced that it would not accept a truce until after the start of face-to-face negotiations to discuss the timetable for the implementation of 598. "A cease-fire cannot stop the war," Iraqi President Saddam Hussein said, "but it can suspend it temporarily, to allow [it to be resumed] worse than before." The Iraqis also demanded that Iran permit freedom of navigation in the Gulf and the Shatt-al-Arab [*The New York Times*, 7/21/88, 22/88].

While stiffening its bargaining position, Iraq pressed its military advantage, recapturing territory on the southern and central sectors and supporting a drive into Iran by the Mojahedin-e Khalq, an insurgent Iranian group based in Iraq. They captured and held for three days the town of Eslamabad, 60 miles inside Iran, before withdrawing to the border. At the same time, the Iraqi air force sent out scores of bombing raids on Iranian economic targets [*Middle East International*, 8/5/88].

In early August, Iran again accused Iraq of using chemical weapons, this time in chemical bombardments that disabled a thousand people in northwestern Iran. One day earlier, a U.N. investigative team had reported Iraq's "repeated utilization" of chemical weapons. After examining Iranian victims, soil samples, and weapons fragments and reviewing seven previous U.N. reports, the investigators concluded that Iraq had been using chemical weapons with increasing frequency since 1984, employing mustard gas, two types of nerve gas, and cyanide gas against Iranian troops and civilians, including a hospital. The report cited the wounding of nine Iraqi soldiers by chemical grenades, leaving open the possibility that the wounds resulted from an accident rather than battle [*The Economist*, 8/6/88]. At the end of the month, the Security Council again condemned the use of chemical weaponry by both parties [SC/5036].

Starting in late July 1988, the Iraqi army reportedly employed chemical weapons as part of a massive campaign by some 30,000 Iraqi troops against **Kurdish rebels** who had assisted Iranian attacks on Halabja in the spring of 1988. The campaign reportedly resulted in the flight of 100,000 Kurds into Turkey. In September the U.S. State Department corroborated these reports, declaring it had proof of "abhorrent and unjustifiable" chemical attacks by Iraq against its own Kurdish population [*The Economist*, 9/3/88, 9/10/88].

In early August, after two weeks of negotiations between envoys of Iran and Iraq and the Secretary-General in New York, Iraq agreed to the cease-fire, to be followed immediately by comprehensive face-to-face negotiations [*The New York Times*, 8/7/88]. After the Security Council dispatched to the Gulf a 350-person, 24-country peacekeeping force to monitor the 740-mile front, the cease-fire went into effect on August 20. Five days later, comprehensive peace negotiations began in Geneva, but talks quickly stalled when Iraq insisted on making the Shatt-al-Arab, unmentioned in Resolution 598, the first order of business. Iraq demanded that Iran guarantee freedom of navigation in the Shatt and reopen the waterway, which was badly clogged with silt and the wreckage of war. Talks broke down in Geneva when Iraq refused to accept a compromise formula presented by the Secretary-General by which Iran would agree to suspend the search and seizure of Iraqi ships in the Shatt, after which both parties would withdraw from enemy territory, exchange prisoners of war, and jointly study the feasibility of reopening the Shatt [ibid., 9/31/88]. Iraq also asserted its right of full sovereignty over the Shatt-al-Arab, while Iran refused to discuss the status of the waterway until Iraq reaffirmed its commitment to the Algiers Accord, which it had abrogated at the start of the war.

Negotiations resumed in late September in New York and again in late October in Geneva, but in both cases sustained mediation by the Secretary-General failed to produce a breakthrough. The parties did agree in early November to exchange 1,500 sick and wounded prisoners of war under the aegis of the International Committee of the Red Cross, but fewer than 100 prisoners were repatriated before each party accused the other of reneging on the agreement [ibid., 11/24/88]. In January 1989, Ambassador Jan Eliasson, the Secretary-General's Personal Representative for the Gulf negotiations, traveled to Baghdad and Tehran, where he secured the agreement of the two parties to a series of **confidence-building measures** on the front. Iraq lifted a ban on civilian flights over its war zone. Iran agreed to cooperate with a U.N. military working group to resolve cease-fire disputes and also to refrain from flooding border areas, which the United Nations considers a cease-fire violation [ibid., 2/4/89].

Negotiations between Iran and Iraq made no headway during the rest of 1989. In November the U.N. Special Envoy spent sixteen days shuttling between Baghdad and Tehran, and Pérez de Cuéllar met separately with the Iraqi and Iranian foreign ministers in New York in December. Iraq proposed in November 1989 that the two foreign ministers hold face-to-face talks in Baghdad and Tehran under the auspices of the United Nations. In January 1990, President Saddam Hussein repeated this offer and further proposed that airlinks between the two countries be restored. Saddam remained committed to the reversal of the Algiers Accord of 1975 and the renegotiation of the Iran-Iraq border in the context of a comprehensive settlement. Iran rejected all these offers as outside the framework of Resolution 598. Iran was willing to engage in an immediate exchange of prisoners if Iraq withdrew from Iranian territory [ibid., 11/19/89, 12/14/89, 1/7/90].

The implementation of the cease-fire in August 1988, supervised by a U.N. peacekeeping force, is a promising development, although given the negligible progress of negotiations since the fall of 1988, the danger remains that Iraq and Iran may become locked into an extended period of "no peace, no war" that could set back a comprehensive settlement and reconstruction effort for years. The resumption of hostilities is highly unlikely but by no means impossible. Iraq is in a much stronger military position but is not likely to risk renewing the war at the cost of alienating its chief creditors and weapons suppliers, especially the Arab countries of the Gulf, France, and the Soviet Union. Under the more prudent leadership of President Hasemi Rafsanjani, elected in July 1989 after the death of Ayatollah Khomeini, Iran is likely to view the exhaustion of its economy and its poor military position as powerful incentives for seriously pursuing peace negotiations.

In pressing its claims to the Shatt-al-Arab before an exchange of prisoners of war and a full retreat to international borders, Iraq seems determined to use its military advantage to win a moral and territorial victory that might justify to its own population the tremendous costs of the war. Article 6 of Resolution 598 requests the Secretary-General "to explore, in consultation with Iran and Iraq, the question of entrusting an impartial body with inquiring into responsibility into the conflict" [S/Res/598]. Iran may hope to use such an impartial war tribunal to condemn Iraq and secure war reparations or at least advantageous terms of international assistance, a process Iraq is certain to oppose. A possible solution may lie in Iraq's forgoing its claims to full sovereignty over the Shatt in return for Iran's dropping the question of a war tribunal. But given the hatred that separates both parties, this kind of solution may be a long way off. With his record of long involvement in the conflict and the respect he still enjoys from both parties, Pérez de Cuéllar is well placed to mediate an eventual settlement.

The Arab-Israeli Conflict and the Occupied Territories

Forty years after the establishment of the state of Israel, the Arab-Israeli conflict persists. During most of the 1980s various U.S. peace plans and inter-Arab initiatives failed to bridge the enormous differences separating Israel and the **Palestine Liberation Organization** (PLO), two parties that had long refused to recognize or even address each other. In December 1987 this diplomatic stalemate was shaken by a massive and sustained **Palestinian uprising**, or *intifadah*, in the **Occupied Territories**, forcing Israelis to confront Palestinian demands for self-determination and pushing the **Palestine National Council (PNC)**—the PLO's parliament in exile—to recognize Israel formally in Algiers in November 1988. But since then Israel's government has declined to reciprocate or even devise a unified negotiating posture capable of advancing the peace process.

Starting spontaneously in early December 1987 in the Gaza Strip and quickly spreading to the West Bank and East Jerusalem, the **intifadah** soon displayed signs of careful organization, combining daily riots by rock-throwing protesters with strikes, boycotts, and piecemeal measures of civil disobedience. Israel reacted by doubling its occupation forces and dispersing the riots with tear gas and bullets. By December 1989, after nearly two years of **intifadah**, Israeli troops had killed 682 Palestinians in the Territories, and some 40,000 Palestinians had been detained without trial, 10,000 of whom remained in detention. During the same period, Palestinians had killed 42 Israelis and some 140 fellow Arabs, most of the latter executed as "collaborators" [*The Economist*, 12/2/89].

The uprising has altered relations between Israelis and Palestinians more profoundly than any other event since the Six-Day War of 1967, when Israel first occupied the Territories. It has demonstrated the fierce and unremitting determination of Palestinians in Gaza, East Jerusalem, and the West Bank to expel Israelis from the Territories and establish a state of their own. It also has pushed the PLO to pursue more realistic policies. In November 1988 the Palestine National Council met in Algiers, implicitly recognized Israel, and endorsed a "two-state solution" to the Palestine Question. The **Algiers declarations**, together with subsequent statements by PLO Chairman Yasser Arafat in December 1988, prompted the United States to open a dialogue with the PLO for the first time in 13 years. But the Israeli government, as well as both the mainstream Labour and Likud parties, have refused to recognize the PLO or the legitimacy of Palestinian aspirations for self-determination.

The United Nations remains at the margins of the peace process in the Middle East. Over the past fifteen years, the General Assembly has relentlessly reviled Israel for its occupation of the West Bank and the Gaza Strip, but Israel has ignored the actions of the General Assembly, protesting the body's strong pro-Arab bias. In the **Security Council**, the United States has continued to veto almost all resolutions critical of Israel, urging its colleagues on the Council to adopt a more "balanced" approach to Middle East issues.

Israel's response to the Palestinian rebellion has spurred a spate of U.N. Security Council resolutions censuring the Jewish state. In January 1988 the Security Council unanimously passed a resolution reaffirming that "the Geneva Convention relative to the protection of civilian persons in a time of war . . . is applicable to Palestinian . . . territories occupied by Israel since 1967, including Jerusalem," and calling upon Israel to refrain from deporting Palestinian civilians from the Occupied Territories [S/Res/607]. The United States had last supported a resolution critical of Israel in 1981, when Israel annexed the Golan Heights [*The New York Times*, 1/6/88]. The United

States abstained on a similar resolution a week later and vetoed a third resolution calling upon Israel "to desist forthwith from its policies which violate the rights of the Palestinian people" [S/19466]. In February 1989, the United States vetoed a further draft Security Council resolution strongly deploring "Israel's persistent policies and practices against the Palestinian people," in particular "the opening of fire that has resulted in injuries and deaths of Palestinian civilians" [S/20463]. The U.S. viewed the efforts of the Council as distinctly anti-Israel, and noted that there had been almost no mention of Palestinian excesses, such as the killing of suspected Arab collaborators.

In July and August 1989, the Security Council passed two further resolutions deploring Israel's deportation of Palestinian Arabs and calling upon Israel to "ensure the safe and immediate return to the occupied Palestinian territories of those deported and to desist forthwith from deporting any other Palestinian civilians" [S/Res/636, 641]. The United States abstained on both resolutions and continued to veto all others critical of Israel's occupation of Arab lands and its policies toward the *intifadah*.

The Palestinian rebellion did, however, inspire U.S. Secretary of State George Shultz to sponsor **a new U.S. peace initiative** in January 1988. Necessarily vague and open ended, the Shultz plan was in essence an update of the defunct autonomy formula of the Camp David Accords signed by Israel, Egypt, and the United States in 1978. Secretary Shultz proposed an international peace conference that would provide a forum for negotiations between Israel and Arab parties on the basis of "land for peace." The international conference he had in mind was to be a cover for bilateral negotiations between Israel and a Jordanian-Palestinian joint delegation acceptable to Israel. In addition, municipal elections would be held on the West Bank and Gaza together with Israel's parliamentary elections scheduled for November 1988. Representatives elected in the Occupied Territories could constitute embryonic institutions of local self-government and civil administration, which would achieve their full form after an interim period of three years rather than the five years originally proposed at Camp David [*The Middle East*, 3/88]. Like previous U.S. formulas, the Shultz plan made no provision for a separate PLO representation in the peace process, nor did it recognize the principle of Palestinian self-determination and the possibility of an independent Palestinian state.

Arab leaders greeted the Shultz plan with skepticism, and only Egyptian President Husni Mubarak endorsed it. On the Israeli side, Prime Minister Yitzhak Shamir rejected it out of hand, insisting that an international peace conference of any kind was out of the question and that negotiations on the basis of land for peace were equally unacceptable. Between February and June 1988, Secretary Shultz made four trips to the Middle East to canvass support for his plan, but Prime Minister Shamir's implacable opposition precluded further refinement of Shultz's ideas. Israeli Foreign Minister and Labour party chief Shimon Peres welcomed the Shultz initiative, which was designed to produce a settlement through talks with a Jordanian-Palestinian joint delegation, a formula Peres had been promoting for some time. Peres's Jordanian option, however, was effectively foreclosed in July, when Jordan's King Hussein severed all formal links with the West Bank, leaving Arab administration of the Occupied Territories as well as negotiation on their behalf to the PLO.

The core of the Arab-Israeli conflict remains the Palestine Question. Israel has never conceded Palestinian rights to self-determination and continues to treat the PLO as a fundamentally illegitimate terrorist organization that operates beyond the bounds of international law and world civilization. Israel is willing to negotiate on the basis of **U.N. Security Council Resolutions 242 and 338**, the former conferring legitimacy and "the right to live within secure borders" on "every state in the area." The Palestinians, for their part, had long refused to recognize the state of Israel without a reciprocal concession from the Israelis. Nor would the PLO accept Resolution 242 as the sole basis for a settlement, since the resolution makes no mention of Palestinian rights and addresses the Palestinians only as a refugee problem.

But this equation of mutual intransigence was radically recast in November 1988 when the Palestine National Council met in Algiers and revised its approach to negotiations with Israel. By a vote of 253 to 36, the PNC approved a document declaring the independence of the Arab Republic of Palestine based on the U.N. partition plan for Palestine in 1947 and also recognized Security Council Resolutions 242 and 338. Taken together these declarations amounted to a PNC-endorsed "two-state solution"—an implicit but clear recognition of Israel's right to exist in conjunction with an assertion of the Palestinians' right to self-determination. The PNC declaration also condemned terrorism (with the implied proviso that resistance in the Occupied Territories and PLO attacks on military targets in Israel proper represented legitimate acts of armed resistance) and called for the withdrawal of Israeli forces from the territories occupied by Israel in 1967, whose security would be guaranteed by the U.N. Security Council pending an international conference to negotiate a comprehensive solution to the Arab-Israeli conflict [*The New York Times*, 11/16/88].

The complex issues surrounding the question of an international peace conference have divided Arabs and Israelis since the Six-Day War. Arabs have long favored a multilateral "comprehensive solution" to the conflict in the Middle East, to be mandated by an international conference that would seat the five permanent members of the Security Council together with all the front-line Arab states (Egypt, Jordan, Syria, and Lebanon), Israel, and the PLO. Israel, unwilling to submit to the collective pressure of the Arabs and the Soviet Union, has preferred to pursue bilateral negotiations with its Arab neighbors in order to exert maximum bargaining leverage on each and avoid the Palestine Question entirely.

The PNC declaration of November 1988 was first and foremost a direct consequence of the *intifadah*. On the one hand, the PNC wished to recognize the uprising and celebrate its achievements with a declaration of independence—a strictly rhetorical gesture. On the other hand, it moved to assert diplomatic leadership of the *intifadah* by offering a dynamic and credible new negotiating stance that made important concessions to Israel while reaffirming Palestinian desires for self-determination. In particular, the PLO hoped that its acceptance of Security Council Resolution 242, with its implicit recognition of Israel, would allow the organization to open a dialogue with the United States, exerting pressure on Israel to come to terms. Salah Khalaf, the second-ranking official in Yasser Arafat's Fatah faction of the PLO, gave further reasons for the timing of the resolution: The PNC was anxious to take advantage of warmer relations between the United States and the Soviet Union and their new-found desire to cooperate on solutions to regional conflicts. Also, Israel's elections in early November, which had strengthened the hand of the rejectionist elements in the Israeli government and the growth of radical Islamic fundamentalism in the Occupied Territories, made a credible PLO diplomatic initiative all the more urgent [ibid., 11/15/88].

Inasmuch as the declaration renewed Palestinian demands for self-determination, it was rejected out of hand by mainstream Israeli politicians. Prime Minister Shamir dismissed the declaration as "ambiguity and double-talk." The United States reacted more favorably but regretted that the declaration, with its "possible or implied recognition of Israel," fell short of satisfying three conditions for a U.S.-PLO dialogue. In 1975 the United States had signed a memorandum of agreement with Israel that the United States would not negotiate or recognize the PLO until the organization recognized Israel's right to exist without reservation and also accepted Resolutions 242 and 338. The Reagan administration imposed a third condition for dialogue: the PLO's renunciation of terrorism. The U.S. Congress has passed all three conditions into law [ibid., 11/16/88, 11/19/88].

During the next month intensive indirect negotiation between the PLO and the U.S. government closed the gap separating PLO statements and U.S. conditions for dialogue. This process was stalled in late November when Secretary of State Shultz denied a visa to Chairman Arafat, who was planning to address the U.N. General Assembly in New York in December. U.N.

Secretary-General Javier Pérez de Cuéllar called the decision "a breach of obligations," specifically the 1947 U.S.-U.N. Headquarters Agreement [ibid., 11/28/88]. Arab delegates quickly marshaled support to move the U.N. General Assembly debate to Geneva for a special three-day session, where Arafat offered Israel a three-part Palestinian peace initiative, which essentially reprised the two-state settlement envisioned by the Algiers declarations. Several days after Arafat's U.N. address, the United States officially opened a **"substantive dialogue" with the PLO.** This dialogue in no way amounted to U.S. recognition of the PLO or of Palestinian rights of self-determination, but it did mean the United States could now mediate between Israel and the PLO.

Shortly after Arafat's speech at Geneva, Israel formed a new coalition government after six weeks of talks following the Israeli elections in early November. The new government marked a shift to the right in Israel's foreign policy. Once again Likud and Labour formed a national unity government, but this time Likud's Shamir no longer shared the prime ministership with the more moderate Labour chief Shimon Peres, who forfeited the foreign affairs portfolio to become Minister of Finance.

Both Labour and Likud gave Arafat's peace initiative short shrift. Both adamantly opposed a Palestinian state, and both refused to recognize the "terrorist" PLO. Nevertheless, in early 1989, growing pressures at home, in the Territories, and abroad prodded Prime Minister Shamir to produce a peace plan of his own. An Israeli newspaper poll in February 1989 revealed that a majority of Israelis favored talks with the PLO; and in March, Israeli military intelligence told the government that negotiations with the PLO could no longer be avoided. At the same time, contacts between Israeli and Palestinian activists grew, several prominent Labour politicians met with West Bank dignitaries in East Jerusalem, and two cabinet ministers publicly endorsed talks with the PLO [*The Christian Science Monitor*, 3/15/88].

In April, Shamir unveiled his new peace plan on a trip to Washington, where he met President Bush for the first time. His plan, which was ratified by Israel's cabinet in May, called for free elections in the Occupied Territories, which would produce a delegation that would negotiate an interim period of self-rule lasting up to five years. Three years into this period, delegates elected from the Territories would form "the central Palestinian component" in talks with Israel, Jordan, and Egypt to decide a final Middle East settlement [*The Economist*, 5/20/89].

Noting that Israel's new peace plan excluded the PLO as well as an independent Palestinian state, the PLO's Executive Committee denounced it as "a farce" in May [ibid., 5/20/89]. But in a landmark policy speech, U.S. Secretary of State James Baker III praised the plan as "a useful and very positive start" to the Middle East peace process. Baker also called upon Israel to abandon "the unrealistic vision of a greater Israel" and to "foreswear annexation, stop settlement activity, allow schools to reopen [in the Occupied Territories], reach out to the Palestinians as neighbors who deserve political rights" [*The New York Times*, 5/23/89].

The flexibility of Shamir's plan was greatly stiffened in July when the Likud's Central Committee met and forced the Prime Minister to issue a **set of public assurances** concerning his peace plan. Shamir pledged never to negotiate with the PLO or accept the creation of a Palestinian state, never to surrender sovereignty over any part of the Territories, and never to restrict new Jewish settlements there. He further stated that the *intifadah* must cease completely before elections take place and that the 140,000 Arabs residing in occupied East Jerusalem could neither vote nor stand for election. The Central Committee voted to incorporate all these restrictions into a resolution that all Likud members in government must honor [*The Economist*, 7/8/89].

In September, **Egyptian President Husni Mubarak** tried to resuscitate Shamir's moribund plan by issuing **"Ten Points"** clarifying possible elections in the Occupied Territories. Seven of the points qualified the actual election process outlined in the original Shamir plan: Israel must allow East Jerusalem residents to vote, accept the results of the election, grant the winning candidates immunity from detention, permit international supervision of the elections, and withdraw its armed forces from polling stations during election day. Three further points required Israel to freeze its settlement activities in the Occupied Territories, set a firm date for negotiations, and accept the four principles of the U.S. policy in the Middle East, including the notion of trading land for peace.

In late September, Israeli Minister of Defense Yitzhak Rabin visited Mubarak in Cairo and publicly approved the idea of sending an Israeli delegation to Cairo to talk to a Palestinian delegation selected by the Egyptians [*The Economist*, 9/23/89]. Meanwhile, President Mubarak held a series of meetings in Cairo with Yasser Arafat, who also blessed the idea of Israeli-Palestinian talks in Cairo, although the PLO was to play no formal part. "We accept this dialogue without any conditions from both sides," Arafat said. But Prime Minister Shamir pronounced Mubarak's Ten Points *treif* ("unclean") and said the proposed Cairo talks "would not be for negotiations but surrender talks" [*The New York Times*, 9/27/89]. In early October the PLO Executive Committee criticized the Ten Points but did not reject them.

In October, President Mubarak drew up a list of Palestinian negotiators, including two Palestinians who had been deported from the West Bank by Israel and another two who resided in East Jerusalem, but once again Prime Minister Shamir, supported by Likud ministers, rejected the list. Secretary of State Baker now attempted to support Egypt by drafting his own "five points," which called for a meeting of Israeli, Egyptian, and

U.S. delegations in Washington to discuss the formation of a Palestinian delegation with which Israel might negotiate plans for elections in the Territories [ibid., 10/19/89]. In October, Shamir rejected the plan, affirming that Israel would not compromise on the issue of the PLO [Facts on File, 1989]. In December, Baker's five points were scrapped.

During early 1990, negotiations over the preelection Israeli-Palestinian talks in Cairo continued between Likud leaders on one side and Labour leaders and Egyptian and U.S. officials on the other. In January, Secretary Baker suggested a further compromise: a list of Palestinian negotiators including one or two West Bank residents "with second addresses" in East Jerusalem [ibid., 3/8/90]. Finally, Shamir agreed to talks with Palestinians in Cairo but only if Labour officials in government accepted two conditions: East Jerusalem Arabs must be excluded from the process, and the Israelis could walk out of the talks if they thought the PLO was manipulating the Palestinian delegation behind the scenes. Labour rejected these conditions and soon withdrew from Israel's national unity government, which collapsed in mid-March [ibid., 3/6/90, 3/7/90]. The new governing coalition cobbled together by Likud has been described as the most conservative in Israel's history [*The Christian Science Monitor*, 6/15/90].

In late May a resurgence of violence in the Occupied Territories and the shooting of seven Palestinians by a purportedly mentally unstable Israeli led to a request by Arafat to address an emergency session of the U.N. Security Council. Heading off the possibility of a U.S. denial of a visa to the PLO leader, the Council moved its deliberations to Geneva on May 25, where the United States vetoed a bid to send a U.N. mission to the West Bank to monitor the treatment of Palestinians by Israeli security forces [*The New York Times*, 6/1/90]. At about this time, the PLO and the Arab states, Jordan in the lead, launched a preemptive verbal strike against the increasing Soviet Jewish immigration to Israel with the expectation that the newcomers would be settled in the West Bank or Gaza Strip. Soviet President Gorbachev warned that he would curtail this exodus if Israel did not pledge to keep the newcomers from the Occupied Territories, and the United States also voiced its opposition to such settlements. In a late-June speech, Israeli Housing Minister Ariel Sharon announced that the government would refrain from moving Soviet Jews into the Territories, leaving open the question of whether immigrants would be permitted to settle there as a matter of personal choice [ibid., 6/25/90]. It was also in late June that the United States suspended its 17-month dialogue with the PLO, citing the PLO leadership's failure to condemn directly the aborted amphibious raid on Israel, May 30, by a radical Palestinian group [ibid., 6/21/90]. With the Mideast peace process at a standstill, U.N. Secretary-General Pérez de Cuéllar asked the Security Council's five permanent members to explore ways of moving it ahead. Washington is said to have given "a guarded response" to the suggestion [ibid., 7/18/90].

This much is certain: The *intifadah* and the PNC's Algiers declarations have dynamically recast the terms of the Palestine Question. In Israel the *intifadah* has shattered the complacent illusion that peaceful coexistence between Arabs and Israelis under the present occupation is still possible. The uprising has vindicated many moderates, both Israeli and Palestinian, who have long felt that peace must be made before Israel's annexation of the Occupied Territories becomes irreversible. As of 1986, Israel controlled, directly or indirectly, 50 percent of the West Bank, where more than 180,000 Israelis lived in some 110 settlements, and East Jerusalem. Israel has also confiscated a third of the Gaza Strip, which Israeli demographer Meron Benvenisti has called the "Soweto of the state of Israel." Benvenisti's figures suggest the Gaza Strip is now as crowded as Hong Kong and will grow in population from its current 650,000 to 900,000 by 1999 [*The Jerusalem Post*, 6/7/86].

The **44th Session of the General Assembly** passed a number of resolutions condemning Israel's occupation of the West Bank and the Gaza Strip. The resolution on "The Situation in the Middle East" [A/Res/44/40] repeated the body's conviction that "the question of Palestine is at the core of the conflict" and that a just solution to the Arab-Israeli conflict must include the PLO "as the sole legitimate representative of the Palestinian people." The resolution demanded "the total and unconditional withdrawal by Israel from all the Palestinian territory occupied since 1967, including Jerusalem, and from the other occupied Arab territories." It also reaffirmed the Assembly's call to convene an international peace conference under the auspices of the United Nations. Following Yasser Arafat's address to the General Assembly in Geneva in December 1988, the General Assembly acknowledged the proclamation of the state of Palestine and changed the name of the PLO's observer office at the United Nations to that of the Palestine Observer Mission to the United Nations [43/177]. Forty-four countries voted against the resolution, including Israel, the United States, and the entire NATO bloc.

Lebanon

Persistent sectarian strife and public disorder have kept Lebanon in a state of virtual anarchy since the outbreak of the Lebanese Civil War in 1975. The situation deteriorated further after Israel's invasion of Lebanon in 1982. Israel's 1985 withdrawal from southern Lebanon to a 6-mile-wide "security zone" north of the Israeli border raised new hopes that Lebanese internal disputes might be peacefully resolved; but without a functioning central government or a national consensus on how to restore one, Lebanon's many private armies continue their bloody turf battles.

Since the start of the civil war, Lebanon has faced the growing threat that the country might be partitioned into two ministates, Christian and Muslim. The process of partition was further advanced in September 1988 when the election of a new Lebanese president was deadlocked, and the Lebanese government split into two rival regimes: a Christian government under General Michel Aoun, commander of the Lebanese army who had been appointed acting president by outgoing president Amin Gemayel, and a Muslim government under former Prime Minister Selim al-Hoss. In March 1989 "President" Aoun launched a new round of civil war by blockading Muslim ports outside Beirut and declaring his intention to chase Syria's 35,000 troops from Lebanon. It was widely reported that Iraq was supplying General Aoun with military equipment, including Soviet FROG surface-to-surface missiles. Intermittent artillery duels and several pitched battles between Aoun's Christian forces and his Muslim and Syrian foes had killed 835 and wounded some 4,000 before an Arab League–sponsored truce took hold in late September 1989. Meanwhile, as many as 500,000 residents had fled predominantly Muslim West Beirut and 175,000 had left East Beirut [*The New York Times*, 9/22/89; *The Christian Science Monitor*, 9/11/89].

In May the Arab League met in Casablanca and created the Arab Tripartite Commission, composed of Saudi Arabian King Fahd, Moroccan King Hassan II, and Algerian President Chadli Bendjedid, to mediate the Lebanese crisis. After numerous shuttles between Baghdad, Damascus, and Beirut, the foreign ministers of Saudi Arabia, Morocco, and Algeria announced in early August they had reached a dead end. In a report prepared for the Arab League, the Tripartite Commission later blamed its failure on Syria, which had refused to pull its troops out of Beirut and the northern Lebanese coast and redeploy them in the Bekaa Valley in return for Arab and international guarantees to embargo arms deliveries to warring Lebanese militias [*The New York Times*, 8/2/89, 9/1/89].

A second effort at mediation by the Tripartite Commission was more successful. In late September, the commission invited the 73 surviving members of Lebanon's Parliament elected in 1972 to Taif, Saudi Arabia. Sixty-three members attended, and 59 approved a new peace plan, which combined a phased redeployment of Syrian troops over two years with reform of the Lebanese national charter. A new constitution would divide power more evenly between Muslims and Christians, reducing the prerogatives of the Christian presidency and changing the allocation of seats in Parliament from the previous 54–45 Christian-Muslim split to an even 54–54. Syria quickly approved the Taif Agreement, but General Aoun and several Muslim groups rejected it. In November, 52 Lebanese members of Parliament met in northern Lebanon to ratify the new Tripartite peace plan and elect René Moawad as the new president of Lebanon. After just 17 days in office, Moawad was assassinated by a car bomb and replaced by Elias Hrawi, another pro-Syrian Lebanese politician.

But without the approval of General Aoun and his forces, the new Lebanese constitution remained stillborn. The new national charter hammered out at Taif had gained the support of many Maronite Christian leaders, including George Saada, head of the Lebanese Front, and Samir Geagea, commander of the Lebanese Forces militias. Eager to unify Christian ranks, General Aoun's 15,000 troops attacked Geagea's 10,000-man Lebanese Forces in late January 1990. By early April, the intra-Christian fighting had killed over 900, wounded some 3,000, and driven about 300,000 abroad [*The New York Times*, 4/9/90].

Syria, which has occupied most of Lebanon for nearly 14 years, has not been able to impose peace on its fractious neighbor. Since the Israeli withdrawal in 1985, Damascus has brokered numerous "national reconciliation" accords and "security plans," but to no avail. In March 1987 escalating violence between several Lebanese militias and the Shiite Amal, Syria's chief client in Lebanon, threatened to upset the country's precarious balance of power, forcing Syria to occupy West Beirut for the first time since the late 1970s. Syria's move into West Beirut was clearly a last recourse, which put its alliance with Iran in jeopardy—Syrian troops dealt harshly with Iranian-backed Shiite fundamentalist Hizbollah—and expanded Syria's already costly and dangerous involvement in the killing fields of Lebanon. But the move did restore relative calm to Beirut for some 14 months, before a new battle erupted between Amal and its Shiite competitor, the Hizbollah, in May. In a week's fighting at least 150 died before Iranian and Syrian negotiators intervened [*The New York Times*, 5/12/88]. Another round of inter-Shiite fighting broke out in southern Lebanon in January 1989, killing at least 70, before Syria and Iran brokered another cease-fire in Damascus. The accord pledged both parties not to harm U.N. troops and workers in the area while permitting the Hizbollah to attack Israeli troops in their "security zone" [ibid., 1/31/89].

The United Nations has also been frustrated in its efforts to push war-torn Lebanon toward peace. The mandate of the **United Nations Interim Force in Lebanon** (**UNIFIL**), which was sent to restore Lebanese sovereignty in southern Lebanon in 1978 after an Israeli incursion, has been thwarted by Israel's refusal to evacuate its "security zone" and also by the harassment of local militias, including the Israeli-backed South Lebanon Army (SLA). UNIFIL has had to contend with the violence of the Hizbollah, which has not been appeased by Israel's withdrawal from most of southern Lebanon in 1985 and remains committed to the "liberation" of Jerusalem and the destruction of Israel.

U.N. attempts to mediate between Israel and Lebanon broke down in 1985. Since the onset of the Lebanese Civil War in 1975, the Security Council has been unable to intervene effectively in Lebanon. Eschewing any association with the larger Arab-Israeli conflict, the Lebanese government has for the most part declared Lebanon's troubles internal and thus unsuited to consideration by the Council. Differences within the Security Council have further hampered its efforts in regard to Lebanon.

Violence has persisted among the militias of Lebanon's many ethnic and religious communities. In the last several years the fiercest fighting has been the intermittent "war of the camps," which started in May 1985 when the Shiite Amal, supported by elements of the Syrian and Lebanese armies, stormed three Palestinian refugee camps in Beirut and southern Lebanon in an effort to impose Shiite hegemony in the area and forestall the return of PLO guerrillas. This campaign did not drive armed Palestinian defenders from their homes, and Amal has renewed its "war of the camps" several times, bringing Palestinian settlements to the brink of starvation and epidemic by February 1987, when Amal lifted its siege and allowed shipments of food and emergency supplies into the Palestinian camps [*Time*, 2/23/87]. The brutal battles between the Shiite Amal and the Palestinians, and more recently the Hizbollah, have underscored Amal's fierce determination to control southern Lebanon, moving other factions in the country to oppose Amal's drive for hegemony and to support a steady revival of PLO power in Lebanon. While 8,000 Palestinian fedayeen fled Lebanon during the Israeli invasion of 1982, up to 11,000, including 5,000 members of Yasser Arafat's moderate Fatah faction, have returned to Beirut and south Lebanon [*The New York Times*, 4/2/90].

Meanwhile, fighting along Israel's "security zone" continues in the south. The Hizbollah, whose power and influence has grown rapidly since its formation in the wake of the Israeli invasion, has fired rockets on settlements in northern Israel and attacked Israeli and SLA positions in southern Lebanon, prompting retaliation in force by Israeli warplanes. Although Yasser Arafat's Fatah group has suspended raids into Israel since the start of the U.S.-PLO dialogue in December 1988, other Palestinian groups have launched nearly 30 rocket attacks and ground raids, according to the U.S. State Department [ibid., 3/21/90]. All of these actions have drawn Israeli reprisals in the form of air and land raids against PLO and Hizbollah positions in southern Lebanon. In December 1988 Israel launched a combined air, land, and sea raid just ten miles south of Beirut. The United States later vetoed a Security Council draft resolution deploring the Israeli attack and demanding Israel withdraw from Lebanon to internationally recognized boundaries [SC/5052]. In January the United States had vetoed a similar Security Council resolution that "strongly deplore[d] repeated Israeli attacks against Lebanese territory and all other measures and practices against the civilian population." The United Kingdom abstained [PR SC/4977/88].

Another war between Syria and Israel in Lebanon is unlikely. In April 1986 allegations that Syria was behind a failed attempt to blow up an Israeli airliner spurred rumors of a new war, but tensions between Syria and Israel quickly subsided. Israel's withdrawal to its security zone in southern Lebanon in 1985 has eased friction between the two countries, restoring Lebanon as a buffer zone separating the Syrian and Israeli armies. At present Israel, Syria, and the Shiite Amal all have an interest in checking the growth of PLO and Hizbollah influence in southern Lebanon. Both insurgent groups threaten to upset the delicate strategic balance that Israel and Syria have struck.

UNIFIL, which has nearly 6,000 troops in southern Lebanon, continues to play its peacekeeping role, although its U.N. mandate proscribes the use of force to stop guerrilla attacks or Israeli countermeasures. Since the establishment of UNIFIL, 156 members of the force have died, 60 as a result of hostile fire and bomb or mine explosions. During the last six months of 1988, 5 UNIFIL soldiers lost their lives in accidents and 17 were wounded, 10 of those from hostile fire or explosions. In February 1988, Colonel William Higgins, a U.S. Marine attached to UNIFIL, was kidnapped, and three more UNIFIL soldiers were kidnapped in December 1988 before being rescued by Amal forces. Colonel Higgins was executed in captivity in July 1989 by the Organization for the Oppressed on Earth, a group thought to be a front for the Hizbollah, after an Israeli commando operation abducted a prominent Hizbollah cleric from his village in southern Lebanon. In December 1988 three more UNIFIL soldiers were kidnapped before being rescued by Amal forces two days later [S/20416].

In his semiannual report of January 1989, the Secretary-General noted that **UNIFIL's finances** "have continued to deteriorate" because some U.N. members have failed to meet their UNIFIL obligations. As of December 1989 unpaid contributions totaled $318 million, against an assessed 1989 UNIFIL budget of $153 million. In 1987 the United States paid only half of its $45 million UNIFIL assessment and it has paid nothing more since. U.S. arrears at the end of 1989 stood at $111.89 million. Soviet arrears stood at $125.13 million, including Byelorussia and the Ukraine, despite a 1986 Soviet announcement that it would start to pay its assessed share.

UNRWA

The United Nations Relief and Works Agency for Palestine Refugees in the Near East (UNRWA) was created in 1949 to provide humanitarian support for some 700,000 Palestinian refugees. Today the agency extends a wide range of welfare services to over 2.1 million eligible refugees in the Middle

East. It provides education to 350,000 Palestinian students in Jordan, Lebanon, Syria, and the Occupied Territories. It also supplies shelter materials, emergency medical supplies, and food relief for more than 108,000 Palestinians it classes as special hardship cases.

UNRWA's operations for 1989 were budgeted at $227.4 million, the largest contributions coming from the United States ($61.3 million) and the European Economic Community ($41.6 million). The agency runs to emergency supplementary budgets—one for Lebanon set at $6.4 million for 1989 and another for the West Bank and Gaza Strip set at $10.6 million for the first half of the year [*UNRWA Report*, 3/89]. In 1985 the agency weathered a severe financial crisis when its proposed budget of $258.2 million faced a sudden and severe shortfall, requiring sharp cuts in educational services, as well as staff and expenditure reductions across the board. The greatest challenge UNRWA faces is how best to use its severely limited resources to serve its large, needy constituency [DPI/NGO/SB/87/4].

As in past years, the anarchy and violence of Lebanon have imperiled both UNRWA clients and personnel, making the agency's work extremely difficult and dangerous. As Secretary-General Pérez de Cuéllar noted, "UNRWA staff members as a group have suffered more arrests, detentions, injuries and even loss of life than the staff of any other United Nations organization" [SG/SM/43481]. Since June 1982, 26 UNRWA workers have been killed in Lebanon, out of a total staff of 2,300. In February 1988 two UNRWA employees were kidnapped near Saida in southern Lebanon, allegedly by supporters of PLO renegade Abu Nidal [*The New York Times*, 2/6/88]. The agency played a vital role in getting emergency food and medical supplies into the Palestinian refugee camps, which the Shiite Amal has besieged at various times since May 1985. Since the start of the Palestinian uprising in December 1987, UNRWA has reported extreme difficulties in meeting emergency demands for food, water, and medical care in the refugee camps of Gaza because of curfews, beatings of refugees, and restrictive economic policies imposed by Israeli occupation authorities [PR DH/85/88].

UNRWA's largest program, education, has been hard hit by Israel's closing of schools in the Occupied Territories. The agency's 98 schools for 40,000 students in the Territories remained closed for most of the 1987–1988 school year. Schools were reopened in December 1988 but shut down again in February 1989. Israeli authorities delayed the start of the 1989–1990 school year until January 1990 [PAL/1724].

3. Africa

The agenda of the 45th Session of the U.N. General Assembly will feature two major categories of African issues. One is the persistent economic crisis in sub-Saharan Africa; the other, the continuing struggle against apartheid in the Republic of South Africa and the peace and security issues associated with the Republic's attempt to destabilize and dominate the region. A number of subissues fall under each category. Related to the economic crisis, for example, are matters affecting humanitarian and emergency assistance to refugees and others who have been displaced by regional conflicts and ecological failures. Under the category of southern Africa, the General Assembly will be reviewing its own role in liquidating South Africa's illegal occupation of Namibia, and it will also be attempting to discourage South Africa from mounting any further attacks on the frontline states, especially Mozambique and Angola.

The African Economic Crisis

Africa is in the throes of an economic crisis of devastating proportions characterized by a precipitous decline in growth rates and real incomes, falling rates of production, internal and external deficits, declining agricultural production, and serious failures in the organization of industrial and agricultural management [John Ravenhill, *Africa in Economic Crisis* (New York: Columbia University Press, 1986), p. 36]. A 1983 assessment of the situation by the U.N. Economic Commission for Africa (ECA) offered a disturbing prognosis:

> The picture that emerges from the analysis of the perspective of the African region by the year 2008 under the historical trend scenario is almost a nightmare. Poverty would reach unimaginable dimensions since rural incomes would become almost negligible relative to the costs of physical goods and services. The conditions in the urban centres would also worsen with more shanty towns, more congested roads, more beggars and more delinquents. The level of the unemployed searching desperately for the means to survive would imply increased crime rates and misery. Against such a background of misery and social injustice, the political situation would inevitably be difficult. The very consequence of extreme poverty would be social tensions and unrest which, in turn, would result in political instability [*ECA and Africa's Development, 1983–2008* (Addis Ababa: ECA, 1983), p. 93].

As late as 1989 most observers were agreed that for all the efforts of the African countries and the various international agencies, the economic crisis had worsened appreciably.

The crisis in Africa is the result of a combination of external and internal factors. Entering the world capitalist system with a legacy of colonial exploitation that placed them on unequal terms with other actors, and forced to depend upon an international political economy that continues to reduce the terms of trade for the continent's export commodities, the states of Africa have been severely limited in their ability to acquire sufficient resources for development. This problem is exacerbated by the internal policies of most African governments, whose attempts to control prices and exchange rates and subsidize some sectors of the economies have contributed to the generally dismal economic performance.

In 1980 the Organization of African Unity (OAU) adopted as a blueprint for development the **Lagos Plan of Action for the Economic Development of Africa, 1980–2000 (LPA)**, based on the concept of collective self-reliance and regional economic integration. The plan concentrated on the development of some nine sectors in order to attain self-sufficiency in food production, eliminate illiteracy, develop indigenous technical manpower, preserve the environment, and integrate development with African sociocultural values. A year later came the World Bank's own blueprint, **Accelerated Development in Sub-Saharan Africa: An Agenda for Action (AD)**. According to the analysis that informed AD, while external factors play a role in the African economic crisis, the main causes were domestic policy deficiencies—specifically, overvalued exchange rates, inappropriate agricultural policies, and excessive government interference in the economy. AD's prescription for economic growth included the eradication of the exchange rate problem (through devaluations), renewed priority on agricultural development, and improvements in economic management.

For the past decade the LPA and the AD were thought to represent two opposing tendencies in the search for appropriate strategies to overcome the African economic crisis. Today many observers agree that these tendencies are far from incompatible and that the World Bank's blueprint can be viewed as a statement of "what should be done now and during the next few years to achieve the longer-term objectives of the Lagos Plan of Action" [S. Please and K.Y. Amoako in J. Ravenhill, *Africa in Economic Crisis*, p. 132]. There is also agreement that whatever strategies are adopted, African economic recovery will require massive transfers of resources in the form of investments and official assistance.

As the discussion continues, Africa has been sinking into almost total economic collapse. Contributing to the situation is a debt crisis fueled by the increasing interest rates and other costs of paying off the huge sums that were borrowed to implement development programs. This debt servicing leaves the African countries with even less revenue for domestic consumption or investment.

One of the issues that the 45th Session will deal with is African industrial development. In 1980 the General Assembly proclaimed the 1980s as the **Industrial Development Decade for Africa** [A/Res/35/66 B] to spur the development of industry through the efforts of the African governments to mobilize domestic resources, with the technical and financial assistance of the United Nations system, especially the U.N. Industrial Development Organization and the Economic Commission for Africa. A midterm evaluation in 1988 concluded that the program has been hampered by the scarcity of foreign exchange. Nevertheless, the 44th General Assembly proclaimed a Second Industrial Development Decade for Africa [A/Res/44/237]. Among the areas for which technical and financial assistance will be provided to aid country programs are the rehabilitation and expansion of existing industries, development of factor inputs, standardization and manufacture of spare parts, and subregional industrial cooperation. The General Assembly requested the Secretary-General to present a progress report at its 45th Session.

The **13th Special Session of the General Assembly** in May 1986 was an important milestone in the General Assembly's involvement in the issue of African economic recovery. It was here that the Assembly adopted the **U.N. Programme of Action for African Economic Recovery and Development, 1986–1990 (UNPAAERD)**, which made specific policy recommendations for governments and established the levels of capital assistance to be provided by the international community. The Secretary-General then set up an interagency committee under the chairmanship of the Director-General of Development and International Economic Cooperation to monitor the implementation of UNPAAERD. In April 1987 the Secretary-General also appointed a 13-member Advisory Group on Financial Flows for Africa, chaired by Sir Douglas Wass (former head of the United Kingdom Treasury), to offer advice on finding the capital assistance called for by UNPAAERD. Despite these efforts, the Secretary-General reported in October 1987 that as a result of debt service and the serious drop in commodity prices, $16 billion more was flowing out of Africa than was being brought in through development assistance and private lending combined. He went on to note that northern protectionism and global economic contraction were among the causes of Africa's worsening economic situation [A/42/560].

By the end of 1987, 33 African countries had embarked on International Monetary Fund-mandated **structural adjustment programs (SAPs)** representing the orthodox view of the causes of the economic crisis in Africa as outlined in the "Accelerated Development" report. These involved currency devaluations, reduction of government deficits, and privatization of government industrial and agricultural enterprises. While most observers agree that the African countries are in need of some form of internal policy reforms, the SAPs have been criticized for their tendency to benefit the commercial elites at the expense of poorer classes, leading to appeals for "adjustment with a human face" [*Africa Recovery* 13, no. 1–2, 10/89].

In September 1988 the Ad Hoc Committee of the General Assembly undertook a midterm review of the progress made by UNPAAERD. This report [A/43/664] and the Secretary-General's own report to the 43rd Session of the General Assembly [A/43/500] noted that the financial assistance from the international community was substantially less than was called for by UNPAAERD. On the basis of these reports the 43rd Session noted that the goals of the Programme of Action were not being met and also expressed doubt that meeting these goals would, in fact, lead to development. The Assembly nonetheless called for a redoubling of efforts to implement UNPAAERD and for structural adjustment programs that would go beyond mere adjustment of the African economies by working toward the sort of fundamental structural transformation that would be conducive to long-term development. Its resolution asked for a final review of UNPAAERD during the General Assembly's 46th Session in 1991 [A/Res/43/27].

On March 8, 1989, the World Bank and UNDP undertook a study of "**African Adjustment and Growth in the 1980s.**" The main thrust of their report was to defend SAPs on the grounds that those African countries pursuing SAPs were showing better signs of economic recovery than were others. One month later the ECA Council of Ministers commissioned a study of the World Bank report. *Statistics and Policies: ECA Preliminary Observations on the World Bank Report "Africa's Adjustment and Growth in the 1980's"* [Addis Ababa: ECA, 1989] took issue with a number of the conclusions of the World Bank report. The most serious objection was that in its eagerness to make SAPs attractive, the Bank had made selective and inconsistent use of its data to arrive at the conclusions of its own earlier report, *Adjustment Lending: An Evaluation of Ten Years of Experience* (1989), and the General Assembly's midterm review of UNPAAERD. Further, the Bank's study had paid no attention to the devastating social consequences of the SAPs.

As a result of this review, the ECA developed its own "**African Alternative Framework to Structural Adjustment Programmes for Socio-Economic Recovery and Transformation**" **(AAF-SAP)**, which called on "African governments to move beyond a narrow preoccupation with short-term adjustment to embrace a range of far-reaching policy reforms that seek to transform the very structures of their economies" [Addis Ababa: ECA, 6/6/89]. At its 44th Session, the General Assembly adopted a resolution urging the international community and international financial and development institutions to consider the "**African Charter**" adopted at the February 1990 International Conference on Popular Participation in the Recovery and Development Process in Africa," held at Arusha, Tanzania, under the auspices of the Secretary-General's Interagency Task Force on African Recovery. The charter sought recognition of the benefits of popular participation in Africa's economic recovery and recommended measures that governments, the United Nations, and donor agencies could take to encourage such participation.

In addition to the general problem of economic recovery the General Assembly has considered a variety of specific problems that affect the economic situation in sub-Saharan Africa. Among the most serious is that of **desertification**—the result of such natural disasters as locust and grasshopper infestations and persistent drought but frequently compounded by such manmade catastrophes as deforestation or armed conflict. The invariable consequences of these occurrences are famine, migrations, and the creation of refugees. At its 44th Session, the General Assembly adopted a number of resolutions urging donors to provide humanitarian and emergency assistance for refugees and displaced persons in Angola, Chad, Djibouti, Ethiopia, Malawi, Somalia, and Sudan. At the same session the Assembly authorized "**Operation Lifeline Sudan**," which coordinated emergency humanitarian assistance—some 120,000 metric tons of food and nonfood supplies at a cost of $78 million—to help alleviate the suffering of those displaced by civil war in Sudan and adjacent countries [A/Res/44/12]. The Assembly will continue to monitor the situation in these regions during its 45th Session.

Southern Africa

As in years past, the Assembly's attention will be directed to several issues that fall under the general heading of southern Africa: apartheid in the Republic of South Africa, developments relating to the independence of Namibia, and relations between South Africa and its neighbors.

Apartheid. Apartheid became the official policy of South Africa in 1948, when the Afrikaner-dominated National party came to power. It was the culmination and formalization of policies from the turn of the century aimed at creating a completely segregated society based on the domination and exploitation of the black population by the minority of whites. This racist policy was met by the opposition of the General Assembly almost immediately. In 1952 the Assembly established the **U.N. Commission on the Racial Situation in the Union of South Africa** and during the rest of the decade adopted a number of resolutions condemning apartheid. These resolutions went unheeded by the Republic of South Africa, which maintained, often with the support of the major Western powers, that apartheid was an internal matter and that General Assembly discussions of the matter were in violation of Article 2(7) of the U.N. Charter.

Then came the Sharpeville massacre of 1960. In its aftermath a General Assembly energized by a group of new African members began to urge more drastic action against South Africa. These included requests for member states to take specific unilateral or collective measures to help dismantle apartheid and calls to the Security Council to take some measures of its own, including sanctions against South Africa. In 1962 the General Assembly established an 18-member **Special Committee against Apartheid,** which became the source of most of the resolutions condemning South Africa. In the two decades that followed the Assembly took even more drastic actions against apartheid. Among these actions were the adoption of a resolution expressing solidarity with the opponents of apartheid [A/Res/2054 (XX)], the adoption of an International Convention on the Suppression and Punishment of the Crime of Apartheid [A/Res/3068 (XXVIII)] and a Declaration of the U.N. Decade of Action to Combat Racism and Racial Discrimination [A/Res/3380 (XXX)], and the many endorsements of "armed struggle" against apartheid. The Security Council, for its part, imposed a voluntary **arms embargo** on South Africa in 1963 and a mandatory embargo in 1977. Throughout this period South Africa remained defiant, generally ignoring the hundreds of resolutions deploring apartheid.

In 1982 the Republic began introducing measures that it claimed were reforms of the system, among them the establishment of a tricameral legislature for whites, Indians, and Coloureds. The General Assembly condemned these reforms because they maintained power exclusively in the hands of the white minority and failed to offer any political rights to black South Africans [A/Res/39/2]. In 1985 the South African government introduced a state of emergency, banning many opponents of apartheid or detaining them without trial. Reactions to the state of emergency were almost universally negative. In 1986 the United States Congress, overriding a presidential veto, voted to adopt unilateral economic sanctions against the Republic. As international pressure increased, the General Assembly stepped up its antiapartheid activities.

At the 44th Session the Assembly adopted several resolutions directed against South Africa. Among these were a bid to exclude the "racist apartheid régime" from participating in meetings of the Antarctic Treaty Consultative Parties [A/Res/44/124 A]; a call for a Special Session on Apartheid and Its Destructive Consequences [A/Res/44/408]; and a catchall resolution that expressed solidarity with the two black antiapartheid organizations in South Africa—the African National Congress (ANC) and the Pan-Africanist Congress (PAC). The resolution called for comprehensive and mandatory sanctions and an oil embargo against South Africa, and condemned South Africa's internal and external terrorist policies, including its aggressive actions to destabilize its neighbors [A/Res/44/27A-L]. The Secretary-General was asked to prepare a report on progress in implementing this resolution for the 45th Session [A/Res/44/27 K].

At the **16th Special Session** (December 12–14, 1989), devoted to the question of apartheid, the General Assembly approved specific **guidelines**

for the peaceful dismantling of apartheid in South Africa. The guidelines—recommendations by the international community for the Pretoria regime—were contained in the "Declaration on Apartheid and Its Destructive Consequences in Southern Africa" and adopted without a vote [A/Res/S-16/1]. After reaffirming its duty to support all those in South Africa seeking to eradicate the crime of apartheid, the declaration cited a "conjuncture of circumstances" that "could create the possibility" of ending apartheid through negotiation, "if there is a demonstrable readiness on the part of the South African regime to engage in negotiations." These negotiations, it said, should be based on acceptance of the fundamental principles that South Africa should be a "united, non-racial and democratic state, where the rights of all citizens will be equally protected through an "entrenched bill of rights," a "legal system that will guarantee equality of all before the law," and an "independent and non-racial judiciary."

To pave the way for negotiations, the Special Session urged the present government to release unconditionally all political prisoners and detainees, lift the bans and restrictions on all proscribed and restricted organizations and persons, remove all troops from the townships, end the state of emergency, and cease all political trials and political executions. Before relaxing existing sanctions, said the Assembly, it would have to have "**clear evidence of profound and irreversible changes**" in the Republic. It will decide the question sometime after July 1, 1990, when the Secretary-General submits his report on the progress made in implementing the Special Session's December declaration.

Events in South Africa have given some hope to the antiapartheid forces. In a speech at the opening of Parliament two months after the Special Session, South African President F.W. de Klerk lifted the ban on the ANC and other antiapartheid movements. Even more dramatic was the release of ANC leader **Nelson Mandela** on February 11, 1990, after 27 years in prison. Talks between de Klerk and Mandela, scheduled for April, had to be postponed after police fired on and killed several antiapartheid demonstrators.

Representatives of the South African government and the ANC met at Cape Town from May 2 to 4. After the meeting they released a joint statement in which they expressed a commitment "toward the resolution of the existing climate of violence and intimidation from whatever quarter as well as a commitment to stability and to a peaceful process toward negotiations." The statement also announced the temporary immunity from prosecution of the National Executive Committee members of the ANC and set up a joint working committee to determine the modalities for the release of political prisoners and the granting of immunity with respect to political offenses. In addition, the government promised to work toward lifting the state of emergency. Talks between the two sides were scheduled to resume in mid-June after Mandela's return from an international trip. In the meantime, President de Klerk lifted the state of emergency in all provinces but strife-torn Natal and also revoked the **Amenities Act** that had directed the segregation of public facilities. Yet to be repealed is the **Internal Security Act,** which gives the government the right to arrest without trial.

Complicating any discussion about dismantling the apartheid system is the three-year-old conflict between supporters of the ANC and those of the Zulu-based **Inkatha,** whose leader, Gatsha Buthelezi, insists on participating in such talks. The continuing bloody confrontation between elements of Inkatha and the ANC could be a serious obstruction to the negotiating process. Another obstacle is the intransigence of elements among the right-wing **Afrikaner Resistance Movement.** The South African weekly *Vrye Weekblad* has reported rumors of a plot by this faction to assassinate Mandela and de Klerk.

Namibia. The United Nations has been dealing with the problem of South West Africa since 1946, when the then Union of South Africa attempted to annex the territory it administered under a League of Nations mandate, claiming that the mandate had lapsed with the demise of the League. Internal opposition to the occupation began with the formation of the **South-West Africa Peoples Organization (SWAPO)** in 1960, and by 1966 SWAPO had become a guerrilla force engaged in armed struggle in the territory and in adjoining Angola.

In the mid-1960s the General Assembly stepped up its challenge to South Africa on the Namibian issue. In 1966 it declared South Africa's occupation illegal, terminated the League mandate, gave the U.N. direct responsibility for the territory, set up the U.N. Council for Namibia to administer it [A/Res 2145 (XXI), A/Res 2248 S–V], changed the territory's name to Namibia in accordance with the wishes of the majority of the population, and recognized SWAPO as the "authentic representative of the Namibian people" [A/Res/3111 (XXVIII)].

In 1975 the Republic of South Africa responded to the challenge by attempting to establish an "independent" Namibia under the leadership of the **Turnhalle Conference,** to which it gave the responsibility of drafting a new constitution. In an effort to break this impasse, the "**Western Contact Group,**" made up of five Western governments with seats on the U.N. Security Council at the time, proposed a plan for a cease-fire in Namibia and tried to work out the basis of a compromise. The world body's response to the South African maneuverings was the now-famous **Security Council Resolution 435** of 1978 setting out provisions for the movement toward Namibian independence. The resolution called for a cease-fire in Namibia, the abolition of apartheid laws in Namibia, the withdrawal of South Africa from Namibia, the election of a constituent assembly, and establishment of the **United Nations Transitional Assistance Group (UNTAG)** to oversee free and fair elections under U.N. supervision. The mandate of this force went far beyond anything ever assigned to previous U.N. peacekeeping missions. It called for UNTAG to participate in nearly every aspect of Namibia's path to independence: monitoring elections, helping the former colony draft a constitution, and overseeing the transition to independent state.

The implementation of Security Council Resolution 435 was resisted by South Africa with the support of the United States, which proposed in 1980 that implementation be linked with the withdrawal of Cuban troops stationed in Angola. The General Assembly accepted Angola's response that the **linkage issue** was fraudulent, since the Cuban troops had been invited by the Angolan government to assist it in its war against the U.S-supported resistance forces of the National Union for the Total Independence of Angola (UNITA) [A/Res/42/24]. In 1985, while continuing to assert its demand for linkage, South Africa announced its final troop withdrawals from Angola and, at the same time, declared its intention of establishing a Multi-Party Conference (excluding SWAPO) as a prelude to a South African-sponsored form of Namibian independence. Between 1985 and 1987, using as a basis Security Council Resolutions 566 and 601, the U.N. Secretary-General made several attempts to start up negotiations with a view to emplacing UNTAG in Namibia.

In 1988 several factors combined to create conditions that led to some movement toward the independence of Namibia: the war weariness of Angola and SWAPO, Angolan fears about a reduction in Soviet assistance, South Africa's unwillingness to accept more casualties, and the development of a new U.S.-Soviet understanding about the need for a peaceful settlement of the conflict. A series of diplomatic meetings with vigorous U.S. participation produced a set of **Principles for a Peaceful Settlement in South Africa** in July; and at a U.S.-Soviet summit, Washington and Moscow set a target date of September 29—coinciding with the tenth anniversary of the adoption of 435—for reaching an agreement on the independence of Namibia. In December 1988 a **protocol on the independence of Namibia** was signed. Cuba began its troop withdrawal, and the way was paved for the deployment of UNTAG.

In spite of the problem of **armed SWAPO guerrillas** crossing into Namibia within hours of the official beginning of the transition period on April 1, 1989, and the controversial decision of U.N. Special Representative in Namibia Martti Ahtisaari to allow elements of the **South African Defence Forces** to interdict them, and in spite of sporadic activity by the South African counterinsurgency group **Koevoet,** plans went smoothly for the election of a constituent assembly in November. In the event, an estimated 97 percent of registered voters turned out at the polls, and the constituent assembly went on to approve a constitution for Namibia. On March 21, 1990, Namibia joined the ranks of independent states, with SWAPO leader **Sam Nujoma** as its first president, and on April 23 it became a member of the United Nations. At its 45th Session the General Assembly will discuss a "detailed performance report" by the Secretary-General on the budget of UNTAG [A/Res/44/191]. The UNTAG forces, having completed their mission, were withdrawn from Namibia at the end of March. The mission had involved 7,900 military, police, and civilian personnel from 109 countries at a cost of $373.4 million.

With the transition to independence of the **last major non-self-governing territory**, an important chapter in the history of the United Nations comes to a close. The Namibian experience was unique—the only time that the United Nations has taken on the role of administering authority in a territory and provided the machinery for its transition to independence.

The Front-Line States. South Africa's strategy for the survival of apartheid has involved a foreign policy of subimperialism for the past twenty years. In 1977, P.W. Botha, then Minister of Defense, presented a white paper in which he introduced the "total strategy" for reaching South Africa's foreign policy objectives. The aim was to keep the Republic's neighbors economically dependent, politically unbalanced, and militarily unstable so as to provide a *cordon sanitaire* against any international opposition to apartheid. The strategy involved coordinated efforts to destroy the regional transportation routes of neighboring states, to control regional trade, to mount a massive diplomatic offensive to gain some legitimacy for a cosmeticized version of apartheid, and to pursue a "strike Kommando" tactic involving the use of surrogates as well as South African forces in overt and covert warfare, sabotage, and terror [Reginald Green and Carol Thompson, "Political Economies in Conflict: SADCC, South Africa and Sanctions," in Phyllis Johnson and David Martin, eds., *Destructive Engagement: Southern Africa at War* (Harare: Zimbabwe Publishing House, 1986)].

It was to reduce their economic dependence on and military vulnerability to the Republic that South Africa's neighbors formed the **Front-Line States** (Angola, Botswana, Mozambique, Tanzania, and Zimbabwe) and, in April 1980, the **Southern Africa Development Coordinating Conference** (Angola, Botswana, Lesotho, Malawi, Mozambique, Swaziland, Tanzania, Zamibia, and Zimbabwe) [R. Green, "The SADCC on the Frontline: Breakdown or Breakthrough?" in Colin Legum, *Africa Contemporary Record* (New York: Africana Publishing Corp., 1988)]. South Africa reacted by stepping up its strategy of destabilization, and this pattern of terror continued until 1988. It is estimated that 1.5 million people, two-thirds of them children, have lost their lives as a result of South African aggression and that the SADCC countries have lost $62.6 billion in revenue [U.N. Interagency Task Force, Africa Recovery Program/Economic Commission for Africa, *South African Destabilization: The Economic Cost of Frontline Resistance to Apartheid*, 10/89].

The two countries that have borne the brunt of South Africa's aggression are **Mozambique** and **Angola.** Their strategic location on the Atlantic and Pacific coastal flanks of the Republic and their importance to the communications and transportation systems of the region are among the reasons. Another is the fact that both countries have been supportive of the ANC and SWAPO, providing sanctuary to its members.

South Africa's efforts to destabilize the two have taken the form not only of direct military attacks but of support for the **Mozambique National Resistance (RENAMO)** and the forces of the **National Union for the Total Independence of Angola (UNITA)**. As a result of this pressure, Mozambique accepted the Nkomati Accords of 1984, according to which the government would expel the ANC from its territory as a condition for withdrawal of South African support from RENAMO. In the same year Angola accepted the Lusaka Accords in an attempt to get South Africa to withdraw its support from UNITA. In spite of such South African assurances, the Republic continued its actions against the frontline states, and Mozambique and Angola in particular. In Angola it saw justification for such actions in the continued presence of 40,000 Cuban troops, which had been helping the government conduct its war against UNITA. The interest of the United States in removing these troops and the introduction of linkage between their removal and negotiations toward the independence of Namibia further complicated the Angolan situation.

By 1987 the devastating effects of war, evidence of the withdrawal of Soviet support, and movement toward an understanding between Moscow and Washington had put the governments of Mozambique and Angola in a mood to negotiate with their enemies and attempt a "reconciliation." With regard to Angola, aggressive diplomacy on the part of the United States produced the New York Agreement of 1988, which arranged for the **withdrawal of Cuban troops** within a 30-month period and peace talks between the Angolan government and UNITA. Lending support to this agreement, the U.N. Security Council established the **United Nations Angola Verification Mission (UNAVEM)** to monitor the pullout of Cuban troops, one-half of which were scheduled to leave by November 1, 1989 [S/Res/626 (1989)]. These developments paved the way for a meeting between Angolan President Edouardo dos Santos and UNITA leader Jonas Savimbi on June 22, 1989. The Gbadolite Accords they signed at this meeting were intended to lead to a transitional government, but plans have fallen through. New talks, scheduled for June 1–3, 1990, were postponed. A meeting between Mozambique's government and the RENAMO resistance, scheduled to be held in Malawi on June 12, was also postponed.

On April 26, 1990, the U.N. Secretary-General convened a conference of donors to secure emergency food aid and logistical support for Mozambique. A thorough in-country review of Mozambique's requirements will be conducted between July and August 1990. The 44th General Assembly adopted a resolution that called for international assistance to aid in the economic rehabilitation of Angola and requested the Secretary-General to consult with the Angolan government to ascertain the level of aid required, reporting his findings to member states, international agencies, and the 45th General Assembly [A/Res/44/68]. Also on the agenda of the 45th Session is the issue of cooperation between SADCC and the U.N. system [A/Res/44/150] and the Secretary-General's Report on U.N. Assistance to the Front-Line States [A/Res/43/209].

4. Central America

The United Nations's successful monitoring of Nicaraguan elections and subsequent disarming of Nicaraguan rebel forces marks one of the more unusual and significant diplomatic victories in the world body's history. Unlike most other U.N. efforts, this one did not begin with the superpowers. Rather, it stemmed from the **Esquipulas peace plan** broached by the five Central American presidents in August 1987. The United Nations skillfully, though quietly, continued to shepherd the plan through 1989 until all Security Council members, including the hesitant United States, signed on.

The major role accorded the United Nations might not have been predicted at the start of 1989, when the superpowers seemed hesitant and the regional states divided over just what the world body would do. But once agreement was reached, the United Nations performed its tasks admirably, proving again how useful a diplomatic tool it can be when nations finally decide to extricate themselves from a situation but are unable to do so alone.

If any evidence is needed that the lesson has stuck, one need simply look at Cambodia, where all parties now agree the United Nations should perform functions similar to those it took on in Central America and Namibia.

Like other peace efforts, the cardinal rule of U.N. initiatives remained constant in Central America: The United Nations can in no way force a settlement; it can only provide a vehicle once the parties to the conflict seem ready. By 1989 the parties in Central America clearly seemed ready, with

Moscow retrenching from support for leftist governments worldwide, Nicaragua battered by years of civil war, Honduras fed up with housing contra rebels, and the new Bush administration facing stiff domestic opposition to continued contra support.

Throughout the spring of 1989 the United Nations gently sought to push ahead with the plans laid out by the **five Central American leaders** at their February summit in Costa del Sol, El Salvador. In addition to giving their imprimatur for a U.N. observer group to verify the security commitments of the Esquipulas plan, they also made known that Nicaragua had agreed to reform its electoral and media laws and to advance the date of elections by more than 10 months, to February 1990. International observers would be invited to verify the electoral process. The group also undertook to draw up, within 90 days, a joint plan for the voluntary demobilization, repatriation, or relocation of the contras.

A March 18, 1989, article in *The Washington Post* pointed out that some in the Bush administration were taken aback by the new agreement to demobilize the contras. The administration announced a plan to allocate $45 million in humanitarian aid to the rebels, but others in the administration, Secretary of State James Baker among them, appeared to be seeking a way to end the contra war, though the United States would not publicly back the U.N. role until later in the year.

On March 15 officials from the five states drafted plans for a 160-member peacekeeping force to monitor the halt in aid to guerrilla groups, the first element of the Costa del Sol plan. But there were still hurdles to overcome. Throughout the spring, **Honduras and Nicaragua feuded** over a Nicaraguan lawsuit against Tegucigalpa in the **World Court**. Honduras said it would back contra demobilization and U.N. peacekeeping only if the lawsuit, over alleged Honduran support for military attacks against Nicaragua, were withdrawn [*The Washington Post*, 5/24/89].

In July, Secretary-General Javier Pérez de Cuéllar and Nicaragua took what may have been the boldest and most creative step toward unblocking the peace process. In a letter to the General Assembly [A/44/375], the U.N. chief formally announced that Nicaragua had asked the United Nations to monitor elections scheduled for February 1990, the first time the organization would perform such a role in a sovereign country. The U.N. observer mission to Nicaragua, known by its Spanish acronym **ONUVEN**, began in late August 1989 when eighteen officers were sent to Managua to watch voter registration and preparation for the elections throughout the autumn. An additional 22 would be sent in early December to keep an eye on the campaign as it began, ensuring that all parties could campaign freely, with equal access to the media and no harassment. An additional several dozen observers, to be matched by officials of the Organization of

American States, would be sent just before the February election to watch the voting, ensure the tally was fair, and certify the results [ibid.].

Pérez de Cuéllar announced on August 30 that he had appointed former U.S. Attorney General (and former UNA Chairman) **Elliot L. Richardson** to lead the U.N. vote-monitoring effort. Diplomats hailed the appointment of Richardson, a Republican, as a shrewd move that would head off U.S. skepticism if the United Nations certified the elections as fair and proper [ibid., 8/31/89].

On July 27 the Security Council adopted **Resolution 637/1989** expressing support for the regional peace plans and calling on the five nations to continue their efforts. But there was still no clear indication the five permanent members of the Security Council would support the emplacement of U.N. military observers as called for in the regional peace plans.

On August 4 the ruling Nicaraguan Sandinistas and 14 opposition parties signed an agreement guaranteeing free and fair elections to be held in February 1990. The Sandinistas agreed to suspend military subscription from September 1 until after the elections and to amend many security and press restrictions. They also provided amnesty for some political prisoners [*Keesing's Record of World Events*, 8/89].

On August 7 the five Central American presidents held another summit in Tela, Honduras. There they called for the creation of a joint U.N.-OAS International Support and Verification Commission (CIAV) to oversee the repatriation or relocation of the contras currently in Honduras within ninety days of September 8. Also, the five called on the Salvadoran rebel **Farabundo Martí National Liberation Front** (**FMLN**) to halt hostilities immediately, a major concession from Nicaragua, which had supported the insurgents for many years. It was proposed that two peacekeeping forces be created: one to patrol borders and ensure a halt in support for rebels and the other to demobilize the contras once they agreed. The Secretaries-General of the U.N. and the OAS announced they had formed CIAV on August 25.

The Security Council approved Pérez de Cuéllar's moves once again on September 21, though there was still no indication when the Council might approve either of the peacekeeping forces.

Meanwhile, little progress was being made in **El Salvador.** Representatives of the government and the FMLN met in Mexico City from September 13 to 15, with the FMLN proposing a cease-fire by November 15, leading to a permanent peace by January 31, 1990. Also they demanded creation of a legal political party on their behalf and constitutional and military reforms. The government agreed to the rebels' demand that international observers and church officials be present at future talks [ibid., 9/89]. Nevertheless, a new outbreak in fighting would soon jeopardize these agreements.

Throughout the autumn, U.N. election monitors increased their activities in Nicaragua, watching voter registration, noting compliance with electoral laws, and ensuring the groundwork was in place for fair elections in February. On October 23 the first ONUVEN report announced that registration appeared to be working well [A/44/642]. Reports leading up to the election noted some problems with slanted election coverage from the pro-Sandinista press and some incidents of harassment, but in general Richardson and his team placed their mark of approval on Nicaragua's handling of the election campaign right up until the February vote [A/44/834, 917, 921].

On October 17 the U.S. Senate agreed to send $9 million in aid to the Nicaraguan opposition UNO, a coalition of parties headed by Violeta Barrios de Chamorro, the widow of a slain newspaper editor who had led the opposition to former dictator Anastasio Somoza [*The New York Times*, 10/18/89]. Also about this time **former U.S. President Jimmy Carter** announced he would bring his own group of election monitors to Nicaragua for the February vote.

A major breakthrough occurred on October 11, when the United Nations formally presented the Security Council with plans for a **600-member military observer group** for Central America. The team, to be known by the Spanish acronym **ONUCA**, would patrol borders in the region and ensure a halt in cross-border raids and government support for neighboring rebels. It would also attempt to end outside interference in the region.

Again, the United States hesitated for several weeks, but on November 7 it and the 14 other Security Council countries formally approved the plan, the first time that Washington has approved placement of peace-keepers in the Western Hemisphere [*The Washington Post*, 11/8/89]. The U.S. Permanent Representative to the U.N., Thomas Pickering, called the creation of the group an "essential step to advance the peace process in Central America." [S/Res/644].

Many veteran U.N. observers were stunned at the quick pace of events. As late as March 1989 former U.S. chief delegate Vernon Walters had bitterly denounced plans to place peacekeepers in the region, saying they would only allow the Sandinistas to "get the contras out of their hair." During her days as U.S. ambassador, Jeane Kirkpatrick had repeatedly said the world body had little role to play in the Western Hemisphere. In approving ONUCA, the United States appeared to have ended its suspicion of most U.N. activities, discovering it could use the world body to accomplish pragmatic foreign policy aims. While differences with Nicaragua's Sandinista party continued, Washington's pro-ONUCA vote appeared to signal that the Bush administration had decided to try to force the Sandinistas out through the ballot box rather than with guns.

Under the plan approved by the Council, 260 soldiers and observers from Canada, West Germany, Spain, and a number of Latin American countries were to patrol the region, assisted by 360 technicians. The force would cost $41 million for its first six months and about $33 million each six months after that. Major-General Agustin Quesanda Gomez of Spain was appointed Chief Military Observer of ONUCA on November 16 [S/20981]. The General Assembly approved funding for the force by consensus on December 7 [A/Res/44/44].

But all was not settled yet. In late October, Nicaragua announced it would step up fighting against the contras, alleging rebels were entering the country from Honduras and violating a de facto cease-fire. The State Department confirmed that 2,000 contras had crossed the border since August, joining 3,500 already inside Nicaragua [*Keesing's*, 11/89]. Nicaraguan President Daniel Ortega Saavedra was harshly criticized in some quarters for his public pronouncement that he would resume fighting, a move that seemed guaranteed to earn world approbation. But others saw his decision as a bold attempt to force contra forces to negotiate and agree on demobilization once and for all. Ortega said he decided to suspend the fragile, and in his words "unilateral," cease-fire to "shock" the world community into action [ibid., 10/89]. Pérez de Cuéllar expressed concern over the new clashes on October 30 [SG/SM/4350].

Whether by chance or intent, Ortega's move did jump-start elements of the peace process. Some speculated that the Bush administration approved ONUCA in early November to encourage restoration of a cease-fire [*The Washington Post*, 11/8/89]. Moreover, the contras did agree to hold several days of talks with Sandinista officials on November 9 and 10 at U.N. headquarters in New York and the following week at OAS headquarters in Washington. Enrique Bermudez led the contra team; Deputy Foreign Minister Victor Hugo Tinoco represented the Sandinista government. But the talks made little progress, partially because a hard-line contra group had seized control in the field in the weeks before Bermudez came to New York [ibid., 11/11/89]. The contras continued to demand the right to set up camps in Nicaragua before agreeing to disband, while the Sandinistas wanted all rebels to return to Honduras and disband there in return for a cease-fire.

Meanwhile, the U.S. administration's right wing, led by Vice-President Dan Quayle, continued to assert support for the contras, and conservatives in the administration effectively discouraged efforts to have the contras demobilize before the February elections [ibid., 11/11/89]. This pattern of "good-cop/bad-cop" pronouncements from Washington, with some U.S. officials defending the contras even as the administration tacitly took a pragmatic course, continued into early 1990.

While progress continued on Nicaraguan issues, fighting in El Salvador heated up. On October 31 a bomb destroyed the headquarters of the National Union Federation of Salvadorean Workers. Eight people died, including the group's leader. Another bomb that day exploded at offices of a group representing relatives of victims of death squads. Other left-wing targets were bombed over the next few days. All of this took place against a backdrop of worsening human rights abuses in El Salvador, with mounting murders by both left-wing and government forces, according to a U.N. study issued November 17 [ibid., 11/18/89; A/44/620].

The FMLN launched a major attack in the capital, San Salvador, on November 11, raiding the presidential palace, Cristiani's home, and several neighborhoods, both wealthy and impoverished. On November 15 the FMLN announced it had "liberated" 6,000 square kilometers of the country [*Keesing's*, 11/89]. Pérez de Cuéllar expressed "grave concern" over developments on November 13 [SG/SM/4365].

The Salvadoran government declared a state of siege and curfew in the capital on November 15 as helicopter gunships and aircraft strafed rebel-held areas, with heavy civilian casualties. Over 2,000 people were killed or wounded after the first week of fighting, according to the army. British correspondent David Blundy of the *Sunday Correspondent* was killed on November 17 [*Keesing's*, 11/89]. One of the most gruesome killings came on November 16, when six Jesuit priests were murdered with two women servants at the University of Central America in San Salvador by 30 uniformed men. Cristiani vowed to find the killers, but there were growing allegations over the next few weeks that investigators were hesitant to uncover evidence that would incriminate right-wing political groups linked to the army and security forces.

The FMLN called for more negotiations on November 19 and demanded the United States halt aid to Cristiani's government. Cristiani rejected these demands on November 23 [ibid., 11/89]. On November 21, 20 guests at the Sheraton Hotel, including OAS chief Joas Baena Soares, and twelve U.S. soldiers, were trapped for several hours by FMLN forces.

Nicaragua became embroiled in the Salvadoran conflict once again on November 25 when an airplane from that country crashed in eastern El Salvador. It was found to have Soviet ground-to-air missiles of the type used by the FMLN on board. Subsequent investigations by U.S. journalists appeared to confirm that the plane had been loaded with arms in Nicaragua, apparently part of a Sandinista effort to aid the FMLN in violation of the regional peace accords. Cristiani suspended diplomatic relations with Nicaragua on November 26.

The Security Council met to hear the two parties on November 30 [SC/5149]. The peace process nevertheless continued, with a December 7 ONUVEN report again stating that election preparations were proceeding smoothly in Nicaragua, despite some conflicts over access to media [A/44/834].

On December 15 the **General Assembly** adopted by consensus a **resolution** expressing its "deepest dismay at the aggravation of the conflict" in El Salvador, as well as "serious concern" over attacks on the nation's economic infrastructure, a reference to FMLN sabotage. The text also criticized indiscriminate attacks on civilian targets and urged all sides to resolve the conflict and respect human rights [A/Res/44/165].

The 44th General Assembly took some action on other Central American topics as well. A consensus resolution of October 23 [44/10] expressed support for the regional peace initiatives. On December 19 the Assembly moved by consensus to "emphasize" the need of Central American states for development aid [44/182]. A December 15 consensus text welcomed a plan put forward at a Guatemala City meeting held in May 1989 to help regional refugees [44/139]. But two of the perennial controversies came up once again in the Assembly. On December 7 the body voted 91 to 2 to demand that the United States comply with the World Court judgment of June 27, 1986, that had found the United States guilty of illegally mining Nicaraguan harbors and called for reparations. And on December 22 the Assembly voted 82 to 2 to deplore the U.S. trade embargo against Nicaragua.

The Assembly appeared ready to adjourn when the U.S. invasion of Panama on December 20 disrupted most delegates' holiday plans. The Security Council went into emergency session, dozens of states criticized the invasion, and the United States, Great Britain, and France vetoed a resolution on December 23 demanding a U.S. withdrawal [SC/5155]. Threats were tossed back and forth as U.S. troops searched the home of the Nicaraguan Ambassador to Panama in violation of diplomatic privilege and surrounded the Nicaraguan embassy in Panama City. Nicaraguan troops did the same to U.S. premises in Managua. Meanwhile, all sides argued over who should represent Panama in the Security Council: a pro-Noriega or a pro-Endara envoy. On December 29 the General Assembly voted 75 to 20 to demand an American pullout from Panama [A/Res/44/240]. The **Commission on Human Rights** "strongly deplored" the U.S. invasion by a vote of 14 to 8, with 17 abstentions, on February 21, 1990 [HR/CN/133].

Some predicted the U.S. invasion would destroy the peace process; others said it would harm the opposition's chances of winning the Nicaraguan elections by strengthening "anti-Yanqui" sentiments. Whatever the long-term effects of the invasion or its justification or illegitimacy, the U.S. attack did little to impede the continuing Central American peace process. There was much shouting but little action. Once again, the United Nations proved itself to be what former Under-Secretary General Brian Urquhart has called an "arena for primal therapy" on a "global scale."

On February 25, Nicaraguans went to the polls. The results stunned the world: Opposition candidate Violeta Barrios de Chamorro beat Daniel Ortega for the presidency by a whopping 15 percent. The opposition UNO coalition won 52 seats in the 91-seat Assembly, while the Sandinistas took 38 and the Social Christian Party took 1. After over a decade of civil war, it appeared that the Sandinistas had been peacefully ousted from power, democracy was nearly restored, and the country was as close as it had ever been to civil peace.

The United Nations, joined by President Carter's election monitors and OAS officials, played an essential role in this effort. Over 200 ONUVEN observers under the command of veteran international civil servant Iqbal Riza and Elliot Richardson had fanned out across the country for the vote, ensuring a fair tally and certifying the election quickly after the count was complete. Just days after the elections, the outgoing and incoming governments and the Nicaraguan National Opposition Union (UNO) requested that a small team of observers remain in the country during the transition period.

But Nicaragua was not in the clear yet. Saber rattling began within hours of the Sandinista loss. Some Sandinista leaders threatened to hold on to the army and the Ministry of the Interior, which controls the secret service, even if Chamorro were to take the reins of government. The contras demanded total disbanding of the largely Sandinista army before they would disarm. And UNO remained a shaky coalition of 14 political parties, from leftists to conservatives, joined only by their opposition to the Sandinistas.

Since the elections all sides appear to be moving toward moderation. On March 22, UNO and Sandinista negotiators said they had reached agreement on a full transfer of power to the opposition, including control over the military and security forces. UNO assured the Sandinistas it would not seek to bring contras into power or conduct a wholesale reshuffling of the armed forces [*The New York Times*, 3/22/90]. And both sides urged the contras to disband and, as UNO's Antonio Lacayo Oyanguren put it, hasten the "firm initiation of a new era" in Nicaragua. On March 23 the contras announced they would agree to disband those forces now in Honduras on Honduran soil, but it remained to be seen whether they would relinquish their demand that rebels now in Nicaragua be allowed to form "transitional bases" there before turning in their weapons. On March 27, the outgoing and incoming Nicaraguan governments signed a transition protocol and agreed to "professionalize" the armed forces and remove them from political influence. On the same day, the Security Council voted to enlarge by 800 the team of armed peackemakers assigned to demobilize the contras in both Honduras and Nicaragua and gave them the task of receiving and disposing of the rebels' weapons and other military equipment [S/Res/650 (1990)]. Meeting in Montelimar, Nicaragua, April 2–3, the Central American presidents requested ONUCA and CIAV to ready themselves for the demobilization and disarmament process. The first contingents of the Venezuelan battalion arrived in Nicaragua on April 10.

On April 18, with Chamorro's inauguration only seven days away, the Sandinista government, government-elect, rebel leaders, and the Archbishop of Managua reached agreement on an immediate cease-fire and a timetable for complete disarmament by June 10. Under the plan, the rebel forces in Nicaragua would move into "security zones," where they would hand over their weapons to U.N. peacekeepers under the watchful eye of Cardinal Obando Y Bravo. The Security Council now expanded ONUCA's mandate to include monitoring the cease-fire and the separation of forces, noting that the entire demobilization process was to be completed by June 10 [S/Res/653 (1990)].

Nicaragua's new president assigned herself the functions of Minister of Defense but agreed to keep General Humberto Ortega Saavedra on as head of the country's army and received his pledge to professionalize the armed forces and reduce them by 50 percent over the next 18 months. In May, Chamorro also gave assurances to the rebels that their forces would be protected and allowed to resettle with dignity.

On May 4 the U.N. Security Council extended ONUCA's overall mandate for six months, until November 7, 1990, on the understanding that the force's authority to carry out its present tasks would lapse with the completion of the demobilization process on June 10 [S/Res/654 (1990)], later extended to June 29 [S/Res/656 (1990)]. On June 29 the Secretary-General announced the completion of the process at all locations, save one in Nicaragua; and that, he said, would be completed the next day. A total of 2,607 rebels were demobilized in Honduras and 19,256 in Nicaragua [S/21379].

As President Chamorro attempts to solidify her governing coalition and address Nicaragua's abiding social and economic ills, the U.N. Secretary-General continues his efforts at bringing together the government of El Salvador and the FMLN. These efforts—part of the broader Central American peace process—have intensified since January 1990. Consulting with both parties, the Secretary-General and his representative, Alvaro de Soto, have worked to establish a framework of negotiations that will call a final halt to the armed conflict in that country and to human rights abuses. On May 21, during direct talks in which de Soto participated, the government of El Salvador and the FMLN agreed to an agenda and a calendar for negotiations. A round of substantive talks was held in Mexico from June 19 to 21.

5. Afghanistan

The completion of the Soviet Union's troop withdrawal from Afghanistan in February 1989 led most observers to believe that an end to the Afghan conflict was at hand. Supporters of the Afghan rebels, including the United States, hoped the *mojahedin* forces would finally defeat the troops of Afghanistan's Marxist government once the Soviets pulled out. Others speculated that Moscow's withdrawal would pave the way for some sort of settlement between the rebel groups and government forces. Still other supporters, prominently neighboring Pakistan, were backing particular rebel factions in the hope of shaping the Kabul government to come.

The **departure of the Soviet troops** and the prospect of defeat by the rebels appear to have had the opposite effect: stiffening rather than weakening the resolve of the **Najibullah government**. Soon after the troop withdrawal, government troops repulsed several rebel attempts to take the key city of Jalalabad and in May 1989 managed to beat back the rebels thoroughly [*Keesing's Record of World Events*, 5/89]. This major blow to rebel morale and infighting among the various **mojahedin groups** have further weakened the insurgents' position.

As the fighting continued, there were stronger calls in the United States for a shift in policy, many urging Washington to abandon its support for a military solution and encourage some kind of **negotiated settlement** [*The Christian Science Monitor*, 1/4/90]. At the same time, there was growing dissatisfaction with **Pakistan's handling of funds** for the rebels, with Islamabad apparently favoring the group led by **Gulbuddin Hakmatyar**, described as a radical Islamic fundamentalist with ties to Pakistani military intelligence [*The Washington Post*, 3/17/90]. The rebels continued to appear dead set against any settlement that would keep Najibullah or other leading members of the Marxist regime in power.

In December 1979, when Soviet troops had entered Afghanistan to install a pro-Soviet leader after months of domestic conflict, nearly every member of the United Nations condemned the invasion. The General Assembly adopted scores of resolutions calling for a Soviet withdrawal and a halt to attacks on civilians. Years of U.N. diplomacy by Javier Pérez de Cuéllar and then by former Under-Secretary-General Diego Cordovez finally produced four agreements, one dealing with the Soviet troop withdrawal: the **Geneva Accords** of April 14, 1988. The rebels vowed to fight on.

In May 1988 the **United Nations Good Offices Mission in Afghanistan and Pakistan (UNGOMAP)**—a force of fifty observers called for by the accords—began monitoring the Soviet withdrawal and the pledges of the United States, Pakistan, and the Soviet Union not to meddle in Afghan affairs. The Soviet Union has been critical of UNGOMAP, saying that it has ignored **Pakistani and U.S. efforts to arm the rebels**. At the same time, Moscow continues its arms supplies to the government forces, worth an estimated $200 million to $300 million monthly [*The Christian Science Monitor*, 7/18/89].

The Soviet invasion and eleven years of civil war have left in their wake a level of destruction unparalleled in recent times. Nearly 10 percent of the Afghan population—1.5 million people—have died as a direct result of the conflict, and three-quarters of the country's 22,000 villages have been destroyed by bombs and shelling. The 5 million Afghans in Pakistan and Iran form the largest **refugee population** in the world; another million internal refugees have flooded Kabul and other major cities seeking food and protection. Health and welfare levels are among the lowest in the world.

Concurrent with its diplomatic activities, the United Nations established **Operation Salaam** in May 1988, naming as its head Prince Sadruddin Aga Khan, a former U.N. High Commissioner for Refugees. Prince Sadruddin is overseeing a massive, system-wide attempt by the world organization to lay the groundwork for the return of the refugees and the rebuilding of their nation. More than $1 billion in money and goods has been raised so far, but Operation Salaam has received mixed reviews. Interviewed in the field by *The Washington Post* [3/21/90], a U.N. official and land-mine specialist accused the program of vastly overstating its success and using its funds ineffectively. He noted that Operation Salaam trains Afghan refugees to **dismantle mines** in their homeland—clearing the way for a wholesale return of refugees and for the renewal of agriculture—but that it does not require trainees to return home or to put this skill to use. Addressing this charge, an official of the U.N. operation in Pakistan expressed the hope, if not the certainty, that mine clearance would increase soon. He asserted that the program is progressing as well as can be expected while the fighting continues [ibid.].

Efforts to provide **emergency care** for victimized Afghans continue as well, and the dozens of U.N. and nongovernmental relief organizations involved are slowly expanding their programs. **UNICEF**, for example, has been able to extend its reach beyond Kabul for the first time in ten years, setting up offices or maintaining a presence in several provinces, and it has also set up the first programs for Afghan refugees in Iran. Other agencies have followed suit with the opening of **new supply routes** through Finnish and Black Sea ports and the Soviet-Afghan border. Nonetheless, the government still depends on Soviet aid for survival; planes trailing missile-diverting magnesium flares provide a daily airlift of food and armaments.

On the political front, little progress has been made since the signing of the Geneva Accords. In what many saw as an attempt to divide the already shaky rebel alliance and promote tribal loyalty over Islamic fundamentalism [*Far Eastern Economic Review*, 7/13/89], President Najibullah opened a Grand Assembly of tribal leaders in late May 1989 at which he urged a political settlement with *mojahedin* commanders and offered to give rebel leaders posts in the army and government. He also proposed autonomy for some regions of the country, as well as a cease-fire.

This was the month that saw the rebels' decisive defeat at Jalalabad, and in the months that followed, as rebel attacks wound down and troop morale improved, the position of Najibullah's government forces grew stronger [ibid., 7/13/89]. On July 7 government forces regained control of areas to the south and southeast of Jalalabad, including the important military garrison of Samarkhel [*The Washington Post*, 7/7/89].

After this defeat, **infighting among the rebels** increased. On July 9 one rebel faction, apparently led by fundamentalist Hekmatyar's Pakistani-backed forces, murdered as many as seven military commanders of a rival fundamentalist group, Jamaat-i-Islami, raising tensions within the rebel coalition's fundamentalist wing.

A three-week **blockade of Kabul** by rebel forces in July caused major food problems for the city, now home to 2 million, including thousands of war refugees [*The New York Times*, 7/27/89]. Soviet airlifts supplied a thousand tons of flour weekly, and a few relief agencies provided some additional foods.

Soviet and U.S. talks on Afghanistan in Stockholm between July 31 and August 1 produced no published results but led to speculation that a recent Soviet-Iranian rapprochement had strengthened Moscow's hand in its demand that Najibullah be allowed to share power with Iranian-based rebel groups. In a summer-long paper war, all sides complained about violations of the Geneva Accords, trading letters of protest through the United Nations [A/44/473, 6].

The **44th General Assembly** opened its fall session with new calls for a political settlement in Afghanistan. And on September 29 the Soviet Union and the United States themselves issued a joint statement calling for a settlement "on the basis of national reconciliation, one that ensures the peaceful, independent and non-aligned status of Afghanistan." The statement went on to note that the two sides differed "over how to translate these principles into reality" but that both agreed on the need for "a **transition period**" as well as "an appropriate mechanism to establish a **broad-based government**" [A/44/578].

On November 1 the General Assembly adopted by consensus a resolution calling on all parties to abide by both the "letter and the spirit" of the Geneva Accords and requesting the Secretary-General to encourage and facilitate the early realization of a comprehensive political settlement in Afghanistan in accordance with the provisions of the accords and the present resolution [A/Res/44/15]. The text had been drafted in October during meetings between Soviet Foreign Minister Eduard Shevardnadze and his Pakistani counterpart, Sahibzada Yaqub Khan. A resolution dealing with the human rights situation in Afghanistan [44/161], adopted by consensus on December 15, also urged a settlement and asked all parties to respect the rules of war. It called on all parties to release their prisoners of war, urged aid for the refugees, cautioned the Afghan government about its treatment of prisoners, and "note[d] with concern the allegations of atrocities committed against Afghan soldiers, civil servants and captured civilians."

As the fighting continued throughout the winter, civilian casualties mounted and accusations were exchanged. The failure of the Security Council to reach a consensus on renewing UNGOMAP's mandate on March 15, 1990, led to the establishment of an **Office of the Secretary-General in Afghanistan and Pakistan (OSGAP)**. The Secretary-General's Personal Representative, Benon Sevan, maintains contacts with all parties in the attempt to achieve an intra-Afghan dialogue. U.N. Secretary-General Pérez de Cuéllar proposed that the United States, the Soviet Union, and Afghanistan's neighbors attempt to reach consensus on an intra-Afghan settlement, noting that this would make it easier for the Afghan opposition to get together and begin playing a political role in shaping Afghanistan's future.

An American observer, writing in *The New York Times Magazine* [2/4/90], described the rebels' failure to topple Najibullah as a sharp blow to U.S. prestige. He suggested that the result might be a fundamental shift in U.S. policy toward a negotiated settlement and went on to note that increasing numbers of the Afghan public are lending their support to Najibullah's government, fearing rule by the Muslim fundamentalist rebels. The **Soviet Union** floated its outline of a political settlement in *Izvestia* on February 15 [reprinted as U.N. document A/45/134]. Here Shevardnadze called for a "broad dialogue among Afghans, with the "participation at the current preparatory stage of the United Nations." Among the elements of the Soviet plan for an "intra-Afghan settlement" were a "suspension of hostilities"; noninterference by outsiders; a "transition period"; rebel "recognition" of the results of elections monitored by U.N. observers; the convening of a conference to include the Soviet Union, Pakistan, Iran, the United States, and representatives of all Afghan factions; an end to arm shipments; and the demilitarization of Afghanistan.

On March 7, Afghan Defense Minister Shahnawaz Tanai, who enjoyed support from both Pakistan's military intelligence and its candidate for Afghan leader Hekmatyar, attempted to topple the Najibullah government. According to reports in *The Washington Post* [3/17/90] and elsewhere, Pakistani officials, misrepresenting the failed coup as a success in their press handouts and enlisting the support of the U.S. embassy, pressed the *mojahedin* rebels to launch a major offensive against Afghan cities. All but Hekmatyar's forces refused. Official Washington disclaimed knowledge of the Pakistani disinformation campaign and the pressure on the rebels. Rebel guerrillas and leaders interviewed by reporters made clear their abhorrence of General Tanai (described as leading a hard-line Marxist faction of the Kabul government) and their suspicion of Hekmatyar (whom they considered an agent of Pakistan). To some observers, noted *The Post*, the entire affair offered the "clearest example to date of the mujaheddin's alienation from their Pakistani and U.S. backers."

According to reports received in May, the United States and the Soviet Union have agreed to the **principle of general elections** in Afghanistan, to be overseen by the United Nations and the Conference of Islamic Countries. They have further agreed that the ruling People's Democratic party of Afghanistan (PDPA) will be allowed to participate, although the United States takes the position that Najibullah must step down before the balloting begins [*The Christian Science Monitor*, 5/21/90]. Still to be negotiated is the matter of who will exercise power during the transition to a democratically elected government. The Pakistan-based resistance groups have rejected a coalition with the present Kabul government and also resist the call for a "transitional broad-based coalition government" comprised of their own and Iran-based rebel groups, various nationalist opposition groups, independent political personalities, and the PDPA [ibid.].

By July 1990 a loose and informal international consensus was emerging about the elements of a transition period, and efforts to refine these elements would be continuing both within and outside the United Nations.

6. Indochina

Negotiations to resolve the Cambodia problem moved ahead during the 44th General Assembly. With the suspension of the **International Conference on Cambodia** in late August 1989, attention turned toward more direct involvement of the United Nations on the ground in Cambodia, in particular through the possible creation of a **United Nations Transitional Authority in Cambodia (UNTAC)**. The five permanent members of the U.N. Security Council agreed to take the lead in brokering the conditions for UNTAC with the Cambodian factions and with the other concerned parties. Yet in spite of these encouraging signs and a highly significant shift in policy by the United States in July 1990, a compromise solution to the Cambodia problem remained elusive.

At the center of the conflict are the four Cambodia parties. On one side is the **People's Republic of Kampuchea (PRK,** rechristened the **State of Cambodia, SOC,** in April 1989), Vietnam's protégé government in Phnom Penh. Opposing it is the **Coalition Government of Democratic Kampuchea (CGDK)**, the anti-Vietnamese resistance movement operating out of Thailand, consisting of three factions: the communist **Khmer Rouge** (titular holders of Democratic Kampuchea's U.N. seat since 1975) and two noncommunist groups, the **National United Front for an Independent, Neutral, Peaceful and Co-operative Cambodia** (FUNCINPEC), headed by **Prince Norodom Sihanouk,** and the **Khmer People's National Liberation Front** (KPNLF), headed by a former Sihanouk Prime Minister, **Son Sann.** The hostility between the Khmer Rouge and their noncommunist "allies" has been as bitter as that directed against their enemies, Vietnam and the Phnom Penh regime of SOC prime minister **Hun Sen.** Cambodia's U.N. seat has been in the name of Democratic Kampuchea (DK), but in practice it is occupied by the three CGDK factions.

In February 1990 the name of the Coalition Government of Democratic Kampuchea (CGDK) was changed to the **National Government of Cambodia (NGC).** As a result, in the General Assembly the coalition now sits behind a sign that reads "Cambodia." The sign "Democratic Kampuchea" is no longer used.

One level removed is the **Socialist Republic of Vietnam (SRV)**, which deposed **Pol Pot's Khmer Rouge** and installed the PRK in January 1979, opposed by the **Association of Southeast Asian Nations (ASEAN**— Thailand, Malaysia, Singapore, Indonesia, the Philippines, and Brunei). ASEAN, with encouragement from China and the United States, organized the CGDK in 1982 and has been the prime mover of the international effort to end Vietnam's military occupation of Cambodia. Refusing to accept Vietnam's claim that the situation was "irreversible," ASEAN for ten years used the CGDK's guerrilla insurgency, plus diplomatic and economic isolation of Vietnam, to drive the Vietnamese and their Cambodian clients to the negotiating table.

Although the United States, Japan, the European Community, and virtually all of the Third World continued to support the ASEAN effort, there were signs during the period that certain key countries (Thailand, Australia, Canada, Great Britain, and France) were closer to according de facto legitimacy to the Hun Sen regime even while peace negotiations continued.

In the outer circle are the **Cambodia conflict's great power patrons.** The **Soviet Union** backed Vietnam's 1978 invasion of Cambodia, and although it has remained the ally of Vietnam and the SOC, Moscow has indicated that levels of material support for Vietnam would be substantially reduced from 1991 onward. Opposing the Soviet Union has been the **People's Republic of China (PRC)**, the primary source of arms and money for the CGDK and the Khmer Rouge in particular, which is the most powerful military force (an estimated 40,000 fighters) of the Cambodian parties. By contrast, the two noncommunist armies together contain perhaps 30,000 fighters of mixed quality. The SOC armed forces number 45,000 well-equipped but spottily trained regulars, plus approximately 100,000 lightly armed provincial and village militia [Congressional Research Service, U.S. Library of Congress, 89-631F, 11/30/89].

The **United States** has been a prime supporter of the CGDK. Washington's role of political support for the ASEAN position, including the enforcement of an economic and trade embargo against Vietnam, is well known. Less public is its role as supplier of nonlethal assistance to the two noncommunist resistance factions (annually up to $5 million overtly since 1985 and several times that amount covertly since the early 1980s), a fact that became increasingly controversial in U.S. politics; and a subject of pointed criticism in the media. Through its support for the noncommunist resistance, the Bush administration was accused of indirectly abetting the Khmer Rouge cause [*The New York Times*, 11/14/89, 11/16/89, 2/4/90; *The Washington Post*, 2/9/90].

Partly in response to this criticism, U.S. Secretary of State James A. Baker III, in a stunning policy reversal, announced in Paris on July 18, 1990, that the United States was withdrawing diplomatic recognition of the CGDK and opening direct negotiations with Vietnam on Cambodia. Baker said the United States would consider humanitarian aid to both Vietnam and Cambodia to encourage a settlement of the conflict and prevent a return to power of the Khmer Rouge [*The New York Times*, 7/19/90]. The administration's abrupt shift was caused by growing anxiety in the international community over a possible Khmer Rouge victory, by the U.S. Congress' disinclination to continue aid to Sihanouk and Son Sann as long as they were associated with the Khmer Rouge in the CGDK, and by Soviet assurances (rendered at meetings of the five permanent members of the U.N. Security Council) of pressure on Hanoi and Phnom Penh to conclude a genuine compromise political settlement with the noncommunist Cambodians.

A significant parallel development is the **growing international consensus for the concept of a major role for the United Nations on the ground in Cambodia** as part of a comprehensive, internationally supervised settlement. The key is the emerging cooperation among the **five permanent members of the United Nations Security Council** in the form of four intensive negotiating sessions during the first half of 1990 (January, February, March, May, and July), all of which seem to be creating the essential underpinning for a settlement. Also important was the first visit since 1964 by a head of government of the PRC to the Soviet Union in April 1990, which marked further **rapprochement between the two communist superpower patrons** of the Cambodia conflict [*Far Eastern Economic Review*, 4/26/89]. There were also indications of rapprochement between China and Vietnam in the form of increased trade and exploratory talks at the deputy foreign minister level.

Less hopeful was the **growing strength on the ground of the Khmer Rouge.** Many observers believe that the military dominance of the Pol Pot forces within the CGDK insurgency, the Khmer Rouge's expansion of cadre networks within Cambodia, and the Khmer Rouge's sophisticated participation in diplomatic negotiations are dangerous signs for the future.

To understand how international momentum developed for a more direct U.N. role in a Cambodia settlement, one must go back to the **Paris Conference on Cambodia** (**PCC**), which opened on July 30, 1989, almost two months before the convening of the 44th General Assembly. An initiative strongly advocated by France (and accepted with serious reservations by the ASEAN states, which felt the meeting was premature), the conference was cochaired by the foreign ministers of France and Indonesia. In attendance were U.N. Secretary-General Javier Pérez de Cuéllar, the five permanent members of the U.N. Security Council, the six member states of ASEAN, Japan, India, Australia, Canada, Zimbabwe (representing the Nonaligned Movement), Vietnam, and Laos. After wrangling initially over the right to represent their country, the four Khmer factions agreed to share the chair for "Cambodia."

At the conclusion of the first plenary session, the conference agreed to establish three committees to pursue negotiations on specific aspects of a comprehensive solution. One was to work out arrangements for monitoring Vietnam's announced military withdrawal in September, a cease-fire, the ending of military aid to the factions, and the modalities of future national elections. The second committee was charged with responsibility for drawing up a blueprint for securing the territorial integrity and neutrality of Cambodia. The third was to examine the problem of repatriation of Cambodian refugees from Thailand and of obtaining reconstruction aid for the country after a settlement.

The conference dispatched **a survey mission to Cambodia** under Lieutenant General Martin Vadset, chief of staff of the **United Nations Truce and Supervision Organization** (**UNTSO**). The fact that the PRK and Vietnam agreed to this involvement of the United Nations—albeit in the context of the Paris conference—represented a change in their position. In mid-August the Vadset mission visited Cambodia and the refugee camps in Thailand and on return provided the conference an outline of the significant logistical problems a peacekeeping operation would face in Cambodia.

Meanwhile in Paris, the three committees continued their negotiations [summarized in *Conference de Paris sur le Cambodge,* documents CPC/89/C.1/COM/2-6, submitted to the Conference by Rafeeuddin Ahmed, Special Representative of the U.N. Secretary-General]. The key conference discussions, however, took place in the fourth, or ad hoc, committee made up of the four Cambodian factions and the two conference chairs who sought to achieve some sort of agreement on the fundamental issues of power sharing, and particularly the role of the Khmer Rouge, in both a transitional arrangement and a future coalition government. In the absence of agreement on power sharing, it was clear that any gains made in the work of the other committees would be of marginal value and that any comprehensive solution would be out of the question.

Initial optimism at the plenary session gave way to a frustration all too familiar to those acquainted with the Cambodia conundrum. Intransigence on the part of all four Cambodian factions, as well as their backers, Vietnam and China, had created an impasse in the ad hoc committee. Sihanouk charged that more than a million Vietnamese civilians had been settled in Cambodia in the ten years following the Vietnamese invasion, and he made their complete removal a condition of any comprehensive settlement. As deliberations dragged on, his demands for inclusion of the Khmer Rouge in a quadripartite regime were met by adamant counter-demands by the SOC and Vietnam for exclusion of the Khmer Rouge. Sihanouk's statements were often contradictory, at one moment seeming to indicate continued full alliance with the Khmer Rouge and the next signaling a desire to separate himself politically from the CGDK in order to move closer to accommodation with Hun Sen.

On August 30, 1989, the conference issued a final communiqué announcing the suspension of negotiations. Although the meeting had "achieved progress in elaborating a wide variety of elements," it was not yet possible to achieve a comprehensive settlement, and therefore the conference would be suspended indefinitely [*The New York Times*, 9/1/89].

The reason for the **inconclusive result of the ICF** was summed up by a member of Sihanouk's delegation: "We are deadlocked here because the military situation is not decisive. If there is no result on the battlefield, there is no result at the negotiating table. . . . Hun Sen thinks he can still win the war. That is why he has made no concessions. When he sees he is weak, he will negotiate." Tommy T.B. Koh, Singapore's delegate to the PCC and Ambassador to the United States, observed: "It will be like Afghanistan; there will be more fighting. The two sides are preparing for war, they're already fighting" [AP, Paris, 8/30/89; *The New York Times*, 8/30/89].

While Sihanouk's insistence that the Khmer Rouge be included in a transition government was a roadblock, the Paris conference actually foundered on several other points:

1. The precise composition of an international control mechanism to supervise the imminent Vietnamese pullout.
2. The organization of a cease-fire.
3. The use of the word *genocide* in describing Cambodia's history in a final declaration.
4. The future of Vietnamese settlers in Cambodia.

Both China and Sihanouk objected to the use of the term *national reconciliation* in the final communiqué, since their position remained that the Hun Sen government remained a Vietnamese puppet without authority.

Although the conference was judged a failure by most participants, some saw it as an essential step in the international diplomatic process. Despite the obduracy of all the Cambodian parties and the hard positions adopted by both Vietnam and China, the Paris conference cleared the air by making ever more stark the realities of the Cambodia problem, in particular the intractability of the Khmer Rouge threat. Moreover, it put in place a new and broader framework for future peace negotiations beyond the Jakarta Informal Meetings (the JIM process) of 1988 and early 1989.

On September 26, 1989, **Vietnam** announced the completion of its **military withdrawal from Cambodia** [press release no. 28/BC, SRV Permanent Mission, 9/30/89]. ASEAN and the United States had made clear that Vietnam's withdrawal should have formal international verification, preferably by the United Nations, and be part of a comprehensive Cambodia political settlement. Although the withdrawal received considerable international media coverage, it was not monitored by the United Nations, ASEAN, or any of the foreign governments critical of Vietnam. Vietnam's offer, made initially in April 1989, to resurrect the 1962 International Control Commission to supervise the withdrawal had been summarily rejected, and ultimately observers came primarily from the socialist bloc. As a result, Vietnam failed to receive all the international credit it had expected, the SOC remained subject to charges of being a puppet, and the CGDK had justification for continued military pressure against the Phnom Penh regime, now bereft of main force Vietnamese army units.

At the 44th General Assembly the **ASEAN draft resolution on Kampuchea** became the focal point for unusual diplomatic maneuvering, partly because the end of the Vietnamese military occupation, though not officially verified, appeared to be genuine and partly because of the threat of a Khmer Rouge resurgence. Vietnam was tossed a flower but not the bouquet it wanted. The resolution noted the "announced withdrawal of foreign forces" but emphasized that this had "**not been verified under supervision and control of the United Nations** and is not within the framework of a comprehensive political settlement." The resolution retained the previous year's statement regarding the "**universally condemned policies and practices of a recent past,**" a reference to the 1975–1978 Pol Pot era, yet implicit in its language was the practical need to include the Khmer Rouge in a comprehensive settlement [*The New York Times*, 11/17/89]. The resolution added a call for "the creation of an interim administering authority" and reiterated Prince Sihanouk's role in the "promotion of national reconciliation among all Kampucheans." On November 16, 1989, the resolution carried by the largest margin in its history [A/Res/44/22; vote 124–17, with 12 abstentions].

With the General Assembly exercise completed, **activity on the battlefields** of western Cambodia picked up tempo. CGDK forces initiated limited offensives in the Battambang-Sisophon area and in December claimed to have captured the small town of Pailin, a gem-mining center a few miles from the Thai border. The two noncommunist factions claimed to have liberated a number of villages around Svay Chek, north of Battambang, but by year-end SOC forces had apparently regained much of the area. There were reports of Khmer Rouge probes near Phnom Penh. The Khmer Rouge moved under duress many thousands of Khmer refugees from camps in Thailand into Khmer Rouge–held zones within Cambodia. From the murky claims and counterclaims, it was difficult to pinpoint precisely what appreciable gains had been made by any of the four factions by the end of the dry season in May 1990.

Three conclusions seemed valid: The Khmer Rouge had given added proof of their superiority on the battlefield, when they cared to demonstrate it, and were building up their political and administrative infrastructure inside Cambodia; the noncommunist groups seemed somewhat better organized and more effective militarily than in previous years but were tainted by their association with the Khmer Rouge and had limited capability to affect events on the ground; and although the SOC armed forces had not collapsed under the CGDK's military pressure, they were nonetheless hard pressed to fend off attacks from a variety of quarters. These were some of the realities that had implications at the negotiating table [*Far Eastern Economic Review*, 12/14/89, 1/25/90, 2/15/90].

Also significant was the fact, admitted by Hanoi's Ambassador to Phnom Penh, that **Vietnam had felt it necessary to reintroduce several thousand troops late in 1989** to stiffen its Cambodian allies' spine [*The New York Times*, 2/22/90; UPI, 3/6/90]. It was not clear whether these troops were sent back to Cambodia as combat units or uniquely as "technicians" or advisers, but their presence in the Battambang area and elsewhere was established.

The fall also saw important diplomatic initiatives. On November 24, 1989, the **Australian Minister for Foreign Affairs and Trade, Senator Gareth Evans,** announced his government's intention to pursue a "possible alternative approach to a comprehensive settlement" in Cambodia [DFAT Canberra news release M201, 11/24/89]. The Evans proposal echoed a similar suggestion put forward a month earlier by **U.S. Congressman Stephen Solarz** (D–N.Y.), chairman of the House of Representatives Foreign Affairs Committee's Subcommittee on Asian and Pacific Affairs. Both proposals addressed the fundamental problem presented by including the Khmer Rouge in a quadripartite interim Cambodian administration and the inevitable threat it posed to the other factions, even as a minority and shorn of its top leaders. To avoid this danger, there would be established a transitional authority built directly around the "supreme authority" of the United Nations and with a special representative of the U.N. Secretary-General at its head on the ground and with considerable power. Thus no single Cambodian party would be in a position to decide the country's destiny pending free and fair elections organized by the United Nations and held under international supervision. This concept would require an **international control mechanism (ICM)** as both a peacekeeping force and temporary administrator of many aspects of Cambodian national life [DFAT Canberra news release M201]; *The Washington Post*, 2/6/90].

In the aftermath of the "failed" Paris conference and amid growing anxiety over the Khmer Rouge, the **Australian plan** received a cautiously favorable reception in the Bush administration and among most other concerned governments. The problem, however, was in the details. There was skepticism regarding how far the idea could be taken absent genuine political agreement among the four Cambodian parties, still the core problem, and concern about how much an ICM would cost the already impoverished U.N. peacekeepers. But Prince Sihanouk endorsed the concept of a **"Namibia-like trusteeship"** for Cambodia [*The New York Times*, 12/3/89]. Both Vietnam and the SOC indicated their acceptance of the principle of a major U.N. role in an interim administration [UPI, 12/13/89; *The New York Times*, 12/14/89], in part because they realized that aid from the Soviet Union would soon be cut and further support from Eastern Europe was doubtful [*The Washington Post*, 11/26/89]. This represented a significant modification of their previous positions.

Inspired by this flurry of "internationalization," the five permanent members of the U.N. Security Council met in Paris, January 15–16, 1990. They issued a **sixteen-point communiqué** that contained some of the Paris conference language and pledges to work harder for a peaceful compromise settlement. But they made few substantive commitments. They agreed on the need for a **special representative of the U.N. Secretary-General** in Cambodia "to supervise U.N. activities during a transition period culminating in the inauguration of a **democratically elected government**" and suggested that "a **supreme National Council** might be the repository of Cambodian sovereignty during the transition process." In this initial meeting they did not address the scope of U.N. authority, saying only that it should be "consistent with the successful implementation of a Cambodian settlement" and that it "should take into account . . . the heavy financial burden that may be placed on member states."

The communiqué made no reference to the auto-genocide committed by the Khmer Rouge, not even the standard pledge regarding a "non-return to the universally condemned policies and practices of a recent past" found in the General Assembly Cambodia resolutions and at the August 1989 Paris Conference. It stated that "all Cambodians should enjoy the same rights, freedoms and opportunities to participate in the election process." This formulation seemed to permit clear sailing for Pol Pot and his cadres in the interim period, or it may have been a realistic acceptance that the Khmer Rouge must be allowed to compete in elections so that their (presumed) defeat would allow China a graceful exit. In any event, this language appeared to be part of the price for China's signing on to further cooperation among the permanent five members [declaration text in *The New York Times*, 1/17/90; A/45/91].

Soon after the first round of these talks, SOC Prime Minister Hun Sen offered his own plan for a **temporary division of the country under two separate administrations** running their own economies and social service and preserving law and order in their areas. The U.N. interim administration would control the implementation of international agreements regarding Cambodia (that is, ensure the cutoff of external arms supplies) and organize national elections. A Supreme National Council with representatives from both governments would represent Cambodia and occupy the U.N. seat pending elections [*Financial Times*, 1/27/90]. The Hun Sen plan did not receive great international applause because it would consolidate the SOC's power in the vast majority of the country and effectively prohibit the other Cambodian factions from competing there during transition.

On January 24, 1990, Prince Sihanouk announced his resignation (for the fifth time) as head of the CGDK and withdrawal from future discussions on a settlement in Cambodia [*The New York Times*, 1/25/90]. Sihanouk said he would remain Cambodia's head of state, a post he claims to have held continuously since the 1950s and despite the 1970 coup that forced him into exile. Observers believed Sihanouk's move was an attempt to parry increasing criticism, especially in the United States, over his dependence on the Khmer Rouge [*The Washington Post*, 2/19/90; *The New York Times*, 2/4/90].

But just a few weeks later, on February 21, the Prince, at the urging of **Thai Prime Minister Chatichai Choonhavan,** met with Hun Sen in Bangkok to discuss a proposal that he break with the Khmer Rouge definitively and return to Phnom Penh, perhaps as the country's president. The two Cambodians had met periodically since November 1987; little observable progress was made on this occasion. The February 21 joint communiqué stated that a "U.N. presence at appropriate levels in Cambodia is essential and should be encouraged" and that "the establishment of a supreme national body is essential in order to symbolize Cambodia's national sovereignty and national unity" [Phnom Penh domestic radio service, FBIS-EAS-90-036, 2/22/90]. After the meeting with Hun Sen, Sihanouk declared his intention to reside permanently within a 250-square-mile "liberated" area in northwest

Cambodia. Sihanouk also declared that his country's name was now "Cambodia" rather than "Democratic Kampuchea" [AP, 2/23/90].

In Jakarta, **multilateral efforts** were pursued on a parallel track. During February 26–28, 1990, meeting within the framework of the PCC, the six ASEAN nations, France, Australia, Vietnam, Laos, and the four Cambodian factions held an **Informal Meeting on Cambodia (IMC)** in an attempt to reach agreement on the Australian plan. France and Indonesia were cochairs. Also attending was the Special Representative of the Secretary-General, Rafeeuddin Ahmed. In preparation, the Australians had sent a **fact-finding mission to Cambodia and the Thai refugee camps** to catalog the assets of the Phnom Penh government and the resistance elements to determine the kind of infrastructure a U.N. interim administration would have at its disposal and how it could be used without compromising political impartiality. The Australians produced a 155-page document suggesting various configurations of an "enhanced role" for the United Nations. The hope was that among these options, the Cambodian parties would find some common ground for agreement. Then, assuming genuine agreement among the permanent five members, the way would be cleared for a reconvened Paris Conference on Cambodia [Cambodia: An Australian Peace Proposal, working papers prepared for the Informal Meeting on Cambodia, Jakarta, February 26-28, 1990. DFAT, Canberra].

Combined with growing sentiment among the superpowers on the need to resolve long-running regional conflicts, the Australians' detailed proposals breathed new life into the moribund Cambodia negotiations. The plan envisages a comprehensive settlement that could be achieved within 18 months and addresses three key issues: how to implement a **cease-fire**, how to run **free elections**, and how to ensure a **politically neutral administration** in the transition period. The plan outlines a **U.N. peacekeeping operation** where the agreement of all combatants is required, along with their commitment to concentrate forces and store weapons in specific areas. An estimated 5,500 U.N. peacekeepers would be needed to monitor the cease-fire and to verify the Vietnamese withdrawal and cessation of outside resupply. A prime task would be to organize and supervise the conduct of free elections, actually registering and educating voters, setting up polling places, and verifying the vote count—all this in a country where truly democratic, free elections are unknown and where brutal civil hostilities have been the rule for more than two decades. To control this process, the Australian plan estimates at least **2,000 electoral officials** would be needed. Even more controversial are the questions of sovereignty and structure of the administration governing the country during the transition period before elections.

It is important to note that Cambodia, unlike Namibia (where the U.N. Transition Assistance Group has played a critical role), is not a trust territory and already possesses sovereignty. The Australian plan offers several options ranging from total dismantling of the SOC's 220,000-man bureaucracy to a selective replacement of key personnel. Taking into account the difficulty of deploying and housing large numbers of adequately skilled administrators, the plan favors selective supervision—finding interpreters from Khmer to English or some other lingua franca would be a formidable task in itself. It suggests that 200 to 500 U.N. staff at the higher ranks could take over from the existing Phnom Penh government and the resistance movements, with perhaps 1,000 others supervising those sectors of the bureaucracy in a position to influence voters. The United Nations would also have to dispatch 2,500 police to assist existing law enforcement agencies. In total, this **"mid-range scenario"** would cost about **$987 million over 12 months,** and most analysts believe the U.N. presence would have to remain longer than that. The Australian plan attempts to finesse power sharing, the key issue, by parking the current factional leaderships in a body called the Supreme National Council (SNC) [*Far Eastern Economic Review*, 3/8/90].

The February 26–28 Jakarta meeting ended in open disagreement among the Cambodians, with a communiqué that skirted the central issue: a role for the United Nations in the administration of the country before elections. The CGDK continued to demand total **dismantling of the SOC,** with the United Nations running Cambodia "from top to bottom" (in the words of Prince Sihanouk's son, **Norodom Ranariddh**) but to be responsible to the SNC made up of three resistance factions plus representatives of the Hun Sen regime—that is, three to one. Hun Sen wanted his administration left intact but was willing to have the United Nations monitor its work with a view to preventing any action that might affect the impartiality of elections. The SNC, in his view, should be made up of only two sides: his and the CGDK.

In the end, the Jakarta conference foundered on exactly the same issues that have plagued the Cambodian factions from the beginning: mistrust over power sharing, refusal to give up any advantage already in hand, and memories of the Pol Pot era juxtaposed against hatred for Vietnam [*The New York Times*, 3/1/90; *The Economist*, 3/1/90; *Far Eastern Economic Review*, 3/8/90].

The permanent five members had met for a second time February 11–12, 1989, in New York to discuss peacekeeping and parameters of an interim administration. They consulted with the Secretary-General regarding the newly established **intra-Secretariat task force** on planning a future U.N. role in Cambodia. At their **third meeting in Paris, March 12–13,** they made public initial guidelines on modalities of a comprehensive political settlement, based on the results of the Jakarta discussions and other developments since broaching of the Australian plan. They addressed the key issues of elections, the Supreme National Council, and the U.N. transitional authority.

Their communiqué stated that the United Nations "should be responsible for organizing and conducting free and fair elections on the basis of genuine and verified voter registration lists of Cambodian citizens" (an attempt to defuse the Vietnamese settler dispute). The electoral process should be guided by the principles of absolute impartiality; administrative simplicity; equality of rights, freedoms, and opportunities to participate; and a commitment of all parties to honor the results.

The permanent five members invited the four Cambodian parties "to agree that a Supreme National Council should be established as the unique, legitimate body and source of authority in which, throughout the period of transition, national sovereignty and unity should be enshrined." The SNC would include "representatives of all shades of opinion among the people of Cambodia." The SNC would delegate to a **United Nations Transitional Authority in Cambodia (UNTAC)** "all necessary powers, including those to conduct free and fair elections, and it would "interface with the United Nations Transitional Authority and be consulted on, and give advice relevant to, the functions of the civil administration and electoral organization." The SNC would occupy Cambodia's seat at the United Nations and other international bodies.

Few details were given on UNTAC beyond the permanent five's agreement that such a body was necessary to create a neutral environment in which free and fair elections could take place. UNTAC would be established by the U.N. Security Council under the direct responsibility of the Secretary-General, whose Special Representative would possess "all necessary powers over Cambodian territory in its entirety" in order to assure Cambodians of freedom from intimidation and the threat of force and corruption, to provide them with protection from economic and social discrimination, and to guarantee their human and civil rights [Statement on Cambodia by the Five Permanent Members of the Security Council, Paris, 3/13/90; *The New York Times*, 3/15/90; *The Economist*, 3/17/90; A/45/167].

The five permanent members met for a **fourth time May 25–26**, 1990, in New York to discuss further the U.N.'s role and "alternative transitional arrangements involving varying degrees of exercise of authority by a Supreme National Council which could include representatives of all shades of opinion in Cambodia" [Summary of Conclusions issued by U.N. in New York, 5/30/90]. At their fifth meeting, July 16–17 in Paris, the permanent five announced "significant progress" on transitional arrangements but gave no details of pre-election modalities or a cease-fire [*The New York Times*, 7/18/90].

Meanwhile, on a **separate negotiating track** organized jointly by **Japan and Thailand**, the Cambodian parties met in **Tokyo**, June 5, 1990, in another try at reconciliation. The talks collapsed quickly when the Khmer Rouge representative, Khieu Samphan, boycotted the meeting because his group was included as part of Prince Sihanouk's delegation rather than as a separate entity. The Tokyo meeting ended in what Sihanouk called a "half success," however, when Sihanouk and Hun Sen signed a joint communiqué calling for the establishment by the end of July of a SNC made up of equal numbers of representatives from each of the two governments rather than equal numbers from all four factions, as demanded by the Khmer Rouge. The communiqué also called for **"voluntary self-restraint on the use of force"** (diplomatic language for a cease-fire that cannot be enforced) whenever the SNC comes into being [*Far Eastern Economic Review*, 6/14/90].

The Tokyo meeting had several implications. The further coming together of Sihanouk and Hun Sen, though by no means conclusive or necessarily permanent, tended to reinforce the isolation of the Khmer Rouge. Hun Sen continued to gain international standing in the peace process, which in turn strengthened the SOC's negotiating position vis-à-vis Sihanouk. The Tokyo meeting marked **Japan's debut on the international peacemaking scene**, in part a reflection of its shift from a passive to a more active role in foreign affairs and in part because Japan is expected to pick up much of the expense for any UNTAC operation ultimately put in place in Cambodia. Yet the fundamental problem of what to do with the Khmer Rouge remained as intractable as ever. It remained to be seen whether the major shift in U.S. policy, which came only six weeks after the Tokyo meeting, would make it possible for Sihanouk and Hun Sen to move closer to agreement.

The **bilateral normalization discussions between China and Vietnam**, underway in earnest at the deputy foreign minister level, were emerging as the essential venue for an understanding that might bring peace to Cambodia. The annual ASEAN ministerial meetings scheduled for July, the post-ministerial consultations with ASEAN's friends, the continuing permanent five discussions, and preparations for the 45th U.N. General Assembly—all will be conducted with one eyed cocked to Hanoi and Beijing's tortuous movement toward rapprochement after more than a decade of bitter hostility.

In order to gather data needed for the on-going negotiating process and the contingency planning for an eventual U.N. operation in Cambodia, the Secretary-General sent **three fact-finding missions to Cambodia** in 1990. These missions conducted preliminary technical surveys focusing on basic infrastructure (March 30 to April 13), civil administration (April 24 to May 9), and the question of repatriation of refugees and displaced persons (May 24 to June 8). A second **Infrastructure Survey Mission** visited Cambodia from June 21 to mid-July.

Beyond these steps to facilitate peace negotiations, the United Nations continued to play an important **humanitarian role** in ministering to the needs of over **325,000 refugees** and displaced persons in Thailand. At the meeting of donors to the **Cambodian Humanitarian Assistance Programmes** on February 28, 1990, five states pledged $3,438,790 to relief activities of the **U.N. Border Relief Operation** and the **International Committee of the Red Cross,** and for humanitarian activities in the interior of Cambodia. Another pledging conference would be held in May [U.N. press release CAM/107, 2/28/90]. The **U.N. High Commissioner for Refugees** has budgeted $27.7 million for its own work in Thailand during 1990. The difficult problems of repatriation of Cambodians from Thailand in the event of a settlement were studied by the August 1989 International Conference on Cambodia and in subsequent missions to Thailand and Cambodia by U.N. agencies and on behalf of the permanent five in the context of the Australian initiative. Free and **unrestricted access to the U.N.-sponsored camps** controlled by the Khmer Rouge faction remained a serious problem. Of even greater concern was the forced movement of tens of thousands of Cambodian refugees under Khmer Rouge control in camps or border areas into "liberated zones" inside Cambodia [*Far Eastern Economic Review*, 2/15/90].

7. Cyprus

The Cyprus conflict has been a stubborn item on the U.N. agenda for nearly thirty years. Numerous negotiations have made progress toward reconciling Greek and Turkish Cypriot factions, only to see the two sides lapse back into disagreement and conflict.

Cyprus has been a divided island since 1974, when Turkish forces invaded following stepped-up persecution of Turks by Greek Cypriots and a coup d'état by Greek-Cypriot militarists who favored Greece's annexation of the island. Roughly 200,000 Greek Cypriots are thought to have fled the occupied portion of the island following the invasion, leaving 100,000 Turkish citizens—about a seventh of its inhabitants—in control of 40 percent of the territory.

The Turkish side is secured by an estimated 30,000 troops and is governed by Rauf Denktash, the Turkish Cypriot leader who declared on November 15, 1983, that this portion of the island was the independent state of the Turkish Republic of Northern Cyprus—recognized only by Turkey. The United Nations and most governments recognize the Greek-Cypriot government based in Nicosia.

The U.N. presence in Cyprus dates back to March 4, 1964, when the Security Council established the **United Nations Peacekeeping Force in Cyprus (UNFICYP)** to separate warring Turkish and Greek factions. Since the invasion, UNFICYP has maintained a buffer zone between the two competing governments, extending about 180 kilometers across the island. The United Nations High Commissioner for Refugees and the World Food Programme run efforts to assist those harmed by the conflict.

For 16 years the United Nations has tried to win both sides' agreement to reunify the island under one government. Both the General Assembly and the Security Council have affirmed numerous times their recognition of the Greek Cypriot government and their opposition to permanent division of the island. The Security Council formally rejected the declaration of any independent northern state three days after Denktash declared one.

Secretary-General Javier Pérez de Cuéllar offered a unification plan, accepted by the Turkish side but rejected by the Greeks, in January 1985. Four months later Denktash rejected a revised peace plan that took Greek Cypriot objections into consideration. In March 1986 the Greek side rejected a third version of the U.N. peace proposal, stating it must first receive assurances that Turkish troops would withdraw from the island and "three freedoms" be granted to Greek Cypriots: the right to move around the island freely, settle anywhere, and own property anywhere. The Turkish side accepted the U.N. proposal but equivocated on the three freedoms. Pérez de Cuéllar tried once more to solve this difficult conflict in late 1989 and early 1990.

The Secretary-General met with the belligerents in Geneva in August 1989. A final push toward settlement was attempted in late February and early March 1990, with several days of talks among Denktash, Greek Cypriot leader George Vassiliou, and Pérez de Cuéllar in New York. Pérez de Cuéllar opened the talks with some concessions to the Turkish side, describing them as an "equal community"—a key Turkish demand. The Greek side also appeared willing to accept some temporary restrictions on the three freedoms to prevent Turkish Cypriots from being swamped by returning Greek settlers. But the talks collapsed when Denktash demanded that his constituents be granted "self-determination," amounting to the right to choose secession. He also demanded that the right to "self-determination" be enshrined in any future constitution, claiming such a guarantee is necessary to prevent future Greek persecution [*The Washington Post*, 3/3/90]. The Greek side balked, and Secretary General Pérez de Cuéllar also criticized the Turkish demand, claiming it was far outside the framework for a settlement long established by the General Assembly and the Security Council. Vassiliou called the results of the talks a "tragedy."

There have been no new peace efforts since then, and it appears this may have been Pérez de Cuéllar's final push for a Cyprus settlement before his term expires in late 1991. Nevertheless, new factors may push the two sides toward a settlement soon after that. NATO members want the Cyprus issue solved as the alliance draws a new military map of Europe with the

Warsaw Pact. The Soviet side remains nervous about this little island state in the Mediterranean, allied to a NATO member (Turkey) but not covered by arms control agreements. And Turkey may push for a settlement as it tries to win membership in the European Community, where Greece may veto its application. Meanwhile, U.N. peacekeepers will remain.

8. Other Colonial and Sovereignty Issues

U.N. efforts to end colonialism remain a controversial topic at the world body, so much so that when the 43rd General Assembly declared the 1990s the International Decade for the Eradication of Colonialism [A/Res/43/47], the United States voted against and the other Western nations abstained. The United Nations considers as colonies only those territories the Assembly or other U.N. organs decide by vote are colonies. Thus Namibia was, until its independence, considered the last colony in Africa, while Eritrea was a nonissue and Western Sahara something in between. Puerto Rico is a territory deprived of the right to self-determination, according to a 9-to-2 vote of the Special Committee on Decolonization [GA/COL/2706, 8/17/89]. But Guadalupe, Tahiti, Lithuania, Latvia, Tibet, and a long list of clearly distinct regions seized by U.N. member states are not. It all comes down to whether a U.N. committee—from whatever political motives—decides to define or not define something as a colony.

Woe to the Secretary-General if he or his assistants even appear to be meddling in powerful member states' "internal" affairs regarding these noncolony colonies. In early 1990 the Soviet Union let it be known it did not look kindly upon meetings between James Jonah, the Assistant Secretary-General for the Collection of Research and Information, and several leaders of Baltic independence movements. Jonah's office was created to gather information about potential trouble spots where U.N. involvement might be necessary, so any contact with the Baltic states implied that here was a place where Soviet sovereignty was in doubt. The contacts ceased immediately after the protests from Moscow.

The official list identifies approximately 18 territories—located mainly in the Atlantic and Pacific oceans—that do not govern themselves (non-self-governing in U.N. jargon) affecting approximately 3 million people. While for years this problem slogged on with little progress, the U.S.-Soviet rapprochement and the general trend toward conflict resolution have again created significant hope that many of these problem areas will see progress by the end of the century.

The standout success of the year was **Namibia,** the largest decolonization exercise ever overseen by the world body. Under the tripartite agreement signed in New York in December 1988, South Africa, under U.S. pressure, would pull its troops out of the territory, while Cuba, under Soviet pressure, would withdraw its soldiers from neighboring Angola. Under Security Council Resolution 435 (1978), more than 4,600 U.N. troops would then oversee the disarming of SWAPO (South-West African People's Organization) guerrillas, while hundreds more U.N. officials would lay the groundwork for autumn elections to choose members of a constituent assembly that would draft a new Namibian constitution and prepare for independence in April 1990.

After a rocky start in April 1989, when SWAPO forces invaded from Angola and broke the cease-fire, calm was restored. The rest of the plan proceeded like clockwork. SWAPO won a commanding majority of seats in the November vote but less than the two-thirds majority needed for it to pass a constitution in the assembly unilaterally. The final constitution, adopted by consensus, bans the death penalty, guarantees basic human rights, and upholds a multiparty system [*U.N. Observer and International Report*, 3/90]. The constituent assembly elected SWAPO leader Sam Nujoma as the nation's first president shortly before independence was declared and the South African flag pulled down for the last time.

The success in Namibia means the process used there may serve as a precedent for U.N. decolonization actions in other regions. Most parties to the Cambodian conflict now agree that some sort of similar decolonization exercise and elections will be needed once a final settlement is reached.

The British-Argentine conflict over the **Falkland Islands (Malvinas)** also melted off the list of hot spots this year after an October 1989 accord between Argentina and Great Britain. Since the 1982 war, the General Assembly had overwhelmingly adopted resolutions urging the two countries to negotiate to solve the problem "in all its aspects," a move Britain opposed because it believes sovereignty is not up for discussion. The two nations moved to settle the conflict in August 1989 at talks held in New York. There the Argentine representative noted that hostilities had ceased and, along with Great Britain, pledged that his country would settle the dispute peacefully and never again resort to force [*The Economist*, 10/28/89]. At the October talks, Britain insisted that Argentina end restrictions on British companies in Argentina. Argentina agreed, anxious to resume cooperation agreements with the European Community. Britain, in turn, agreed to shrink the 150-mile military protection zone around the islands, from which it had barred Argentine ships, as well as the right of merchant vessels to sail freely in the zone [ibid.]. Finally, both countries agreed to resume full diplomatic relations, which they did in February 1990.

At the beginning of the year, progress seemed possible in the **Western Sahara**, the region seized by Morocco in 1975 and since colonized with hundreds of thousands of troops and settlers. In August 1988, Morocco's

King Hassan II recognized the existence of the guerrilla movement Frente Popular para la Liberación de Gaguia el-Hamra y de Rio de Oro (**Polisario**). The fighters represent the descendants of 200,000 nomads who do not recognize the King's right to rule their territory. Also that month the two sides approved the Secretary-General's peace plan for the region, under which elections would be held to allow Western Saharan residents to vote and choose independence or union with Morocco. A September 1988 unanimous Security Council resolution asked the world body to appoint a special representative to begin talks toward the vote.

On January 3, 1989, a three-member Polisario team flew to Marrakech to meet King Hassan. In February 1989 the King indefinitely postponed another meeting with the Polisario representatives. A June trip by Pérez de Cuéllar to the region failed to move the process along. Essentially the two sides could not agree who should vote in any referendum: only native Saharans or settlers moved in by Hassan. Polisario also wanted Moroccan troops removed from the territory, or otherwise confined to barracks, to ensure a free vote.

For the rest of 1989 and much of 1990 the situation remained stalemated. The rebels found themselves in a precarious position, isolated militarily and politically. The Moroccans, by constructing huge walls of sand, had isolated the Polisario from most of the disputed territory. And the rapprochement between Hassan and Algeria deprived the rebels of their chief ally. The peace process resumed, however, when on June 27 the **Security Council** unanimously approved a **peace plan** for the region and called on the two sides to end the fighting [S/Res/658]. The next day the Secretary-General announced that he would meet with representatives of Morocco and the Saharan guerrillas on July 5 in Geneva to extend indefinitely a temporary cease-fire agreed to in March.

The peace plan, first proposed by the Secretary-General in August 1988, calls for the creation of a special **Identification Commission** to determine who in the area will be eligible to vote for union with Morocco or independence. The plan notes that the approximately 100,000 Moroccan settlers in the disputed area will not take part. The Secretary-General will then set a date for a permanent cease-fire and will send **U.N. peacekeeping troops** to monitor the withdrawal of most of the 150,000 Moroccan troops in the area over a three-month period. The U.N. troops will supervise the remainder of the Moroccan troops and the approximately 8,000 armed Polisario. The Identification Commission is scheduled to complete voter registration a month later. Polisario guerrillas wanting to vote will be disarmed. The actual vote is expected to take place six weeks later.

The Assembly passed several other resolutions on small territories. On **New Caledonia**, a resolution noted the "positive measures being pursued in New Caledonia by the French authorities" to help develop the Pacific territory so it may comfortably choose self-determination or continued union with France in 1998. The Matignon Agreement, adopted by France and New Caledonian factions in August 1988, commits France to that time schedule [A/AC.109/100].

On **Tokelau**, administered by New Zealand, the Assembly noted progress in the preparation of a legal code to conform with the traditional laws and cultural values of the Tokelau people [A/Res/44/90]. It urged New Zealand to continue to respect fully the wishes of the people of Tokelau and to preserve their heritage.

Resolutions on the **Cayman Islands, Bermuda**, the **Turks and Caicos Islands, Anguilla, Montserrat**, and the **British Virgin Islands**—all administered by the United Kingdom—raised several issues, such as illegal operation of foreign fisherman off the Virgin Islands, drug trafficking in the Caribbean, and the need for development. All the resolutions stated that these regions have a "right to self-determination and independence" and called on Great Britain to ensure that their peoples will be able to "exercise this right."

Similar resolutions were passed on **American Samoa, Guam**, and the **U.S. Virgin Islands**, all belonging to the United States. In several political referendums on Guam, just short of half the island's residents have voted for commonwealth status with the United States. The U.S. Congress must approve a draft commonwealth act for the territory, but problems arose when an August 1989 congressional report concluded that provisions of the act are unconstitutional because they recognize only the right to self-determination of the Chamorro people, grant certain rights to native Guamians, and grant Guam control over immigration [A/AC.109/1017]. The Assembly resolution noted that Guam must be granted self-determination regardless of its importance as a U.S. military base.

On **Gibraltar**, a consensus resolution noted that British and Spanish foreign ministers have met annually and urged them to continue these talks to reach a "definitive solution to the problem of Gibraltar." A consensus on **Pitcairn**—the rocky Pacific outcrop peopled by the mutineers from the famous HMS *Bounty*—urged Britain to "respect the very individual life-style that the people of the Territory have chosen" and "promote the economic and social development of the Territory."

A resolution on **Mayotte** [A/Res/44/9] urged France to accelerate negotiations with the Islamic Republic of the Comoros with the aim of turning the territory over to it.

East Timor has been a source of contention since Indonesia annexed the Portuguese colony in 1976. The problem is all the more disturbing because Indonesian forces have been said to carry out vast human rights abuses against natives, allowing at least 100,000 to die from disease, malnutrition, and war. The United Nations still regards Portugal as the administering power. On May 9, 1989, Indonesia and Portugal agreed to resume talks under U.N. auspices to establish the terms of reference, the timing, and "other indispensable aspects" of a visit by a Portuguese parliamentary delegation to the territory. Little progress has been made since then.

The strategic **Trust Territory of the Pacific Islands**—made up of the Federated States of Micronesia, the Marshall Islands, the Northern Mariana Islands, and Palau—is overseen by the **Trusteeship Council** on behalf of the Security Council. Each year the Committee on Decolonization examines the question, although the United States maintains that under Article 83 of the Charter, only the Trusteeship Council and Security Council have jurisdiction.

In 1986 the Trusteeship Council recommended that the United States as the administering authority had discharged its obligations under the Trusteeship Agreement and that it was appropriate for the Trusteeship Agreement to be terminated on the entry into force of the Compacts of Free Association for the Marshall Islands, Palau, and Micronesia and the Commonwealth Covenant for the Northern Mariana Islands. In the same year the Council noted that the people of the four regions had freely exercised their rights to self-determination in plebiscites, choosing either free association or commonwealth status, as is the case with the Northern Mariana Islands [A/AC.109/998].

The agreements have come into effect everywhere except Palau, where the draft compact would allow the United States to place nuclear weapons on the territory, in violation of the Palauan constitution. Several referendums have failed to garner the 75 percent majority needed to alter the constitution in favor of the terms of the compact. The most recent referendum in February 1990 yielded 60.2 percent in favor.

Under Article 83 of the U.N. Charter, termination of the Trusteeship Agreement would have to be approved by the Security Council. A problem may arise if the Soviet Union attempts to block final resolution of the territories' status over concern about U.S. military usage of the region.

II
Arms Control and Disarmament

Since the 44th General Assembly, a continuing revolution in East-West relations has transformed ongoing arms control and disarmament efforts at the strategic and European theater levels, shaped the course of negotiations over chemical weapons, and eclipsed other multilateral arms control efforts. At their June 1990 summit meeting, Soviet President Mikhail Gorbachev and U.S. President George Bush agreed on a format for the **Strategic Arms Reduction Treaty** (**START**) and declared their intention to complete the treaty by the end of the year. They agreed on verification measures for the **Threshold Test Ban Treaty** (**TTBT**) and the **Peaceful Nuclear Explosions Treaty** (**PNET**), agreed on bilateral **Chemical Weapons** (**CW**) limitations in the hopes of spurring action on a multilateral treaty, and stated their agreement to speed negotiations in Vienna so that an agreement could be signed limiting **Conventional Forces in Europe** (CFE) later in 1990.

At a meeting in Moscow in June, following the summit, Warsaw Treaty Organization (WTO) members declared that they no longer considered the Western alliance to be an "ideological enemy," and that "[m]odern development in Europe creates conditions for overcoming a bloc security model and the division of the Continent" [*The New York Times*, 6/8/90]. In turn, North Atlantic Treaty Organization (NATO) foreign ministers meeting in Scotland began publicly to discuss the transformation of NATO into a more political, less military grouping, given the disappearance of East-West confrontation [*The New York Times*, 6/8/90].

Upheaval in the East-West structure of military confrontation overshadowed important developments in other parts of the world. Tensions rose between India and Pakistan over the Kashmir issue and were exacerbated by development of potentially significant nuclear weapons capabilities on both sides. In the Middle East the spread and further development of chemical weapons and missile delivery systems heightened threats of carnage in that region and demonstrated that countries could respond to nuclear weapons development by building alternative weapons of mass destruction for deterrence. Nuclear, chemical, and weapons delivery technologies were actively transferred internationally despite various efforts to limit their proliferation, giving credence to commentators' warnings that

East-West détente might result in increasing levels of armaments flowing to Third World states.

Following the 44th General Assembly, multilateral and bilateral negotiations over chemical weapons continued fruitfully at the technical level, but bedrock concerns about verification and weapons stockpile destruction threatened to thwart final achievement of meaningful agreements. U.S. and Soviet positions converged toward bilateral agreement, but the United States held that it would not destroy all its chemical weapons stocks until a multilateral regime was in place. Progress toward that regime in the **Disarmament Commission** was made on technical issues, but movement toward completion of a CW treaty has been sluggish. A call for renewed vigor is likely to be issued by the 45th General Assembly.

Parties to the **Treaty Banning Nuclear Weapon Tests in the Atmosphere, in Outer Space and under Water** (or Partial Test-Ban Treaty, **PTBT**) pressed the depositary states to convene a conference on its amendment to upgrade it to a **Comprehensive Test Ban (CTB)**. The nuclear weapon states viewed the conference as of secondary importance to the **Fourth Review Conference of the Parties to the Treaty on the Non-proliferation of Nuclear Weapons** to be held in August-September. The U.S. remained opposed to negotiation of a **CTB** in the **PTBT** context and declared its intention to continue nuclear testing.

The supersession of the Cold War by mutual East-West interests in global conflict resolution by nonmilitary means transformed both the European and Third World security environment during 1989–1990. Arms control arrangements appear to add to the irreversibility of the changes, although some groups within the two societies remain skeptical of the long-term prospects for cooperation in the security field. Third World states have responded cautiously to the rapprochement: Some fear a new age of major-power "condominium," while others are pressing for more rapid dismantling of the two sides' military structures and the channelling of resources thus freed to global economic development and other constructive purposes. At the 45th General Assembly both tendencies should be in evidence, as the major powers are congratulated for accomplishments already attained and urged to quicken the pace.

1. Nuclear Arms Control and Disarmament

During their summit meeting in June, Presidents Bush and Gorbachev declared their intention to sign a **Strategic Arms Reduction Treaty** by the end of 1990. Concessions made by both sides over the preceding year were written into an agreement on the outlines of the planned treaty. During 1989–1990, the two sides moved toward the overall agreement by making concessions that limited cuts in certain weapons categories valued by one or the other side.

Progress toward the agreement picked up speed in the summer and fall of 1989. Just before meeting, Soviet Foreign Minister Eduard A. Shevardnadze and U.S. Secretary of State James A. Baker III announced that the United States would abandon its demand that long-range mobile land-based ballistic missiles (which the Soviets sought to preserve) be banned [*The Economist*, 9/23/89]. At the September 22–23 meeting, Shevardnadze dropped the Soviet demand that space weapons and sea-launched cruise missiles had to be dealt with in START negotiations. In addition, in a letter, Soviet President Mikhail Gorbachev indicated that he would order dismantling of the **Krasnoyarsk radar system**, which the United States contends violates the **Anti-Ballistic Missile (ABM) Treaty** [*The New York Times*, 9/23/89].

At the Malta Summit in December 1989, Presidents Bush and Gorbachev agreed to meet again in early June for a summit at which a strategic arms treaty could be resolved in principle, enabling signature of the treaty by the end of 1990. Progress continued during the winter and spring as the two sides reached agreements on counting rules for air-launched cruise missiles, telemetry encryption, and counting rules for "nondeployed" missiles [*The New York Times*, 2/11/90]. At the June summit the two sides publicly agreed on the treaty's framework. Because of the compromises reached on counting rules, cuts in numbers of warheads will be much smaller than the originally proposed 30 to 50 percent, prompting the two sides to begin discussing a START II process [*The Christian Science Monitor*, 3/16/90]. The U.S. will reduce its strategic nuclear warhead inventory from approximately 12,000 to 9,500. The Soviet Union will reduce from just over 11,000 to about 7,000. Agreed counting rules will mean less of a reduction in bomber-based warheads than originally envisioned, and sea-launched cruise missiles (SLCM), which the Soviets sought to limit, will not be constrained by the treaty at all. Instead, the two will issue an annual, politically binding declaration of their SLCM policies. The treaty is to remain in force for 15 years or until superseded. It will allow modernization of weapons within the numerical limits [*The Economist*, 6/9/90].

Just before the 44th Session, the **Review Conference of the Parties to the Treaty on the Prohibition of the Emplacement of Nuclear Weapons and Other Weapons of Mass Destruction on the Sea-Bed and the Ocean Floor and in the Subsoil Thereof** took place in Geneva. The 44th Session welcomed the positive assessment of the treaty in the review conference as indicated by its final declaration [SBT/CONF.III/15], called for further accessions to the treaty, and proposed that the matter be reconsidered at the 47th Session [A/Res/44/116O].

The 44th General Assembly placed prevention of an arms race in outer space on the agenda for the 45th Session [A/Res/44/112]; encouraged and supported bilateral U.S.-Soviet nuclear arms negotiations [A/Res/44/116B]; and called on the United States and Soviet Union to take the lead in halting the nuclear arms race and to accelerate negotiations toward nuclear arms reductions, placing these item too on the 45th Session's agenda [A/Res/44/116D]. It further urged the United States and Soviet Union to seek a 50 percent reduction in strategic offensive arms, a comprehensive nuclear test ban, and an agreement on keeping outer space free of nuclear weapons, and it invited them to keep the General Assembly and Conference on Disarmament informed of their progress [A/Res/44/116K].

In review of the concluding document of the **Twelfth Special Session of the General Assembly**, the 44th Session reiterated its request to the **Conference on Disarmament** (CD) to negotiate toward an international convention prohibiting the use or threat of use of nuclear weapons and requested that the CD report to the 45th Session on the results of the negotiations [A/Res/44/117C]. The General Assembly called on the nuclear weapon states, led by the United States and Soviet Union, to agree to a comprehensive nuclear arms freeze, and placed the item on the agenda for the 45th Session [A/Res/44/117D].

In review of the recommendations of the **Tenth Special Session**, the 44th Session noted the importance of the declarations made by two nuclear weapons states, the Soviet Union and the People's Republic of China, that they would not use nuclear weapons first; expressed the hope that other nuclear weapon states would issue the same assurance; asked the Conference on Disarmament to negotiate toward a binding instrument obligating states not to be the first to use nuclear weapons; and put the item on the agenda for the 45th Session [A/Res/44/119B]. It requested the Conference on Disarmament to set up ad hoc committees in 1990 on the cessation of the nuclear arms race and on nuclear disarmament and prevention of nuclear war to analyze how the CD can best progress on these matters and to report to the 45th Session [A/Res/44/119E].

2. European Security

Events in Eastern Europe developed so rapidly in 1989–1990 that ongoing negotiations in the CFE talks repeatedly seemed obsolete. Responding to the changes, President Bush, in his January 31 State of the Union message, called for U.S. and Soviet troop levels to be reduced to 195,000 each in the central zone (in September, Bush had called for a 275,000 limit). When Secretary of State Baker met with President Gorbachev and Foreign Minister Shevardnadze in Moscow on February 10, agreement was reached on the 195,000 limits, with a further allocation of 30,000 U.S. troops in other North Atlantic Treaty Organization (NATO) areas. This marked the first time that the Soviets accepted asymmetrical force reductions in Europe and also the first time they acknowledged a U.S. claim that due to the distance from home bases, U.S. troop levels should be permitted to exceed the central zone limits. Counting rules for and definitions of aircraft in the European theater remained the most difficult issue [Ted Greenwood, "CFE-Taking Aim at Aircraft," *Arms Control Today* 20, no. 2 (3/90): 13–18].

At NATO–Warsaw Treaty Organization (WTO) ministerial meetings February 12–13 in Ottawa, the Soviets formally agreed to the 195,000/30,000 troop limit proposal. NATO and WTO ministers agreed to pursue the **"Open skies" approach to mutual verification and surveillance** previously proposed by President Bush. During the two weeks of the Ottawa conference, Soviet and U.S. views of the open skies proposals clearly remained quite different, with disagreements over permissible sensor types, aircraft basing and provision, intelligence sharing, and limits on numbers of flights. Soviet proposals to add an open seas and open space proposal to the open skies concept were rejected by the United States [see *Arms Control Today* 20, no. 2, (3/90): 20].

Impending German unification created uncertainties for the CFE negotiations, the primary issue being whether the new Germany would be part of NATO, neutral, or somehow part of both NATO and WTO. As 1990 progressed, it became increasingly apparent that the neutrality and dual-membership options were very unlikely. At Ottawa agreement was reached to proceed with the "two plus four" negotiations over Germany (the two being East and West Germany and the four being the four occupying powers of World War II—France, Great Britain, the United States, and the Soviet Union). Long-range issues brought up at the Ottawa ministerial conference included a proposal especially favored by the West Germans to convert the **Conference on Security and Cooperation in Europe** (CSCE) into an institutionalized body for dealing with all-European security issues, eventually to replace NATO and the WTO [*The Christian Science Monitor*, 3/14/90]. At the sixth round of the CFE discussions in March and April, foreign ministers of West Germany, Italy, and France supported creation of successor CFE II talks in which the force balance in all of Europe could be addressed. The Soviets proposed that overall limits on the two sides' troop levels be set somewhere in the 700,000–750,000 range, with individual country limits as well. NATO initially rejected the proposal, but discussions on the idea of overall and country limits will continue.

The declaration of the London NATO summit meeting of July 6–7 indicated fundamental transformation of the Alliance's defense and political stance. It stated that "NATO will prepare a new Allied military strategy moving away from 'forward defense,' . . . towards a reduced forward presence and modifying 'flexible response' to reflect a reduced reliance on nuclear weapons." It proposed a NATO-WTO nonaggression agreement and a series of measures to strengthen and institutionalize CSCE, and it endorsed the idea of a CFE II negotiation immediately to follow agreement on CFE I. The NATO heads of state invited WTO leaders to address future NATO meetings. Immediately following the summit, NATO Secretary-General Manfred Werner delivered the invitation and discussed the new NATO policy in Moscow [*The New York Times*, 7/7/90, 7/8/90].

The NATO summit paved the way for consultations in Moscow, July 17–18, during which the Soviets assented to membership in NATO of a united Germany. West German Chancellor Helmut Kohl agreed with Soviet President Gorbachev on a framework for the transition from current Soviet troop deployments in East Germany to a limited deployment of German troops on the eastern front. This cleared one major international political obstacle to German unification.

During a one-day meeting of the "two plus four" group and representatives of Poland on July 17, the second major obstacle was overcome when East and West Germany promised that upon their unification, Germany would sign a treaty guaranteeing the postwar German-Polish frontier at the Oder-Neisse line. The agreement was to be submitted for approval to the CSCE meeting scheduled to begin in Paris on November 19 [ibid., 7/18/90].

As the unification of Germany became a certainty, the United States softened its position with regard to its development and deployment of the short-range Lance II missile, which had been intended for West Germany, targeted on the East. In early May the U.S. announced its readiness to negotiate reductions of short-range nuclear systems in Europe, including missiles and artillery. Such negotiations were originally proposed by the Soviets and supported by some NATO members following agreement on the **Treaty between the United States and the Union of Soviet Socialist Republics on the Elimination of Their Intermediate-Range and Shorter-Range Missiles (INF treaty)** [see *Issues Before the 44th Session of the General Assembly*, p. 60]. However, the U.S. was not willing to proceed with negotiations until further progress was made with a CFE treaty.

No matters specifically referring to Europe are on the agenda for the 45th General Assembly, although progress in the CFE talks will likely be cited once again in the report of the Conference on Disarmament.

3. Chemical Weapons

Momentum toward completion of a multilateral chemical weapons (CW) treaty slowed during the year. The Conference on Disarmament continued work in its 1989 and 1990 sessions elaborating its draft CW treaty. Its report to the 44th General Assembly included draft provisions amounting to over 230 pages, and the 1990 session's report will be considered at the 45th General Assembly. Difficult problems of timing and verification remain. Progress slowed because the major technical questions being largely resolved, the political-military issues remain to be dealt with. President Bush announced that the United States would no longer maintain the right to produce binary chemical weapons after completion of the multilateral convention, if the Soviets agree to bilateral measures of control. However, the United States also announced that it would keep 2 percent of its chemical weapons arsenal until all CW-capable countries signed the multilateral agreement. Soviet disclosures of CW stocks (at 50,000 tons) appeared to converge with U.S. intelligence estimates, increasing trust between the two sides.

At the June summit meeting, the U.S. and Soviet Union agreed to destroy chemical weapons stocks in excess of 5,000 tons of chemical agents by the year 2002, beginning in 1992 or as soon thereafter as permitted by safety and environmental considerations. The agreement set an interim goal of destroying 50 percent of CW stockpiles by the end of 1999 and announced the two sides' intentions to cease production of chemical weapons when the accord goes into effect. They further declared that they would reach agreement on verification methods by the end of 1990 and that they would take measures to encourage conclusion of a global CW ban [*The New York Times*, 6/2/90].

In the spring of 1990 reports indicated that the Libyan chemical plant at Rabta had resumed production of CW agents. Court proceedings in Germany resulted in admissions that the suppliers of the plant knew that it would be used for production of CW agents and that their exports were in violation of German law. A fire at the Rabta plant was at first thought to have destroyed its production capabilities but was later viewed by intelligence sources as a hoax [*The New York Times*, 6/19/90]. In April, Iraq's President Saddam Hussein announced that his country had acquired CW capabilities, and he declared that Iraq would use CW against Israel in retaliation against aggression [*The New York Times*, 4/4/90].

The 44th General Assembly urged the CD on in the chemical weapons negotiations; called for the reestablishment of its ad hoc CW committee [A/Res/44/115A]; renewed its call for states to observe the 1925 Geneva **Protocol for the Prohibition of Use in War of Asphyxiating, Poisonous or**

Other Gases and of Bacteriological Methods of Warfare; called for further accessions to it; asked the Secretary-General to investigate any reports on CW use; and placed the issue of chemical and bacteriological weapons on the agenda of the 45th Session [A/Res/44/115B]. It further called upon states party to the **Convention on the Prohibition of the Development, Production, and Stocking of Bacteriological (Biological) and Toxin Weapons and on their Destruction** to share information annually as called for in the declaration of the Second Review Conference of the Parties to the Convention, and called for the Third Review Conference on the Convention to be held in 1991 [A/Res/44/115C].

4. Nuclear Nonproliferation and Nuclear Weapon–Free Zones

During 1989–1990, preparations continued for the **Fourth Review Conference of the Parties to the Treaty on the Non-proliferation of Nuclear Weapons,** which will take place in Geneva August 20–September 14, 1990. The second meeting of the Preparatory Committee adopted the agenda of the Third Review Conference as the agenda for the Fourth. The 45th General Assembly will likely receive a report or final document from the conference under a standing agenda item created by the **10th Special Session on Disarmament** to review the status of multilateral disarmament agreements [A/Res/36/92H].

The 44th General Assembly reiterated previous condemnations of Israel's refusal to renounce possession of nuclear weapons and of its cooperation with South Africa. It demanded that Israel subject its nuclear facilities to International Atomic Energy Agency (IAEA) safeguards, and called for states to terminate nuclear cooperation with, and assistance to, Israel, placing the issue on the agenda for the 45th Session [A/Res/44/121]. It once again called for the establishment of a **nuclear weapon–free zone in the Middle East.** The 45th Session will review the report of an expert group on the conditions needed to facilitate consideration of a nuclear weapon-free zone in the Middle East [A/Res/44/108].

Concern over nuclear proliferation in the Middle East increased during the year with reports of attempted purchase of nuclear weapons trigger components by Iraq and the general spread of ballistic missile systems to states not before having the capabilities [*Newsweek*, 4/9/90; Janne Nolan, "Ballistic Missiles in the Third World," *Arms Control Today* 19, no. 9 (11/89): 9–14].

Press reports indicated once again that **South Africa** was close to signing the **Treaty on the Non-proliferation of Nuclear Weapons,** following discussions with the three depositary governments (United Kingdom, United States, and Soviet Union) [*The New York Times*, 3/21/90]. The 44th General

Assembly received a report from the Secretary-General on South Africa's nuclear capabilities [A/Res/44/655] in conjunction with its call for establishment of a **nuclear weapon–free zone in Africa** [A/Res/44/113A]. The General Assembly condemned South Africa's military and nuclear buildup and collaboration with South Africa by other countries, particularly noting cooperation with Israel; requested that the Secretary-General again report on South African nuclear capabilities to the Disarmament Commission and to the 45th General Assembly; and demanded that South Africa submit all its nuclear installations to inspection by the IAEA [A/Res/44/113B].

The 44th General Assembly reiterated previous sessions' calls for France to sign **Protocol I of the Treaty for the Prohibition of Nuclear Weapons in Latin America** and placed the issue on the agenda for the 45th Session [A/Res/44/104]. It reiterated prior calls for establishment of an **Indian Ocean Zone of Peace**, a move still opposed by the major maritime powers of the area—France, Japan, the United Kingdom, and the United States. It continued to seek the convening of a conference in Colombo, Sri Lanka, on the zone of peace and renewed the mandate of the ad hoc committee established to meet during 1990 to prepare for such a conference in 1991 [A/Res/44/120].

Unlike General Assembly resolutions regarding nuclear weapon–free zones and denuclearization in the Middle East and African regions, the General Assembly mentioned no countries by name in its resolution calling for a nuclear-free zone in South Asia [A/Res/44/109], Pakistan's and India's apparent nuclear arms race notwithstanding.

The 44th General Assembly urged the Conference on Disarmament to pursue negotiations to strengthen the security of nonnuclear weapons states against the use, or threat of use, of nuclear weapons and to assure them against such use or threat, placing these "security assurances" on the agenda once again for the 45th Session [A/Res/44/110, 111].

5. Nuclear Testing

Bilateral U.S.-Soviet negotiations and verification experiments continued for nuclear weapons test monitoring pursuant to the unratified, but still observed, U.S.-Soviet **Threshold Test-Ban Treaty** (TTBT) of 1974 and for the **Peaceful Nuclear Explosions Treaty** (PNET) of 1976. At the U.S.-Soviet summit in June 1990, an accord on verification measures for the two treaties was signed by Presidents Bush and Gorbachev [*The New York Times*, 6/2/90]. With completion of the verification protocols, the U.S. administration declared its intention to submit the treaties for Senate ratification, although the schedule for doing so remained unclear.

Calls for amendment of the **Partial Test-Ban Treaty** by more than a third of the treaty's signatories to convert it into a Comprehensive Test Ban

(CTB) [see *Issues Before the 44th Session of the General Assembly*, pp. 66–67] resulted in discussions at the 44th Session regarding the timing of an amendment conference. After extended debate, the General Assembly resolved that a preparatory meeting for the conference should be held at U.N. headquarters in May–June 1990, followed immediately by an initial substantive meeting, with another substantive meeting in January 1991.

Two of the depositary states, the United Kingdom and United States, opposed the resolution [A/Res/44/106], seeking to postpone the conference until after the **Review Conference of the Parties to the NPT** in August–September 1990. The depositaries, including the Soviet Union, announced in December that the conference would be held in January 1991, initiating a dispute with the supporters of the General Assembly resolution. At the preparatory meeting held May 29–June 8, 1990, agreement was reached on the agenda, speakers list, and cost-sharing for the Conference.

The 44th Session urged discontinuance of nuclear testing, recommended that the Conference on Disarmament set up an ad hoc committee to work on a CTB, and placed the issue on the agenda for the 45th Session. It also placed on the agenda discussion of the PTBT amendment issue [A/Res/44/106] and reiterated the urgent need for a CTB [A/Res/44/107].

6. Special Sessions on Disarmament

Under agenda items calling for review of the concluding documents of the **Twelfth and Tenth Special Sessions on Disarmament**, the 44th Session reiterated a series of general calls for international progress in arms control, disarmament, and peace and security and made recommendations to streamline the Conference on Disarmament.

In a review of measures initiated in the Twelfth Special Session, in addition to those already mentioned, the 44th Session endorsed the Secretary-General's efforts on behalf of the **World Disarmament Campaign**, calling for a pledging conference to raise money for the campaign at the 45th Session, and placed the issue on the agenda of the session; encouraged states to seek regional implementation of arms reduction and disarmament efforts and requested the Secretary-General to formulate a report on such actions and present it for consideration on the agenda of the 46th Session [A/Res/44/117B]; noted that the program of **United Nations Disarmament Fellowship, Training and Advisory Services** had already trained an appreciable number of public officials, commended the Secretary-General for the diligence with which the program was carried out, and asked that it be continued and put on the agenda of the 45th Session [A/Res/44/117E]; sought support for **United Nations Regional Centres for Peace and Disarmament in Africa and Asia** and the **U.N. Regional Centre for Peace, Disarmament and Development in**

Latin America and the Caribbean; and asked the Secretary-General to report to the 45th Session on the implementation of the resolution [A/Res/44/117F].

In addition to matters already mentioned regarding the Tenth Special Session, the 44th Session called upon the Conference on Disarmament to consider at its 1991 session resumption of efforts to develop a **Comprehensive Programme of Disarmament** and to place the matter on the agenda of the 46th Session of the General Assembly [A/Res/44/119A]. It noted the importance of the declarations made or reiterated by the Soviet Union and the Peoples' Republic of China at the Twelfth Special Session not to use nuclear weapons first, hoped that other nuclear weapon states would consider making **no-first-use** declarations, requested the Conference on Disarmament to start negotiating an international instrument on the obligation not to be the first to use nuclear weapons, and included an item on "non-use of nuclear weapons and prevention of nuclear war" on the agenda of the 45th Session [A/Res/44/119B]. It also placed items on the agenda of the 45th Session concerning the advisory board on disarmament studies [A/Res/38/183O], the United Nations Institute for Disarmament Research [A/Res/39/148H], a review of the implementation of the 1980s Second Disarmament Decade [A/Res/40/152L], and implementation of the guidelines for confidence-building measures [A/Res/43/78H].

The 44th Session reviewed, reaffirmed, and renewed the mandate of the Disarmament Commission, noting consultations on ways to improve its functioning, and attached an annex to the resolution [A/Res/44/119C] entitled **Ways and Means to Enhance the Functioning of the Disarmament Commission**. The annex proposed that the working agenda focus on a maximum of four substantive items and be retained on the agenda for not more than three consecutive years. For items on which no agreement was reached, the commission should report a summary of the proceedings reflecting different views. It recommended that not more than four subsidiary bodies of the commission be established at one time. Meetings should not exceed four weeks but could be shorter. Plenaries should be limited to three days, and except on new items, general exchanges of views should be limited. The chair of the Disarmament Commission should continue consultations year round.

The 44th Session expressed regret that the Conference on Disarmament was unable to establish ad hoc committees or to commence negotiations on the nuclear issues on its agenda in 1989 and hoped that recent progress in disarmament would enable it to move forward. It noted progress in the draft convention on chemical weapons and urged intensification and completion of the negotiations as soon as possible, asking for a report to the 45th Session [A/Res/44/119D]. The 44th Session noted progress in signature and ratification of the **South Pacific Nuclear Free Zone Treaty** (Treaty of Rarotonga) [A/Res/44/119F]; endorsed the Disarmament Week activities of governments, nongovernmental organizations, and the United Nations; requested the Secretary-General to report on implementation of the resolution at the 47th Session [A/Res/44/119G]; and placed on the agenda of the 45th Session an item on **Declaration of the 1990s as the Third Disarmament Decade** [A/Res/44/119H].

7. General and Complete Disarmament

A list of 21 items was considered under the 44th Session's deliberations on **General and Complete Disarmament.** Ten resolutions were adopted without vote and 11 with two or fewer negative votes. The 44th Session asked the Secretary-General to report to the 45th Session on the **prohibition of the development, production, stockpiling, and use of radiological weapons,** noting that attacks against nuclear facilities were tantamount to the use of radiological weapons. It requested that the Conference on Disarmament intensify efforts to reach an agreement prohibiting such attacks [A/Res/44/116A] and to pursue work on cessation and prohibition of the production of fissionable materials for weapons [A/Res/44/116H], prohibition of the dumping of radioactive wastes, and prohibition of development, production, stockpiling, and use of radiological weapons. It placed waste dumping and radiological weapons issues on the 45th Session's agenda [A/Res/44/116R,T].

The 44th Session welcomed the progress in CFE efforts, urging further negotiations on conventional disarmament, and placed the issue on the agenda for the 45th Session [A/Res/44/116C]. It sought implementation of an international system of reporting military expenditure, inviting states to communicate to the Secretary-General the measures adopted toward this end; requested the Disarmament Commission to take up the issue in 1990 and to consider conventional disarmament, naval armaments and disarmament, international arms transfers, and the role of the United Nations in the field of disarmament; and included these issues on the agenda of the 45th Session [A/Res/44/116D,F,M,N,Q]. It urged progress in implementing prior General Assembly calls for conventional disarmament [A/Res/44/116G], expressed satisfaction with and urged continued progress in the **confidence- and security-building measures and conventional disarmament in Europe,** and welcomed and urged similar progress in such matters in other areas of the world [A/Res/44/116 I,U].

The 44th Session invited states to report their views to the Secretary-General on the topic of **conversion of military resources to civilian purposes,** placing it on the agenda of the 46th Session [A/Res/44/116J]. It asked the Secretary-General to report to the 45th Session on measures taken in accordance with the final document of the **International Conference on the Relationship between Disarmament and Development** and placed the issue on the agenda for the 45th Session [A/Res/44/116L]. The Session invited states to intensify their dialogue on defensive security concepts and politics, including it on the agenda for the 45th Session [A/Res/44/116P]. It included in the 45th Session's agenda an item on conventional disarmament on a regional scale [A/Res/44/116S]. The 45th Session will also consider matters regarding notification of nuclear tests [A/Res/42/38C] and the comprehensive U.N. study on nuclear weapons [A/Res/43/75N].

8. Other Issues

The 43d Session included in the agenda of the 45th a general item on special sessions on disarmament [A/Res/43/77A] and a discussion of verification in all its aspects [A/Res/43/81].

The 44th Session urged states to comply fully with arms limitation and disarmament agreements and to resolve questions of noncompliance, noted the utility of verification experiments, and included in the provisional agenda for the 46th Session an item on such compliance [A/Res/44/122]. It invited states and organizations to inform the Secretary-General about efforts taken in the area of disarmament education and put an item on this issue on the agenda for the 45th Session [A/Res/44/123]. An agenda item was included for the 45th Session on security and cooperation in the Mediterranean region [A/Res/44/125]. The 44th Session reaffirmed, and placed on the agenda for the next session a series of statements in support of the **Declaration on the Strengthening of International Security** [A/Res/44/126].

No action was taken on the Convention on Prohibitions or Restrictions on the Use of Certain Conventional Weapons which May be Deemed to be Excessively Injurious or to Have Indiscriminate Effects, but the 44th Session noted the receipt of a report from the First Committee and placed the item on the agenda of the 45th Session [A/Res/44/430].

III
Global Resource Management

1. Food and Agriculture

Neither the 44th General Assembly nor the year since witnessed much attention to or progress in the world food situation. The dramatic political changes in Eastern and Central Europe took center stage, especially for the leaders of industrialized world, and crowded out other questions.

The 45th General Assembly, however, should see more action. The report of the **World Food Council (WFC)**, the highest policy body at the United Nations in this area, will be on the agenda, via the Economic and Social Council (ECOSOC), and the specter of hunger continues to haunt sub-Saharan Africa and those regions of the world that contain sizable numbers of refugees, now approaching 15 million [*FAO Food Outlook*, no. 3, 1990].

The Second Committee's December 20, 1988, report to the General Assembly [A/43/915/Add. 3], adopted on that date, described global food security in terms that could be repeated today, changing only the year: "Despite some slight improvements in 1987, the economies of developing countries continue to suffer from depressed international commodity prices, protectionism and worsening terms of trade, growing debt service burden and net outflow of financial resources from developing countries as a whole."

This sober assessment is borne out once again by the World Food Council's report on the work of its fifteenth session [Suppl. No. 19: A/44/19]. The report, which is introduced by "The Cairo Declaration" (venue of the meeting), is unusually blunt: "Our discussions," the ministers said, "were not free of some frustration and impatience with an international community that has not yet succeeded in turning its energies sufficiently towards a problem that morally must be solved and practically can be solved. . . . Hunger continues to grow, because we have not tried hard enough to eradicate it, even though we have the resources to do so." The declaration continues:

> The tragedy of hunger has many faces: the starvation caused by famine, often associated with violent conflict or war, and natural disasters; the silent suffering of the growing number of undernourished; the millions of malnourished children, women and elderly who are unable to meet their special food and health needs; and the many lives lost to or ruined by disorders caused by deficiencies of micro-nutrients, such as vitamin A and iodine. Hunger is concentrated in the rural areas of Asia, Africa and Latin America and the Caribbean. However, it exists everywhere, including in the more advanced countries of the developing world and in many developed countries. While different forms of hunger have specific causes requiring appropriate responses, they are generally rooted in poverty and a failure to share food and wealth adequately within and between countries.

This description, now a year old, is distressingly familiar and still accurate. After four regional meetings—in Costa Rica, for Latin America and the Caribbean [WFC/1990/3/Add.1]; in Cairo, for Africa and western Asia [WFC/1990/3/Add.2]; in Bangkok, for the Asia region [WFC/1990/3/Add.3]; and in Paris, for Western Europe and other countries [WFC/1990/3/Add.4]—the World Food Council, in its basic agenda document for the Sixteenth Ministerial Session, in Bangkok, May 21–24, 1990, concluded that "there is no reason to assume that the rate of growth in the number of hungry people has declined significantly [since 1980]" [WFC/1990/2, para. 17]. The council estimates the current total at about 550 million, the most conservative estimate available. "More Africans, Latin Americans and West Asians ended the decade [of the 1980s] suffering from poverty and hunger than began it [ibid., para. 34].

The **Food and Agriculture Organization (FAO)**, the major U.N. operating agency in this sector, reported in its "Assessment of the Current World Food Security Situation and Outlook," a document prepared for the Committee on World Food Security [CFS: 90/2, January 1990], that it expected world production of staple foods to be below utilization for the third straight year. This would hold world food stocks at the minimum (17 percent of consumption) the FAO considers necessary to avoid widespread starvation. FAO's March forecast [*Food Outlook*, no. 3, 1990] is for a very tentative 4 percent increase in cereal production for 1990, which would permit an increase of 2 percent in utilization, but consumption in the poorer countries may decline further. Most of the countries experiencing famine, as well as unfavorable prospects for current crops, are those where there is civil strife: Ethiopia, Sudan, Afghanistan, Angola, and Mozambique. Both the FAO and the World Food Council consider that the outlook for world food security is "critically dependent on the outcome of 1990 crops" [WFC/1990/7]. Actually that is true every year.

At the Bangkok session, the World Food Council's ministers unanimously agreed to work together toward their common objective with an increased sense of urgency in order to ensure that the opportunities presented by the new decade will not be lost. Important developments such as efforts towards disarmament, efforts directed at political reconciliation in the two German states and the two Yemen states, and the momentous changes in Eastern Europe were cited as among those important opportunities.

In reviewing the progress made in the implementation of the Cairo Declaration, the WFC meeting revealed a growing convergence among countries in the perceptions of more human-centered development priorities. The discussions highlighted the following issues: raising food production by extending the potential of the "green revolution" to more developing countries; increasing access to food supplies to boost nutritional status among vulnerable groups, particularly women, whose importance to the development process deserved greater recognition; a more open and fair world trading system for agricultural products to boost the foreign exchange earning capacity of developing countries; and increased and better coordinated aid flows to developing countries.

The major operational response to hunger by the international community has been food aid; the **World Food Programme** represents the U.N. share of this cooperative activity. The FAO estimates that total food aid (including bilateral) will reach 11.6 million tons in the upcoming year, an increase from 10 million tons in the previous year. This increase is almost entirely accounted for by the 2.3 million tons to be allocated to Poland and Romania, though early estimates for the 1990 crops in those countries are favorable. Shipments to low-income food-deficit countries will remain near 8.5 million tons, roughly the same as the previous year and well below the quantities shipped in 1987–1988. Actual commitments to the World Food Programme by the end of 1989 amounted to about 72 percent of the pledges of $1.4 billion, three-quarters of which consists of commodities [WFC/1990/7]. The target for the 1991–1992 biennium is $1.5 billion, a modest 7 percent increase.

More and more in recent years, the debate on food and agriculture has moved beyond that sector and taken place in the context of the total global economic structure. In some measure this change reflects the perception that hunger is a symptom of poverty and underdevelopment and that the agricultural sector, however crucial it may be in the developing countries, has to be dealt with in relation to the overall economy. This brings several other items into the debate: the prevailing development model ("structural adjustment," for short); the profound effect of the problem of external indebtedness; the impact of trade and trade policies (especially in the light of the current General Agreement on Tariffs and Trade [GATT] negotiations, which must conclude in 1990); and the growing concern about environmental issues—deforestation, desertification, soil and water pollution, erosion—that are particularly affected by agricultural practices and the social and economic pressures underlying them.

Although these environmental considerations have been moving to the forefront of international policy for some years, it was the report of the **World Commission on Environment and Development** (the **Brundtland report,** "Our Common Future," 1987) that triggered the latest round of concentration. Other issues aside (like global warming, acid rain, and the ozone layer), it is clear that ecological damage to water and soil is mainly attributable to agricultural practices. Forests are destroyed by slash-and-burn agriculture and intensive logging; deserts expand as growing herds consume vegetation; soil washes downstream as peasants try to scratch out a living farther up the mountainsides; surface water is polluted by agricultural runoff; groundwater is contaminated by chemical fertilizer and pesticide residues; and downstream flooding leaves thousands of people hungry, homeless, or dead. All of these problems are driven by profit, survival, or desperation. None can be solved within the agriculture sector itself.

The World Food Day ceremonies in 1989 were notable for their attention to this theme. The Secretary-General specifically linked it to the overall problems of the global economy. "Two years after the World Commission on Environment and Development called for intensified international action to achieve sustainable development," he said, "billions of people continue to live in absolute poverty without adequate food and are frequently forced to ravage their environment in the desperate search for food and fuel for survival. The ensuing degradation of the land further accentuates their poverty" [U.N. press release SG/SM/4342; FAO 3464, 10/17/89]. The FAO issued a detailed statement on what an international response to this problem would entail [I/T6425], and the president of the World Bank has called for a separate fund to protect the environment.

Related to these questions of environmental integrity and sustainability is the increasing attention being paid both on farms (mainly in the developed world) and in research institutions to alternatives to the intensive use of chemicals, capital-intensive irrigation, and heavy production equipment. The 1989 publication of *Alternative Agriculture* by the U.S. National Academy of Sciences gave this movement a significant boost, helping at the same time to revive the earlier small voice of the advocates of what was then called appropriate technology.

Another indication of the broadening of the debate on these issues is the increasing contention about what constitutes development. Generally this discussion revolves around the development model known as structural adjustment. A conceptual invention of the World Bank, this model reflects the conviction of the traditional development community (the World Bank, regional banks, U.S. Agency for International Development, Organization for Economic Cooperation and Development, and the International Monetary Fund) that development will not take place in the developing countries until they restructure their economies so that they will achieve measurable economic growth. In other words, individual projects, however successful, will not deal with the essential macroeconomic problems: fiscal deficits, overvalued currencies, inflation, imbalance of payments, and others.

Agriculture is rarely a central ingredient of the prescriptions for cure of these economic ills, except to "get prices right" and increase production for export in order to earn foreign exchange.

Although its proponents are uninhibited in their enthusiasm, the evidence as to whether this model works, even in the macroeconomic sense, is neither clear nor convincing. Statistics are presented to show increased exports, greater ability to service external debt, reduced fiscal deficits and inflation, increased gross national product, and sometimes even return of flight capital. Statistics are not available, however, on how structural adjustment affects the poor, but most anecdotal evidence (from missionaries, local grass-roots organizations, and fieldworkers) is almost uniformly negative. As the Executive Director of the World Food Council delicately put it, "Frequently, the adjustment period coincided with substantial falls in real wages and incomes and an increase in poverty and food insecurity. . . . It is also the poor and hungry who have most often been directly hit by reductions in Government spending associated with adjustment. Social services such as health and education have often borne a disproportionate share of cuts [WFC/1990/3, para. 4].

As has been generally emphasized in the development community, Africa continues to be the area of most intense hunger, chronic underdevelopment, and dismal economic prospects [*Issues Before the 43d General Assembly of the United Nations; Issues Before the 44th General Assembly of the United Nations*]. In the latter document, attention was called to the dispute between the World Bank and the Economic Commission for Africa about the comparative impact of structural adjustment lending on various African countries. That dispute was resolved diplomatically and a later World Bank report, *Sub-Saharan Africa: From Crisis to Sustainable Growth* [11/89] appears to have taken a more balanced view of the subject. Nevertheless, the insistence of the African countries on having their alternative program (African Alternative Framework to Structural Adjustment Programmes for Socio-Economic Recovery and Transformation) considered as a basis of discussion at the April 1990 General Assembly Special Session on international economic cooperation almost derailed the preparatory process mainly due to the objections of the United States, one of the major proponents of structural adjustment. No doubt many of these questions will come up again as the General Assembly discusses the results of the **U.N. Programme of Action for African Economic Recovery and Development 1986–1990 (UNPAAERD).**

African food production lagged behind other world regions again in 1989, and prospects are not encouraging for 1990. Although South Asia continues to have nearly twice as many hungry people as Africa, the development situation in the latter is much less hopeful. Structural adjustment programs in Africa have led to declining yields; the prices farmers receive have not kept up with input costs, farm-to-market roads have not been maintained, and cuts in food subsidies have worsened the nutritional situation of the poor. "Production performance in many countries was severely affected not only by drought but also by lack of investment, inputs, and yield-augmenting technology. . . . Adverse developments in the international environment, including falling commodity prices, increasing protectionism, a growing debt burden and a reduction in external financial flows" have exacerbated the situation [WFC/1990/3/Add.2, para. 7, 8].

One sign of hope in this rather gloomy picture is the increasing attention being given to the role of women in the development process as a whole and in agriculture in particular. There appears to be a growing appreciation of the fact that the so-called women in development problem is not, in the end, a "women's" problem but a problem of development itself. Until women enjoy equal rights with men, genuine development is unlikely, if not impossible:

> In recent years there has been an increasing recognition of the need to integrate women into mainstream development efforts. The economic rationale behind this approach is that the full productive potential of human resources—male and female—cannot be realized if women, who make substantial contributions to food output and provisioning, do not have adequate access to resources, productivity enhancing inputs and services. . . . The crucial importance of women's contribution to food security in developing countries is widely recognized. In most developing countries, rural women are the mainstay of small-scale agriculture, farm labour force and day-to-day family subsistence. [FAO, CFS:90/4, 1/90]

As noted in *Issues Before the 44th General Assembly of the United Nations*, the interdependent problems of hunger, poverty, and underdevelopment are crucially affected by the dynamics of the global economy and by how resources are transferred within that economy, that is, via trade, finance, investment, and aid. (It is customary to speak of "externalities," but what can be external to a global market?) In all four of these transfers, the poorer developing countries are seriously disadvantaged.

Foreign investment is largely a memory, especially in sub-Saharan Africa; concessional development assistance has been in decline for some years, despite rhetoric; loans are periodically rescheduled in the Paris Club, but debts are not reduced; and the terms of trade continue to worsen.

The major disadvantages arise out of trade and finance. The more crucial of these two clearly is finance; the debt hovers intractably around $1.3 trillion. Although the effective policy debates on this question do not generally take place in U.N. bodies but in the World Bank and the International Monetary Fund (IMF) and do not relate directly to the agricultural sector, they nevertheless have a decisive bearing on that sector, as well as on food security itself.

Here again sub-Saharan Africa is the worst off; Latin American countries and other debtors to commercial lenders appear to have some negotiating room, although progress, if any, has been slight. There has been much discussion of forgiveness by governments of the bilateral debt owed them by African countries, but action has not matched it. African commercial debt is relatively small (about 15 percent of the $140 billion total), but obligations to the international institutions are substantial, and neither the World Bank nor the IMF has so far been willing to reduce or forgive them.

The other major resource transfer affecting food security in developing countries is international trade. The FAO and the World Food Council have repeatedly pointed to the adverse impact of exporting countries' policies and practices in this area on the food-deficit countries in particular. That link has become increasingly clear as the major trading countries move toward the conclusion of the Uruguay Round of trade negotiations in the General Agreement on Tariffs and Trade. The major relevant debate concerns the exporting countries' competitive subsidies aimed at obtaining or retaining their shares of the international market. The United States has proposed to phase out all subsidies by the end of this century, and the European Community and other groupings have tabled alternate plans for subsidy reduction, but the two sides are far apart on this issue.

Although the outcome of this debate is crucial for the developing countries, they are marginal players in the game. Yet it now appears clear that—as the World Food Council and the FAO have often warned—a food war between the giants (the European Community and the United States) would spell further hardship for the developing countries by driving prices down for their already impoverished producers. Some private groups in Europe and North America have been calling for less "free trade" in order to protect the poor—or at least for trade that is not managed almost exclusively by private trading companies accountable to no one. The contention of these advocates is that it is not availability of food but access to it through income that draws the line between hunger and food security—that is, that the underlying problem is poverty and the kind of development that perpetuates it.

All of these matters, many of which can be expected to influence any U.N. General Assembly consideration of food and agriculture, are in a sense overshadowed by the dramatically new international political (and therefore economic) matrix emerging swiftly but unpredictably by the rapid changes in the political map of Central and Eastern Europe. Once the prospect of foreign military intervention was clearly removed from the unpopular regimes and command economies of that region, the forces of popular democracy took control but with little history or planning to guide them. New representatives of those governments, with new approaches to the United Nations and its agenda, will change the character of the debate. The industrialized world understands these countries and their cultures better than it does those of the developing countries, even after 30 years of foreign aid. Resources, especially from the private sector, which have been drying up for the South anyway, can be expected to flow even more strongly to the East, further depriving the South. The Director-General of FAO, among others, while welcoming the improvement in East-West relations, has warned against the effects of a second lost decade in the development of the South. The same concern was expressed in the final declaration of the **18th Special Session of the General Assembly on International Economic Cooperation**, in Particular the Revitalization of Economic Growth and Development of the Developing Countries [A/S-18/14, 4/30/90].

Although official attention to the food problem has generally languished in this second year of the 1989–1990 biennium at the United Nations, the interest of private organizations and individuals has continued as have declarations of various kinds from international conferences, food prizes, and other manifestations of concern. On February 20, 1990, for example, the **Declaration of Geneva** was signed by 30 persons from Europe, Japan, and the United States, declaring that every nation has the right to achieve food security through efforts of its own choice. On December 8, 1989, the **Bellagio Declaration** was "produced and adopted by a group of 23 planners, practitioners, opinion leaders, and scientists" at a conference at that site, which declared that "it is possible to end half of all world hunger by the year 2000." It spoke of new opportunities, described the technical possibilities, and called for action. "For the first time in history," the declaration said, "the end of famine is achievable." At a World Food Congress in Washington, D.C., in 1963, President John Kennedy, making the same point, noted that only the will was lacking.

The year 1990 may well mark a watershed in the often contentious relationship between **the United States and FAO.** For more than a decade

U.S. government representatives have complained about the organization's increasing budgets and what it regards as an unresponsive management. Like most U.N. specialized agencies, FAO has been under pressure to adopt budget and management reforms that reflect the views of the major contributor(s)—a process referred to as "consensus-based budgeting." Meanwhile, the U.S. has amassed substantial arrears to FAO, which threatens its very membership in the organization.

The United States currently owes $195 million to FAO—$70 million for calendar year 1990 dues and some $125 million for arrears dating to the mid-1980s. The arrears equal two years' obligations and thus could trigger a provision of the FAO charter revoking the U.S. seat on its Governing Council. According to the FAO charter, no member state can be more than two years in arrears, not counting the amount still owed for the current year. Technically, then, the United States must contribute its 1988 assessment of some $65 million before December 31, 1990, in order to avert the automatic loss of its Governing Council seat on January 1, 1991. Loss of the seat would be followed by a loss of the vote in the FAO General Conference, which takes place in November 1991.

The current, modified version of the U.S. Congress' Kassebaum amendment requires presidential certification of progress by U.N. specialized agencies on consensus-based budgeting before 20 percent of the final U.S. contribution can be paid. Although the Bush administration has requested the full $70 million FAO assessment for 1990, State Department officials are debating whether they can certify that FAO has made progress on budget reform.

Failing certification, some have suggested a waiver of the Kassebaum requirement when the U.S. stands to lose its vote. While supporters of the proposed waiver believe that it would defuse a potentially divisive debate over U.S. membership in FAO, others believe that such an exemption would send the wrong signal to those organizations in the U.N. system that have already implemented budgetary reform.

FAO argues that it has already met U.S. calls for budget reform. The 1989 budgeting process initiated by FAO provides for early consultation between the Finance and Program committees on the size and priorities of the biennial budget. Then Assistant Secretary of State for International Organization Affairs Richard Williamson had written to **FAO Director-General Edouard Saouma** in 1988 that such a procedure was among "the minimum steps we expect of the FAO as a measure of progress on reform." In 1989 the U.S. voted against the 1990–1991 budget, citing a 3 percent increase over the previous biennium's spending.

In the end, the fate of U.S. participation in FAO may hinge on the dynamics of U.S. government relations with the agency's controversial

Director-General. Reelected to a third six-year term in 1987, Saouma finds more support for his organization's programs within the Department of Agriculture than within the Department of State. His relations with U.S. officials continue to be encumbered by the State Department's decision to back an alternative candidate for FAO Director-General in 1987 and by long-time U.S. displeasure with his management style.

Some other countries also fail to see the relation between paying their dues and getting the United Nations to take necessary action on world problems. Nevertheless, food security continues to be a real and necessary, though increasingly distant, goal. Fifteen years after 134 governments at the U.N. World Food Conference of November 1974 called attention to this problem, concluded that the best solution was to increase agricultural production in the food-deficit countries, and pledged their best efforts to solve it, more people are hungry than ever before: "In 1989, food production in the developing countries as a whole hardly increased. . . . In the low-income food-deficit countries, production growth was about the same as population growth" [WFC/1990/2, para. 45]. The measured language of this document goes on to note that "consumption . . . grew more slowly than production" and that "even the positive growth in average consumption per person in most developing regions has been too modest in the 1980s as to suggest any significant improvements in the food-security situation of those people most in need of it" [ibid., para. 48]. In other words, the world produces enough food to feed everyone, but about a fifth of the world's population has little or no access to it.

During the 45th Session of the General Assembly, developed countries will be assessing the impact of their development assistance upon hunger and will report to the World Food Council's 17th session in 1991.

2. Population

The 1990s will be a critical decade in the search for solutions to the global population problem. The decisions of individuals, families, communities, and nations will determine whether world population triples or only doubles before stabilization in the next century. They will decide whether the pace of damage to the environment accelerates or declines and may answer the question of whether Earth will be fit for habitation in the future.

That the next ten years will decide the shape of the twenty-first century is the central finding of *State of World Population 1990*, issued by the United Nations Population Fund (UNFPA) in May. More people will be added to the world's population during the 1990s than any decade in history. Global population, currently at 5.3 billion, will grow by 90 million to 100 million people per year. By the year 2000 the world will have added a billion people—the equivalent of another China.

The largest increases will be in the poorest countries, which by definition are the least capable of meeting the immediate needs of their citizens or investing for the future. Virtually all of the population growth—94 percent—is taking place in the developing countries of Africa, Asia, and Latin America. The remaining 6 percent of the growth will occur in the developed nations of Europe, the Soviet Union, Japan, and North America [UNFPA, Report of the Executive Director, *State of World Population 1990*, p. 1].

Progress in **reducing birth rates** has been slower than expected. According to the latest U.N. medium projection, world population is now predicted to exceed the 10.2 billion level for eventual population stabilization calculated in 1984, and is likely to be closer to 11 billion. In 15 countries, 13 of them in Africa, birthrates rose between 1960–1965 and 1980–1985. In another 23 countries, the birthrate fell by less than 2 percent. Without steep birthrate declines, global population could grow to 14 billion before stabilizing in the next century [ibid., p. 2].

In addition to urgent efforts to reduce population growth rates, the report calls for decisive action to eradicate poverty and to adopt cleaner and more energy-efficient technologies and greater resource conservation measures to protect the environment.

The most recent report from the U.N. Conference on Trade and Development noted that the growth in gross domestic product (GDP) in most of Africa and the less developed countries of Asia remained below that of the rate of population growth, while in Latin America the rate of growth in GDP per capita declined in 1987, again in 1988, and is expected to have declined further in 1989 [*Trade and Development Report 1989* (UNCTAD/TDR/9), p. 3].

As populations have expanded and developing country economies have stagnated, the number of poor, hungry, and illiterate people has risen despite additional investments to increase the availability of health care, education, and other social services. The demographic treadmill forces developing countries to run faster just to stay in place. For example, although the incidence of malnutrition declined from 27 percent in developing countries in 1970 to 21.5 percent in 1984, the number of malnourished stands at 512 million, up from about 460 million in 1980. Similarly, the number of adult illiterates is estimated to be 889 million, up from 742 million in 1970, and people without access to clean water and proper sanitation increased from 1 billion in 1970 to 1.7 billion today [ibid., p. 2].

Population growth is directly related to the **decline of global environmental quality**. The unprecedented magnitude of demographic change in the last few decades is changing the relationship between human populations and the environment. In the rural areas of many developing countries, increasing numbers of poor families can survive only by destroying their own natural resource base.

At the second Rafael M. Salas Lecture (named for the late UNFPA executive director who served from 1969 to 1987), Prince Philip, the Duke of Edinburgh and International President of the World Wide Fund for Nature, succinctly described the interconnections of population, poverty, and the environment: "Since it is the poor and disadvantaged who are most directly affected by the degradation of the natural environment, as resources become scarce and the quality of the environment declines still further, even more people are bound to become poor and disadvantaged" [*The Washington Post*, 5/8/90].

Poor people, many landless, are forced to cultivate erodible hillsides and to denude upland watersheds needed to prevent flooding and erosion of topsoil. An estimated 26 billion tons of topsoil are lost each year, resulting in declines in agricultural productivity. The overcropping and overgrazing of fragile lands contribute to the process of desertification, which claims about 15 million acres annually [*The Christian Science Monitor*, 4/17/90].

In many countries the conversion of forest to cropland and pasture and the harvesting of wood for fuel threaten large remaining areas of tropical rainforest. Each year some 20 million hectares of forest are destroyed. The Food and Agriculture Organization (FAO) of the United Nations estimates that 1.1 billion people are affected by fuelwood scarcities and that by the year 2000 the number could reach 2.4 billion [FAO, *Fuelwood Supplies in Developing Countries*, Forestry Paper 42 (1983)]. In the absence of affordable alternatives to the burning of biomass fuels, increased populations put additional strains on forests, thus affecting both future levels of greenhouse gas emissions and the sustainability of carbon dioxide–absorbing forests.

New data on environmental trends demonstrate the ways in which global warming may be exacerbated by future population growth through increased production of greenhouse gases. Total emissions of carbon dioxide from developing countries will amount to 16.6 billion tons annually by 2025—over four times as much as the industrialized nations produce today—given current energy use and demographic trends. Under the Montreal Protocol and assuming current trends continue, developing countries could account for a 70 percent increase in the emissions of chlorofluorocarbons by 2040 [*State of World Population 1990*, p. 12].

Better understanding of the linkages between rapid population growth and environmental degradation comes at a time of growing concern about the global environment on the part of the general public and policymakers. One illustration of this broad interest was the massive worldwide observance of Earth Day 1990 on April 22.

A number of recent international conferences on the environment have highlighted the need to address rapid population growth as an integral part of strategies to combat global warming and to promote sustainable development. The declaration of the Global Forum on Environment and Development for Human Survival, held in January in Moscow and attended by more than 1,000 religious and political leaders from 83 countries, concluded that "a population policy is an essential component of any effective, long-range environmental strategy" [*Population* (UNFPA newsletter), 2/90]. An international meeting on the environment sponsored by the American Assembly decided that population growth, along with tropical deforestation and loss of biological diversity and global atmospheric change, are "three indivisibly linked global environmental trends [which] together constitute an increasingly grave challenge to the habitability of the earth" [*Preserving the Global Environment—The Challenge of Shared Leadership,* Final Report of the Seventy-seventh American Assembly, p. 5]. And legislators from 42 countries attending the Interparliamentary Conference on the Global Environment in Washington in May advocated the creation of a global Marshall Plan to assist developing countries in addressing environmental problems and included a call for additional resources to bring about population stabilization [*The New York Times*, 5/3/90].

Global population stabilization at 10.2 billion can be achieved if family planning users in developing countries increase from 326 million couples today (45 percent) to 535 million (56 percent) by the end of the century [*State of World Population 1990*, p. 19].

The concept of family planning has gained acceptance and widespread political support among governments in recent years. In 1978 only 45 developing country governments considered their population growth too high. Today 67 governments—accounting for more than 85 percent of the developing world population—have policies to reduce population growth. In Africa alone the number of governments that consider their population growth rates too high almost doubled, from 16 in 1978 to 30 in 1988. The number of governments worldwide that fund domestic family planning programs rose from 97 to 125 in just 12 years. Governments limiting access to family planning fell from 15 in 1976 to only 7 in the same period [ibid., p. 3].

One of the most dramatic examples of a nation that has reversed its position on family planning is Romania. Under the regime of dictator Nicolae Ceausescu, both contraception and abortion were banned, and women were expected to bear at least five children for the good of the state. The desired growth in population did not occur, but rates of maternal mortality (much of it due to illegal abortion) and infant death mushroomed [*The Washington Post*, 1/5/90]. The first law passed by the legislature after Ceausescu was deposed in December 1989 legalized contraception and abortion. Government clinics now provide abortion free of charge, and the Ministry of Health has encouraged the creation of a private organization to distribute and promote birth control. Abortion is the most frequently used method due to the lack of contraceptives, which are not locally manufactured and impossible to purchase because of a shortage of hard currency. A needs assessment team composed of officials from the World Health Organization (WHO) and UNFPA visited Romania in March and formulated a project for the introduction of family planning services, including training of staff and provision of equipment and contraceptive supplies. The government is expected to require large-scale international support for family planning, estimated at about $5 million.

In countries with supportive governments, efforts to expand availability and use of family planning services on an individual level can be approached from two directions: by meeting existing demand for birth control or by working to increase the level of demand. Data from the World Fertility Survey provide evidence that of all married women in Africa who currently want no more children, 77 percent are not using contraception; in Asia the proportion is 57 percent; in Latin America it is 43 percent [*State of World Population 1990*, p. 19]. The figures would be higher if they included unmarried but sexually active women; couples who are using unreliable, traditional methods of birth control; and couples who want to delay but not prevent another birth.

The number of women of reproductive age will grow from around 717 million now to 874 million in the year 2000. In order to maintain the current level of contraceptive use, the number of women using family planning would have to rise by 157 million and total global spending on birth control would have to reach a minimum of $9 billion in current dollars. To meet that target by the end of the century, an annual increase of 7 percent per year is required [ibid., p. 28].

The goals and targets for the expansion of family planning outlined in *State of World Population 1990*, including the level of expenditure necessary for population stabilization, were adopted by consensus by the representatives of 79 governments at the **International Forum on Population in the Twenty-first Century**. The conference was organized by UNFPA in cooperation with the government of the Netherlands and held in Amsterdam in November 1989 [*Population*, 12/89]. The **Amsterdam Declaration**, entitled "A Better Life for Future Generations," states that the attainment of population goals and objectives rests on seven main pillars: strengthening political commitment; developing national population policies and programs; accelerating and expanding resource mobilization; strengthening the role and status of women; improving the quality, effectiveness, and coverage of family planning services in both the public and private sectors; expanding community participation in the planning and implementation of programs; and intensifying international cooperation in the population field.

The U.N. General Assembly adopted a separate resolution on the future needs in the population field and directed UNFPA to analyze the implications of the Amsterdam Declaration for population programs and for resource requirements for population assistance and to submit a report on these findings to the General Assembly in 1990. The resolution also stressed the importance of the declaration in the drafting of the strategy for the Fourth Development Decade, to begin in 1991 [ibid., 1/90]. The proposed international strategy includes human resource development as one of its top priorities. Family planning and population programs are expected to be given due weight in the document as a result of prodding from the Nordic countries [U.N. press release (DD/168), 3/21/90].

Of the seven "pillars" of the Amsterdam Declaration, mobilizing the resources required for population stabilization is the most urgent priority for the 1990s. To meet the goal of $9 billion annually for population activities, governments and consumers in most developing countries must increase expenditures on family planning substantially over the coming decade, but the largest increases are needed from outside donors.

The **multilateral development banks,** now the largest source of official development assistance (ODA), provided only $85 million in 1988 to population and family planning programs. The banks have come under increasing criticism for their failure to play a major role in international population efforts. At the annual members' assembly of the **International Planned Parenthood Federation (IPPF)** in Ottawa in November 1989, World Bank President Barber Conable committed the Bank to boosting its loans for population, health, and nutrition from a $100 million average over the past five years to a $266 million average in the next three years [*The Washington Post,* 11/8/89]. But at least one report states that the support of multilateral development banks should rise over the coming decade to $1 billion a year, an amount that is less than 5 percent of total 1988 development bank loans [Population Crisis Committee, *1990 Report on Progress toward Population Stabilization*].

The same report argues that industrialized country governments should increase annual contributions to international population efforts from an estimated $534 million in 1988 to $4 billion in the year 2000. This target can be achieved by doubling total ODA to all sectors (as occurred between 1977 and 1987) and by allocating 4 percent of this larger total to population and family planning. Despite the mounting evidence that world population could almost triple to 14 billion by 2100 without a large infusion of resources, **political controversies in the United States** continue to threaten to undermine the global consensus on the need for expanded family planning and population programs. Ignoring calls for improved international cooperation in this area, the United States no longer contributes to UNFPA, an institution it was instrumental in establishing over 20 years ago, because of UNFPA's program in China. In 1985 the U.S. Agency for International Development (AID) withheld $10 million of an earmarked $46 million for UNFPA, claiming the organization was co-managing China's population program and that the Chinese program relied on coercive abortion and involuntary sterilization to implement its one-child-per-couple policy. In the four years since, AID has withheld the entire $25 million to $30 million budgeted annually for UNFPA. In February 1990, AID announced that it would not contribute to UNFPA for fiscal year 1990, a refusal for the fifth year in a row.

As the basis for its decisions to withhold funds, AID has cited what has come to be known as the Kemp-Inouye amendment, originally part of the supplemental foreign aid appropriation in 1985. The amendment prohibits U.S. funding of any organization that "supports or participates in the management of a program of coercive abortion or involuntary sterilization." AID established the conditions under which U.S. contributions could be resumed: China must prevent coercion by punishing abuses or UNFPA must "radically change its assistance to the China program . . . such as by supplying only contraceptives" [AID Administrator M. Peter McPherson to Senator Mark Hatfield, 9/25/85]. AID has continued to maintain that the activities of the Chinese government and UNFPA have not changed sufficiently to warrant renewed U.S. support. UNFPA has repeatedly denied the allegation, pointing out that it does not support abortion in China or anywhere else in the world since it does not consider abortion to be a method of family planning. In addition, UNFPA denies the allegation that it co-manages China's program. The size of UNFPA's contribution relative to the Chinese government's expenditures ($10 million versus $1 billion annually, or 1 percent of the total) and the number of UNFPA staff in Beijing compared to the employees of the State Family Planning Commission (4 versus 160,000 family planning workers, plus numerous volunteers, scattered throughout the countryside) suggest that this allegation is farfetched [Foreign Broadcast Information Service, China Daily Report (FBIS-CHI-89-74), 4/19/89, p. 36].

Critics of U.S. policy have long maintained that proponents of the status quo have never been able to produce evidence of UNFPA complicity, a fact confirmed by a 1985 review of UNFPA's assistance to China, which concluded that UNFPA "neither funds abortions nor supports coercive family planning practices" [AID, "Review of UNFPA Program for Compliance with US Law and Policy" (executive summary), 3/85]. Prior to 1989 the United States had never formally expressed any concern about the China program in the UNDP/UNFPA Governing Council, the appropriate institutional forum. The Governing Council approved five-year programs for China in 1980 and 1984, and subsequent annual meetings were notable for the absence of any expression of concern by the U.S. about the China program. Many critics of U.S. policy marshal such facts to support the contention that the withdrawal of U.S.

funding from UNFPA was primarily a concession to a vocal domestic political constituency rather than an expression of concern about alleged human rights violations in China.

Defenders of UNFPA believe that the organization plays a positive role by strengthening voluntarism in the Chinese population program. Since 1980, UNFPA has supported modern contraceptive production to improve the typically low quality of contraceptives manufactured in China. Its funds have provided production equipment, analytical instruments, and technical assistance to 18 factories and two training institutions. The wide availability of higher-quality contraceptives promotes voluntary participation in the population program by reducing the incidence of unplanned pregnancies resulting from contraceptive failures and discontinuation of use. For example, one study of the impact of Chinese women replacing primitive steel rings with modern copper-bearing IUDs, manufactured by two factories built with UNFPA support, estimates that 324,000 unplanned pregnancies, many of which would be aborted, are prevented each year [personal communication, 11/89].

UNFPA is now in the first year of a new $57 million assistance program to China for the period 1990-1994, which was presented for approval to the 48-member Governing Council in June 1989. The new program concentrates on three priority areas: contraceptive production and research, maternal and child health programs, and the training of demographers. Assisting in the implementation of major components of the new program will be UNICEF and WHO [DP/FPA/CP/48].

The composition of the new program eliminates some of the activities that the U.S. government found most objectionable in the past, such as technical assistance in census taking and other demographic data collection and analysis. Despite these UNFPA and Chinese efforts at accommodation, the U.S. delegate to the Governing Council expressed strong opposition to the new cycle of U.N. assistance to China. Acceding to the demands of antiabortion legislators and pressure groups, the Bush administration stated that the United States "strongly oppose[s] the program as currently formulated and dissociate [sic] ourselves unequivocally from any interpretation of this body's consensus that suggests we approve the family planning program in the People's Republic of China" [AID press release, 6/7/89]. No other country rose to criticize the new program. Four nations—Australia, Bangladesh, Romania, and the Federal Republic of Germany—spoke in favor, and the program was approved by consensus.

In response to the Bush administration's refusal to restore U.S. support to UNFPA, family planning supporters in the U.S. Congress unsuccessfully attempted to pass legislation in fall 1989 to force AID to fund UNFPA. An amendment to the fiscal year 1990 foreign aid appropriation bill, sponsored by Senator Barbara Mikulski (D-Md.), earmarked $15 million for UNFPA and stipulated that UNFPA was to maintain the U.S. funds in a segregated account, none of which could be used in China. The Mikulski amendment was adopted by both houses of Congress as a reasonable compromise to break the impasse over UNFPA funding. It was sent to President Bush as part of a $14 billion foreign aid appropriation bill. President Bush vetoed the legislation, refusing to fund UNFPA's program, which he described as "inconsistent with American values" and contrary to the "human rights character of our foreign policy around the world" [*Congressional Quarterly*, 11/25/90, p. 3266]. In the summer of 1990, members of Congress were again attempting to obtain some funding for UNFPA, but President Bush once again indicated his intention to veto any such legislation. Despite the absence of U.S. participation, contributions from other donor governments in 1990 will push UNFPA income over $200 million for the first time [*Population*, 1/90].

ECOSOC approved in principle in July 1989 the convening of an international meeting on population in 1994. This conference will occur 20 years after the first such gathering in Bucharest in 1974, which adopted the World Population Plan of Action. At the International Conference on Population in Mexico City in 1984, 88 recommendations for realizing the goals of the plan were adopted. The main purpose of the 1994 conference will be to assess the progress that has been made in achieving these goals, to adopt an updated set of recommendations, and to increase international awareness of population issues [ibid., 8/89].

In March 1990 came the announcement of the two winners of the annual U.N. Population Award: Alfred Sauvy, a noted French demographer, and the Mauritius National Family Health and Population Council [U.N. press release (POP/408), 3/9/90].

3. Environment

"As the cold war recedes, the **environment is becoming the No. 1 international security concern,**" noted scientist Michael Oppenheimer [*The New York Times*, 3/27/90]. He was not alone. Leaders of the world's seven major democracies met in Paris in summer 1989 for an economic summit but spent most of it calling for "decisive action" on the environment [*UNEP North America News*, 8/89].

The American Assembly, a nonprofit public policy think tank, brought together leaders from government, business, academia, and the professions from 18 countries, and all agreed that three "indivisibly linked global environmental trends"—population growth, the loss of species and forest habitat, and the changing atmosphere—"threaten nations' economic potential, therefore their internal political security, their citizens' health (because of increased ultraviolet radiation) and, in the case of global warming, possibly their very existence. No more basic threat to national security exists" [Final Report of the 77th American Assembly on "Preserving the Global Environment: The Challenge of Shared Leadership," April 19-22, 1990].

An expert on climate change, Oppenheimer warned that the prospects for environmental destabilization threaten to be just as dangerous as the perceived imbalance in armaments during the cold war. To him, **"global warming, ozone depletion, deforestation, and overpopulation are the four horsemen of a looming 21st century apocalypse."**

This growing perception led a number of people, from citizen activists to U.N. officials, to call for a reallocation of money previously spent on the military. The proposed **"peace dividend"** would finance solutions to a staggering array of environmental dangers. (Figure III-1 shows how 1989 U.S. tax dollars were spent.)

The Executive Director of the **United Nations Environment Programme (UNEP)**, Mostafa K. Tolba, urged that an environment fund—"not of millions but of billions of dollars"—be set up in this decade to confront "the closely linked environmental crises that threaten our future." "This is not a daydream," he said. "It can be done and indeed it has been done. The United States in per capita terms channeled more assistance to the shattered economies of Europe than the world now spends on development assistance. Norway has already offered to contribute some $100 million every year and the Netherlands 250 million Dutch Guilders (about $112 million). If the major economic powers and oil-rich nations follow suit, we will then be in business. That is the type of commitment and responsibility all nations have to display to face the challenge of the climate crisis and the closely linked environmental crises which threaten our future" [*UNEP North America News*, 10/89].

It was a commitment the Bush administration seemed loathe to make. At an April 1990 **White House conference on climate change**—the payoff of a campaign promise to hold a global environmental conference at which, the President had said, "we will talk about global warming"— Bush never once mentioned the words *global warming* or *greenhouse effect* as he called for more research into the scientific and economic ramifications of climate change [*The New York Times*, 4/21/90]. This go-slow approach infuriated the officials of several other countries, especially in Western Europe. Instead of stressing the uncertainties of the greenhouse effect, as the White House wanted, most delegates agreed the threat is real and potentially serious. In the end, the President reconfirmed a U.S. pledge to cooperate in a U.N. effort to forge an international agreement on dealing with climate change [*Time*, 4/30/90].

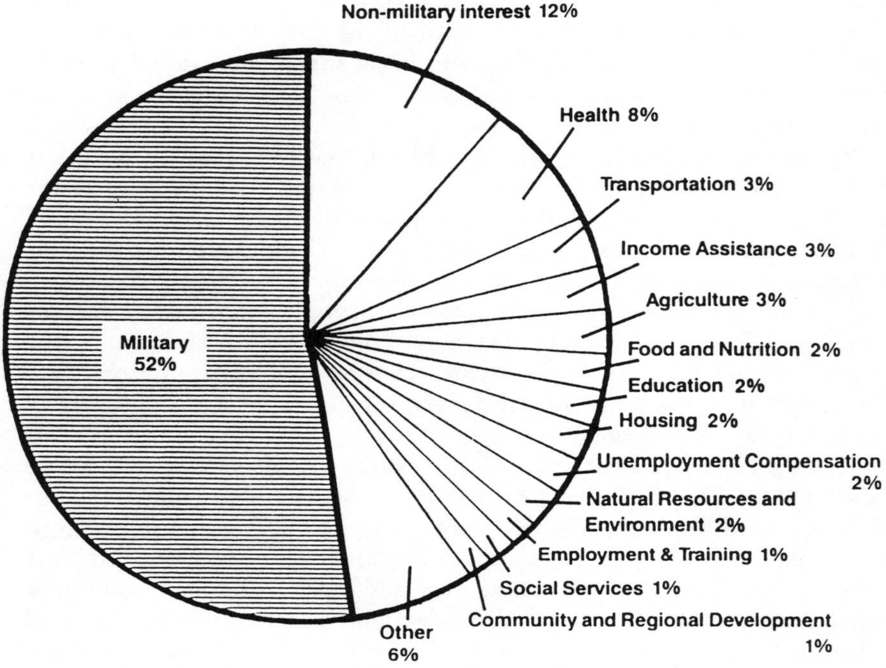

*Pie differs from U.S. government figures because (1) many costs usually kept separate are combined here to reflect the costs of total military spending (e.g., Department of Energy's budget for nuclear warhead production and veterans benefits) and (2) revenues from trust funds, such as Social Security, which are not funded by the income tax, are excluded.

Source: Connecticut SANE/FREEZE

Figure III-1 Division of U.S. Income Tax Dollar

Three weeks later, the U.S. administration stunned world governments by reversing an earlier decision to support an agreement among industrialized countries to provide financial assistance to developing countries to help them phase out use of the chemicals—primarily halons and chlorofluorocarbons (CFCs)—that are **destroying Earth's ozone layer.** International financial experts estimated the change-over to substitutes would cost developing countries $400 million a year for the next ten years. Due to the high price tag, very few developing countries—only 13 by 1989—had ratified the 1987 UNEP–sponsored "Montreal agreement" to control production and use of the ozone-depleting chemicals [*UNEP North America News*, 10/89]. Weeks later—after having received much criticism from within the

U.S. and abroad—the administration again reversed its position, now stating that it would support the agreement to provide assistance.

This support for a new fund (with the United States supplying $40-$60 million of the $240 million total for the first three years), and last-minute agreement in principle to the poorer countries' demand for technology transfers in phasing out CFCs, cleared the way to a new international accord on ozone-depleting chemicals. The "landmark" treaty, signed by 93 nations in London on June 29, 1990, calls for a halt in CFC production by the end of the century—a major step beyond the Montreal treaty's demand for a 50 percent reduction by 1998. China and India, nonsignatories to the 1987 treaty, signaled their satisfaction with the latest agreement. As with the Montreal Protocol, the new treaty gives the poorer nations an additional ten years to carry out its conditions [*The New York Times*, 6/30/90].

This conflict between critical economic and ecological issues was mirrored in the 44th General Assembly debate at the United Nations. It was, according to one U.N. environmental official, "the most difficult General Assembly ever," not only because environment had risen to the top of the political agenda but because "it is also becoming an increasingly politicized—and even polarized—issue." This emerged clearly, he said, on three major resolutions adopted last year: on climate, the illegal traffic in toxic and dangerous products, and, especially, the forthcoming U.N. conference on environment and sustainable development. On all, a major sticking point was North-South conflict over the economic ramifications of protecting the environment [*UNEP North America News*, 2–4/90].

The 45th Assembly will follow up by dealing with just three main environmental issues: the report on preparations for the 1992 U.N. conference by the conference preparatory committee chairman, Tommy Koh of Singapore; a report on UNEP's special Governing Council session, called to coincide on August 1–3, 1990, with a meeting in Nairobi of that committee; and the U.N. Secretary-General's report on implementing the resolution on climate change [private briefing].

Brazil 1992

Well before Earth Day sounded its worldwide call to environmental action on April 22, international organizations, governments, and grass-roots groups in every country were getting ready for one of the biggest assemblies of environmental activists ever: the **United Nations Conference on Environment and Development, to be held in June 1992 in Brazil.**

Launched by the 44th U.N. General Assembly [A/Res/44/228] with a $13.8 million budget, its purpose is to elaborate strategies to halt, or even reverse, the effects of environmental degradation by strengthening efforts that promote sustainable, environmentally sound development in all countries. After protracted debate in the General Assembly, member states agreed the conference would tackle ways to:

- Combat climate change, ozone layer depletion, and transboundary air pollution.
- Prevent the illegal international traffic in toxic and dangerous products and wastes and manage them in an environmentally sound manner.
- Protect freshwater resources.
- Protect oceans, seas, coastal areas, and marine resources.
- Protect and manage land resources by combating deforestation, desertification, and drought.
- Conserve biological diversity.
- Improve the living and working environment of the poor and eradicate poverty through measures that integrate environmental and developmental concerns.
- Protect human health conditions and improve the quality of life.

The General Assembly also outlined **23 conference objectives,** among them, a report on the state of the global environment since the first U.N. environment conference in 1972, regional and international strategies for cooperation, new ways of financing technology transfers, the further development of international environmental law, a review and examination of the role of the U.N. system in dealing with the environment, the development of human resources, environmental education, and an exchange of information on national environmental policies, situations, and accidents.

A **complicated preparatory process** finally emerged. The conference will be run from an ad hoc secretariat in Geneva with one unit in New York to act as liaison with U.N. bodies and the missions to the U.N., and a second unit in Nairobi to act as liaison with UNEP, which is headquartered there. The conference preparatory committee, a body made up of all 159 U.N. member states, was to meet five times—twice in New York and Geneva and once in Nairobi [*UNEP North America News,* 2–4/90].

Governments began preparing for Brazil at **U.N.-sponsored regional meetings.** A meeting for Africa was held in Kampala, Uganda, in June 1989. A high-level meeting for Europe and North America took place in Bergen, Norway, May 8–16, 1990 (U.S. EPA chief William K. Reilly was ordered not to attend by the White House) [*The New York Times,* 5/10/90]. Conferences for Latin America and the Caribbean were set for the second week in August in Santiago, Chile, and October 10–16 in Bangkok for the Asian region [*Brundtland Bulletin,* Centre for Our Common Future, 3/90].

Grass-roots organizations began coordinating with the United Nations and with each other well before the General Assembly gave its December 1989 green light to the conference. A thousand representatives of nongovernmental organizations (NGOs) in 44 countries attended the annual conference of the U.N. Department of Public Information September 13–15, 1989. Its theme, "Environment and Development: Only One Earth," drew the largest NGO gathering ever at U.N. headquarters [DPI conference final report]. In February, NGOs in the field of development met at the United Nations to learn how they could get more involved. In Europe in mid-March, 350 grass-roots organizations planned their role in the Bergen regional meeting in May. And at the same time, NGO leaders from around the world met in Vancouver, Canada, at the behest of **conference Secretary-General Maurice Strong,** to develop a grass-roots agenda for consideration by the U.N. conference and to start planning their own, parallel "people's conference" in Brazil. Initial estimates were that it might draw as many as 20,000 NGO representatives.

There was, however, an immediate problem for NGOs. Although the U.N. Secretary-General had specifically requested "the active involvement of the NGO community"—environment and development groups and such constituencies as industry, trade unions, scientists, educators, indigenous peoples, and women's and youth organizations—"in all aspects of conference preparations," calling them "essential for its success," involvement in the U.N. preparatory process was limited to those NGOs in consultative status with the U.N. Economic and Social Council (ECOSOC).

To talk directly with NGOs, Strong flew from the official organizational meeting of the U.N. conference in New York to Vancouver, where representatives of 115 NGOs from 40 countries met March 15–18. He told them he was committed to ensuring the participation of all NGO constituencies, both in the preparatory process and in the conference itself. The same message was delivered to the European NGOs preparing for the Bergen regional meeting [Report on Vancouver Meeting, Centre for Our Common Future].

Conference Secretary-General Strong organized and led the first U.N. Conference on the Human Environment in Stockholm in June 1972, and went on to become Executive Director of the newly created U.N. Environment Programme. Today he heads the World Federation of United Nations Associations, and is Chairman of Strovest Holdings in Canada and of the Geneva-based World Economic Forum. In his no-nonsense remarks at the conference preparatory committee's first meeting, Strong cautioned that,

> The U.N. and its system of agencies and programmes will be on display in 1992 and must validate the confidence of the international community in its capacity to deal effectively with the key issues on the Conference agenda.

> The road to Brazil 1992 will thus be an especially challenging one. The debates in the 44th Session of the General Assembly which resulted in agreement on resolution 44/228 made clear the substantial differences which continue to exist in the perspectives and the priorities with which member states approach many of the main issues to be addressed at the Conference, especially those affecting the relationship between less developed and more developed countries.

Strong argued that the principle challenge of the conference will be to ensure that developing countries have access to the technologies and additional funding necessary for environmentally sound development policies and for full participation in multilateral environmental efforts. "There has been little progress toward consensus on these critical issues as yet," he said, "but the need is inescapable" [remarks by Maurice F. Strong, 3/5/90].

A Critical Climate for Change

If the atmosphere did not act as a greenhouse, life on earth would be impossible. Sunlight heats the sea and land, the warmed earth radiates heat back into space, and some infrared radiation is absorbed by trace gases.

Recent human activities in industry, transportation, and agriculture and an expanding population have inexorably increased carbon dioxide (CO_2), methane, CFCs, nitrous oxides, and other greenhouse gases. The major sources of these gases are energy use (56.2 percent), agriculture (21.2 percent), refrigeration and cooling (15 percent), natural causes (6.5 percent), and industry (1 percent) [*The New York Times*, 11/19/89]. Today almost half the world's 5 billion people cut trees for firewood for energy [*World Resources 1988-89*]. This not only adds CO_2 to the atmosphere; since trees absorb CO_2, their loss adds even more of the major greenhouse gas to the heat trap.

U.N. scientists say climate change will have devastating effects on millions of people, animals, and plants over the next century unless emissions of CO_2 and other greenhouse gases are quickly cut by more than 60 percent [*The Guardian*, 5/22/90]. Three draft reports—on the scientific aspects, economic and social impacts, and possible strategies for coping with climate change—were distributed to governments by the **Intergovernmental Panel on Climate Change (IPCC)** in the spring of 1990. Their grim conclusions indicated that governments will be faced with difficult decisions when they meet in November at the **second World Climate Conference** in Geneva to start work on a strategy and an international convention to slow global warming. The reports will also go to the 45th General Assembly, where they will be the foundation for intergovernmental negotiations. **The goal is to have a fully negotiated treaty on global warming ready for signing by leaders at the 1992 U.N. Conference on Environment and Development in Brazil.**

The IPCC was established by UNEP and the World Meteorological Organization in November 1988 to coordinate and unify the world's scientific and policymaking communities for effective, realistic, and equitable action on climate change [*UNEP North America News*, 2–4/90].

When the first report, on the science of global warming, was finally approved on May 25, British Prime Minister Margaret Thatcher broke with the Bush administration's skeptical, more-research-and-see position and said that if other countries did their part, the United Kingdom would reduce projected CO_2 emissions by 30 percent over 15 years. The Chairman of the IPCC, Bert Bolin, describe Thatcher's offer to stabilize emissions at 1990 levels by the year 2005 as "very useful" but said, "It is not enough in the long term." Dr. John Houghton, Britain's chief meteorologist, said that "to stop [global warming], you have to cut by 60% immediately." Dr. Houghton, who chaired the scientific working group, said that only a few of its 90 scientists from 39 countries disagreed with the findings. He called the findings dramatic confirmation of how rapidly greenhouse gases have changed the Earth's atmosphere since the end of the eighteenth century [*The New York Times*, 5/26/90].

If nothing is done, global mean temperature could rise 5.4 degrees Fahrenheit by the end of the next century, the IPCC reports said. Oceans would expand, polar ice would melt and sea levels would rise more than 2 feet (25.6 inches)—enough to submerge the Maldive Islands and coastal plains and cities. Millions of people will be forced to migrate. While some fertile land would become desert, parts of the northern hemisphere could benefit, probably Canada and the Soviet Union, because grain will grow in areas currently too cold to produce cereals. This could have long-term political consequences for the United States, whose influence in the international arena is based in part on its grain surplus. Drinking water supplies will be disrupted, the report said; New Yorkers, for example, can expect a 28 to 42 percent shortfall, which will cost $3 billion to rectify. The Great Lakes may drop by as much as 8 feet. Northern forests, unable to cope with rapid temperature change, will be damaged and perhaps die. Air pollution, especially in cities, is expected to get worse, and ozone layer depletion will cause more skin cancers and cataracts in fair-skinned people [*The Guardian*, 5/22/90].

The United States, with 5 percent of the world's population, currently produces a quarter of all manmade atmospheric carbon dioxide, and it uses more energy relative to its economic size than any other Western country except Canada. Any international policy to tackle global warming will mean a radical reduction and restructuring of U.S. energy consumption. It will require hard political and economic decisions.

Some financial analysts estimate that slowing global warming could cost the United States $300 billion a year—the same amount it now spends on the military—with the eventual price tag in the trillions worldwide [*The New York Times*, 11/19/89]. However, the Union of Concerned Scientists (UCS) maintains, "Such estimates are designed to convince the public that it is too costly to fight global warming." The UCS says the reality is that an energy efficiency program could cut carbon dioxide emissions 20 percent from projected levels in the year 2000 and save $75 billion a year. If the U.S. government put just $1 billion a year into renewable energy technologies during the 1990s, the group concludes, renewable sources could meet half of the country's energy needs within 30 years.

A UNEP–Lou Harris international survey of environmental issues in May 1989 found people everywhere—no matter what their economic standing or education—acutely worried. The poll revealed broad, worldwide concern about the quality of drinking water; chemical pollution of the air, lakes, and rivers; loss of farmland and forests; and unsafe disposal of toxic wastes. People in every country said they believe pollution will get worse. And in each country surveyed, more than 75 percent of the people believe stronger government action is needed to fight pollution. A majority of people also believe that "international organizations like the United Nations" must play a major role in that fight [*UNEP North America News*, 8/89].

Natural and Unnatural Disasters

The events that rivet the world's attention generally are manmade disasters; often they have dreadful environmental consequences. As Eastern Europe opened up, the extent of environmental devastation from unconstrained industrial development became increasingly obvious. An avalanche of reports emerged documenting damage done to lives and landscapes, from Sofia to Siberia.

Speaking at the United Nations, the Soviet Union's leading ecologist said that 15 years ago, his country's environmental problems were already as bad as the West's are today—if not worse. **Fallout from the Chernobyl nuclear accident was "at least several times" greater than had been officially announced,** Alexei Yablokov said, with more than 300,000 people evacuated from the contaminated area [*UNEP North America News*, 12/89]. Soviet President **Mikhail Gorbachev proposed establishing a "Green Cross"** to provide emergency assistance to countries struck by environmental disasters [*UNEP North America News*, 8/89]. The United Nations agreed the idea was a good one and gave the proposed Global Centre for Environmental Emergencies priority consideration [Earth Day speech by Dr. Noel J. Brown of UNEP, 4/22/90].

One such environmental disaster, the *Exxon Valdez* tanker accident of March 24, 1989, spilled nearly 11 million gallons of crude oil into Prince William Sound, Alaska, severely damaging the region's bird, marine, and economic life. One positive result, however, did emerge. A coalition of national church and environmental organizations, labor unions, city and state pension funds, and other socially conscious investors began putting financial as well as moral pressure on corporations to adopt standards of environmental accountability.

In the wake of the *Exxon Valdez* disaster, more than 30 major organizations formed the Coalition for Environmentally Responsible Economics (CERES). Their more than 150 billion investment dollars ensure that corporations listen when they talk.

The coalition formulated **the Valdez Principles,** ten ethical guidelines:

1. Protection of the biosphere.
2. Sustainable use of natural resources.
3. Reduction and disposal of waste.
4. Wise use of energy.
5. Risk reduction.
6. Marketing safe products and services.
7. Damage compensation.
8. Disclosure.
9. Environmental directors and managers.
10. Assessment and annual audit.

Shareholders can use these principles to evaluate corporations, and corporations are being urged to adopt them as their own. By the spring of 1990, 24 shareholder resolutions had asked major corporations such as Exxon, Kodak, and Texaco to report on compliance with the principles, and legislation had been proposed in the California and New Jersey legislatures. Among the responsibilities proposed for corporations is an annual self-evaluation of worldwide operations with the findings released to the public. In the future, CERES hopes these corporate ecological assessments will be reviewed by an outside evaluator or auditor [*UNEP Environmental Sabbath Newsletter,* 6/90].

At the same time, **UNEP's Industry and Environment Office** in Paris has been working with leaders in industry, government, and local communities to prepare response plans for both natural and manmade emergencies. The goal of the program—Awareness and Preparedness for Emergencies at the Local Level (APPELL)—is to develop a coordinated response plan for the entire community. UNEP's industry office is also working with industries to develop a Cleaner Production Program with a computerized information exchange system of model case studies, a directory of experts, training opportunities, and a bibliography available to anyone with a personal computer and modem [IEO fact sheets].

Not all environmental afflictions are of human origin. Natural disasters like earthquakes, volcanic eruptions, tidal waves, landslides, and avalanches have also taken a toll. In an effort to improve U.N. systems to deal with such unexpected and often overwhelming disasters, **the 44th General Assembly decided to make the 1990s the International Decade for Natural Disaster Reduction**—a resolution proposed by 155 countries. Its 1990–1991 budget is $602,000 [GA/EF2423,12/11/89]. Among the projects proposed are:

- Development of a historical database on natural disasters.
- A review of lessons learned from previous efforts at disaster relief.
- A system for technology exchange on natural disasters.
- Guidelines for hazard-resistant construction techniques.
- An international mobile early-warning system for volcanic eruptions.
- Safety education programs for schools.
- Training for developing country geoscientists.
- Improving telecommunications for disaster and emergency operations.
- Developing an integrated international electronic information and communication network for disaster management.

Pilot projects were being planned to work on such African problems as the extent of drought in the Sahel, the consequences of health epidemics, and a cyclone warning system for the continent's east coast [A.44/322/Add.2; E/1989/114/Add.2, 10/18/89].

4. Law of the Sea

The slow but steady pace of ratification of the 1982 United Nations Convention on the Law of the Sea (LOS) brings closer the day of reckoning when each nation will have to choose the course most likely, in its view, to contribute to the long-term acceptability and stability of the international legal regime for use of the oceans. Now that the Law of the Sea Convention has been ratified by 42 of the 60 nations needed to bring it into force, the resolve of nations to address the need for improvements in the treaty's deep seabed mining regime grows increasingly apparent.

Dissatisfaction on the part of a number of the major industrialized nations with aspects of the treaty's provisions on mining the deep seabed beyond national jurisdiction has led them to defer adherence to the treaty.

At the same time, despite the fact that the broad outlines of the treaty's provisions governing other uses of the oceans are widely supported by most nations and followed by them in their national practice, the nations of the world are increasingly eager to affirm as international treaty law subject to compulsory, binding dispute settlement both the treaty's general principles and its more detailed rights and obligations in such areas as navigation and overflight, marine scientific research, species conservation, and protection and preservation of the marine environment.

Evidence that the Bush administration is quietly exploring the possibilities of accommodation on the deep seabed mining regime continues to mount. The rest of the world's nations have long been pursuing possible accommodations in the Preparatory Commission for the **International Seabed Authority (ISA)** and the **International Tribunal on the Law of the Sea (ITLOS)** and are urging the U.S. government to lend support to these efforts. The possibility that the 60 ratifications required for the convention's entry into force may be obtained within two to three years places renewed pressure on these nations to fashion widely acceptable solutions to the deep seabed mining issues in order to achieve a universally supported convention.

To date the Preparatory Commission has deferred controversial issues in implementing the deep seabed mining regime to allow promising solutions to emerge and a spirit of compromise to develop. On September 1, 1989, the chairman of the Group of 77 developing nations made a formal statement indicating that the group remained prepared to enter into a dialogue with any and all nations to ensure the universality of the convention, "be they currently involved in the work of the Preparatory Commission, or not, whether signatories or nonsignatories of the Convention." The group also denied that it was in favor of establishing large, bureaucratic, and costly institutions, noting its desire for an efficient and cost-effective ISA whose growth would be dictated by the functions it was called upon to perform. A similar spirit of accommodation was reiterated by the other regional and interest groups represented in the commission. The call for dialogue to ensure the universality of the convention was reaffirmed in the annual resolution on the law of the sea adopted by the General Assembly on November 20, 1989 [A/Res/44/26].

Other developments in the commission indicate widespread support for the establishment of strict financial controls over the ISA budget and granting special representation to the major contributors to its budget until the time when the ISA can support itself from deep seabed mining revenues [LOS/PCN/L.82, 3/29/90]. Similarly, substantial support has emerged for establishing a small, transitional structure for the **Enterprise,** the mining arm of the ISA, until economic and market conditions warrant its full-fledged operation [LOS/PCN/L.80, 3/30/90], and for streamlining the administrative expenses of the ITLOS. The negotiations over the obligations of the four registered pioneer investors (RPIs)—France, India, Japan, and the Soviet Union—indicate that they will reinforce the commission's trend toward taking account of the implications of the delay in commercial mining brought about by altered economic circumstances. They contemplate an emerging compromise where the payments due from the RPIs upon entry into force of the convention would be merged with RPI obligations to train personnel and explore a mine site for the Enterprise, thus reducing the overall burden of RPI obligations. The commission in August 1989 adopted a general framework for the execution of RPI training obligations.

The commission continues to develop rules of procedure for the ISA and the ITLOS and draft agreements related to the establishment of their headquarters, relevant privileges and immunities, and relationships with other international organizations. It has also made progress in identifying a number of functions in monitoring information on minerals market and technological trends and how these may be carried out in collaboration with existing organizations. These activities will be essential if the ISA and the Enterprise are to make well-founded decisions once the convention enters into force—with respect to both establishment and operation of the Enterprise and regulatory decisions on the financial, technical, and environmental rules that will apply to deep seabed mining once it commences. Mining code discussions during 1990 focused primarily on draft environmental regulations for deep seabed mining prepared by the Secretariat [LOS/PCN/SCN.3/WP.6/Add.5, 2/8/90].

Despite a trend toward accommodation in the commission, there is some frustration. The developing nations believe they have made a significant effort to demonstrate that they are open to discussing the concerns of the industrialized mining nations, and they are growing more and more impatient with the delay in agreement on timing and the modalities to implement RPI obligations. All nations are increasingly under the gun from pressures brought to bear by the convention's impending entry into force. They are concerned over national funding obligations and the assessed contributions they will be required to pay for establishment of the institutions called for in the convention, particularly if many of the major industrialized nations are not party to the convention when it enters into force. The countries interested in sponsoring pioneer ventures in deep seabed mining are, in addition, affected by certain deadlines imposed by entry into force. These would deny to their mining entities eligibility to retain pioneer investor status and thus secure title to specific seabed mine sites in which they have already invested significant funds. Both the four pioneer investors registered in 1987 and several other Western nations whose companies form part of multinational consortia that may yet apply to preserve their pioneer mine site rights—including the United States—would be affected. The Federal Republic of Germany would, in addition, lose its right to host the ITLOS if it has not become a party to the convention by its entry into force. Finally, those nations interested in improving the mining regime take the view that their ability to affect that process is greater prior to entry into force. Once it is in force, it will be more difficult to take part in modifying the convention if they are not parties to it.

The Office of Ocean Affairs and the Law of the Sea (OALOS), administered by Under-Secretary-General Satya Nandan, is involved not only in servicing the Preparatory Commission but also in monitoring trends in implementation of the 1982 convention's many other provisions and informing states of these developments. Through publication of the LOS *Bulletin* and other descriptive and interpretive reports, the convening of a special expert group and U.N. interagency consultations, and provision of advice to state members, OALOS helps ensure consistent implementation of all aspects of the LOS Convention regime. In addition to the annual report of the Secretary-General on the Law of the Sea [A/44/650, 11/1/89}, a special report on the marine environment was prepared in 1989 [A/44/461, 9/18/89], which is to be updated in 1990 and issued along with another specialized report on marine scientific research as dealt with in the LOS Convention [*Oceans Policy News*, 12/89].

Another issue of growing importance in the law of the sea was addressed separately during the 44th General Assembly: use of large-scale pelagic drift nets for fishing. On December 22, the Assembly adopted a resolution [44/225] that (1) calls for immediate reduction in drift-net fishing activities in the South Pacific and cessation by July 1991 as an interim measure, pending further agreement on appropriate conservation and management arrangements for tuna resources; (2) bans expansion of such fishing in the high seas of the North Pacific and elsewhere, subject to review in the light of effective conservation and management measures taken on the basis of scientifically sound analysis; and (3) calls for a moratorium on all high seas drift-net fishing by June 1992 as long as no effective conservation and management measures based on sound scientific analysis have been agreed upon.

5. Antarctica

The seventh year of the Antarctica debate in the General Assembly again produced a resolution in two parts that failed to achieve consensus support, with most parties to the Antarctic treaties not participating in the voting.

Australia continues to act as spokesman for the Antarctic Treaty parties, urging that consensus handling of the agenda item be reestablished.

The first part of the resolution appealed again to the Antarctic Treaty Consultative Parties (ATCPs) to exclude the racist apartheid regime of South Africa from participation in treaty meetings [A/Res/44/124 A]. The second part responded to developments in the biennial XV Antarctic Treaty Consultative Meeting (ATCM) in relation to the 1988 Convention on the Regulation of Antarctic Mineral Resource Activities (CRAMRA). It also reiterated previous calls for the Secretary-General to be invited to all meetings of treaty parties and for establishing the United Nations as the repository of all information on Antarctica to serve the international community's right to know [A/Res/44/124 B].

The Australian statement on behalf of the treaty parties indicated that the resolution was unacceptable to them, particularly as it attempted to issue directions on how their deliberations should be conducted, who should be involved, and how they conduct their scientific research in Antarctica and protect the environment, with the underlying premise that something is wrong with the Antarctica Treaty system. Other speakers argued once again that Antarctica should be managed as a common heritage of mankind, the claims and counter claims dispensed with, and criticized CRAMRA and the Antarctic Treaty for the distinction made between decision-making and nonconsultative states parties. They also advocated that documentation for Antarctic meetings be made public in advance for international review and comment with the aim of establishing a more universal framework for consultation on Antarctic matters.

Voting in the General Assembly went as follows: Resolution A (apartheid) 114 in favor and 0 against, with 7 abstentions and 31 nonparticipating; Resolution B, 101 in favor and 0 against, with 8 abstentions and 44 nonparticipating. [The report on voting in the First Committee is contained in document A/44/819, 12/1/89].

The Secretary-General's two reports on Antarctica address follow-up from the 44th General Assembly debate. On the issue of apartheid the report contains the Australian response on behalf of the treaty parties, which references their earlier responses on this question [A/44/518, 9/19/89]. In relation to other issues raised in 1988, the Secretary-General's report contains the ATCP reaction that consideration of Antarctica should proceed on the basis of consensus and reference to the press release from the Preparatory Meeting for XV ATCM, circulated as a U.N. document [A/44/383]. It indicates in addition that the Secretary-General, not having been invited to Antarctic meetings, is not in a position to provide an evaluation of them [A/44/586, 10/3/89]. Additional documents before the General Assembly included a letter from the representative of Malaysia of February 13, 1989, on behalf of 14 other nations, expressing concern for environmental protection in Antarctica and urging reconsideration of support for the 1988 CRAMRA, following the *Bahia Paraiso* oil spill incident [A/44/125; see Issues *Before the 44th General Assembly of the United Nations*, pp. 131–132]; an Organization of African Unity Council of Ministers resolution of July 1989 [A/44/603, Annex I]; documents related to the ninth conference of nonaligned heads of government in September 1989 [A/44/409-S20743 and corr. 1 and 2 and A/44/551-S/20870]; and the Commonwealth heads of government communiqué of October 1989 [A/44/689-S/20921].

In October 1989, Ecuador, Finland, and the Republic of Korea achieved ATCP status, bringing the ATCP total to 25. There are another 14, nonconsultative parties to the Antarctic Treaty. At XV ATCM in Paris, October 9–20, 1989, the states parties were joined by representatives of nine international organizations, which had been invited to attend in an observer or expert capacity [Report on Antarctica, World Resources Institute, 11/89 (WRI 1989)].

The most prominent issue on the agenda of XV ATCM was that of comprehensive measures for the protection of the Antarctic environment. As a result of views expressed by the governments of Australia and France, this issue was also linked to future support for the 1988 Antarctic minerals treaty. XV ATCM decided to convene a special ATCM in 1990 on comprehensive environmental protection, to be held in conjunction with a meeting on the liability protocol envisaged under the minerals treaty. These meetings will take place in Santiago, Chile, November 12–30. All proposals in relation to both items will be explored, including the possibility of a new comprehensive treaty on environmental protection, as proposed by France and Australia. Australia has supported a ban on minerals development in Antarctica and replacement of CRAMRA by a new comprehensive convention; most of the other ATCPs have indicated that while they are in favor of further elaboration of comprehensive measures for environmental protection, they see CRAMRA as an essential component of such measures because it establishes a means to deal with interest in conducting minerals activities should such interest emerge. All the Antarctic Treaty parties continue to support the three Antarctic treaties already in force: the 1959 Antarctic Treaty and its associated measures, the 1972 Convention for the Conservation of Antarctic Seals (CCAS), and the 1980 Convention on the Conservation of Antarctic Marine Living Resources (CCAMLR) [WRI 1989].

CRAMRA has been signed by 17 of the 22 ATCPs eligible to sign it; but to enter into force it must in the long run be adhered to by all of the claimant nations, which include Australia and France, as well as by the United States and the Soviet Union. Growing worldwide concern with environmental protection has led several nations to express the view that minerals development should not take place in Antarctica. The critical question for the special Santiago ATCM is whether alternative proposals to protect Antarctica from the possibility of minerals development will be more effective and durable than CRAMRA, if they can achieve the consensus necessary to be adopted.

In addition to its relationship to the fate of CRAMRA, the Santiago meeting's focus on comprehensive environmental protection will entail consideration of principles to govern all Antarctic activities; supplemental measures required to protect the Antarctic environment and the elaboration of existing measures; the establishment of additional institutional arrangements, such as a secretariat and an environmental-technical advisory panel; environmental monitoring and data management; better coordination and integration among the different Antarctic legal instruments; a strengthening of the binding legal nature of recommendations adopted under the Antarctic Treaty; and the application of compulsory, binding, dispute-settlement procedures and other means of ensuring compliance with governing measures.

U.N. General Assembly Resolution 124B incorporated recent developments in Antarctic policy by urging all members of the international community to support a ban on minerals prospecting and development in Antarctica and expressing the conviction that any regime to be established for the protection and conservation of the Antarctic environment and its dependent and associated ecosystems must be negotiated with the full participation of all members of the international community, if it is to benefit humanity as a whole and to gain the universal acceptance necessary to ensure full compliance and enforcement with it. It endorses establishment of Antarctica as a nature reserve or world park as a means to this end and supports the idea of international scientific research stations to reduce the environmental impacts caused by the increasing number of Antarctic stations and expeditions.

Several important initiatives on the Antarctic environment resulted from XV ATCM. These will, once approved, establish legally binding requirements in the area of waste management and control of marine pollution in the region, and they establish an agenda for the future. On that agenda are such items as waste handling and disposal, vessel construction and manning, marine charting and weather services, contingency planning for marine pollution response, and a liability regime for marine pollution damages from scientific support operations. The initiatives awaiting approval include a call for the establishment of environmental monitoring programs to take into account local impacts of human activities as well as indications of global environmental change, and for a further meeting of experts to deal with the management and effective utilization of Antarctic scientific and environmental data. Still others call for elaborating the system for designating protected areas in Antarctica, with the ability to protect areas of recreational, scenic, and wilderness value, and for addressing conflicts of use and cumulative impacts in high-use zones. And these XV ATCM initiatives would establish additional procedures through which those with less Antarctic experience can obtain information on potentially valuable scientific research undertakings and where they might be carried out and benefit from advice and training in research activities. Finally, the process of declassifying all documents from previous ATCMs was completed; henceforth each ATCM will consider the public availability only of documents from the previous ATCM.

Major developments at the annual CCAMLR meetings on marine living resources conservation, November 6–17, 1989, included the entry into force of a system of observation and inspection, additional limitations on fin-fishing, and more detailed reporting requirements. There is growing concern over excessive fishing and the need to develop a reliable methodology to avoid the overharvesting of krill [Report of the VIII Meeting of the CCAMLR Commission].

IV
Human Rights and Social Issues

1. Human Rights

At the outset of the 1990 session of the Commission on Human Rights on January 29, the outgoing chairman asked everyone to observe a moment of silence for a champion of human rights who had recently died: **Andrei Sakharov**, the famed Soviet dissident and Nobel laureate. The irony of this moment was felt by the human rights advocates present, who knew how little the commission or the United Nations had done to aid the dissident physicist when he was exiled and vilified by the Soviet government. But they also saw the brief observance as a sign of how much things could change in any country, validating the continuing effort to expose human rights abuses and seek improvements worldwide. It is precisely the fact that one can achieve the seemingly impossible in human rights that gets the United Nations so much attention from the world's human rights defenders.

As with past General Assemblies, the 45th will address a wide array of topics when it considers human rights issues in its Third (social and humanitarian affairs) Committee. In so doing, it will build upon the achievements of 1989–1990, a bumpy year for the Organization's human rights bodies but one that, in the end, brought a number of important changes. The dominant issue at the 44th General Assembly, the 46th Commission on Human Rights, and the spring Economic and Social Council (ECOSOC) meeting was the issue of enlarging the commission, the highest specialized political body that addresses human rights. The Third World nations had called for an increase in their representation on the commission—a move that both the Western and Eastern blocs saw not only as an effort to diminish their own influence in the commission but as a potential threat to the further development of effective human rights mechanisms.

In fact, in the last decade, the U.N. human rights program has developed an impressive array of new enforcement machinery—machinery that is not widely known but has fundamentally changed what the United Nations can and does accomplish to aid individual victims of human rights violations. This marks a departure for the United Nations in the field of human rights and has been viewed with considerable dislike by the many countries that violate human rights and do not wish those violations publicized at the United Nations or elsewhere.

The new U.N. human rights machinery includes the following:

- Establishing a variety of specialized theme mechanisms (a Working Group and several independent rapporteurs) to take effective action (often on an emergency basis) wherever there are problems regarding several critical human rights problems that affect individuals: disappearances, summary executions, torture, and religious intolerance.
- Appointing numerous Special Rapporteurs (or Representatives) to examine conditions in individual countries. Afghanistan, Chile, El Salvador, Iran, and Romania are among the current ones.
- Establishing and expanding the activities of new supervisory committees that monitor compliance with human rights treaties, several of which have new optional complaint mechanisms through which individuals can seek redress.
- Substantially expanding the advisory services program that provides technical assistance in human rights.
- Developing a major initiative to expand U.N. public information on human rights in a new world campaign designed to advance awareness of rights and awareness of the U.N. machinery through which individuals can claim their rights.

This progress has come about fitfully over the past decade, but the result has been an arsenal of newly developed enforcement machinery that can accomplish an enormous amount to diminish human rights violations worldwide if its political backing remains strong, if an increasingly vocal backlash is kept under control, and if its resources continue to grow.

The bid to enlarge the Commission on Human Rights has been viewed as a major effort to reverse the direction of the human rights program. At the same time, observers readily note that a good argument can be made for enlargement on the grounds of equity: All past enlargements have been based on existing membership, which served to increase the proportion of members belonging to the Western and Eastern blocs—today only a small minority of the U.N. membership. The Western and Eastern blocs' response was to link the call for enlargement—which would cost more and involve more speakers and time—with the need to rationalize U.N. programs and increase their efficiency. All this soon received the diplomatic name **enhancement**, and the stage was set for an attempt to link enlargement and enhancement. An early initiative at the 44th General Assembly to link the two received only a glancing reference in the resolution that recommended enlargement [44/167]. The real debate came at the Commission on Human Rights—the body that has always set the terms for such matters as enlargement and agenda-structuring, which established a Working Group (or, more accurately, two groups: a public one and a closed, private one) to discuss the issues. Instead of proposing ways to expand the effectiveness of the commission, however, India and Pakistan launched an initiative—soon supported by the whole Nonaligned Movement—that would have had the triple effect of eliminating the independence of the theme mechanisms (by rendering them all regionally balanced groups staffed by diplomats rather than experts), foreclosing the possibility of timely intervention (by routing all complaints about individual cases through the closed-session, confidential **1503 procedure** of the subcommission and commission, which takes a year at best and must be approved by a majority of commission members voting in confidential session), and curtailing the already modest capacity of nongovernmental groups to present oral interventions before the commission. The Western group, for its part, launched an initiative for a **new emergency mechanism** that would enable the commission to be called into session following a major event, such as the Beijing massacre of 1989. It did go on to propose ways to restructure and prune the commission's agenda.

Going right down to the wire, the Working Group at the commission failed to reach agreement on any of the enhancement proposals and refused to link them with enlargement. In an atmosphere that seemed to put at peril the U.N.'s still-fledgling underfunded human rights program, ECOSOC met to proceed with plans for the General Assembly-endorsed enlargement. To everyone's surprise, at these meetings at New York headquarters, representatives of a moderate group of nonaligned states hammered out the compromise [E/1990/L.26] that had eluded the commission in Geneva: a ten-seat, all–Third World enlargement of the commission, to be elected in 1991; and the "understandings" that (a) exceptional sessions of the commission could be convened if a majority of its members agree and (b) beginning in 1992, the mandates of the thematic mechanisms should be extended by three years (instead of the current two) and all governments should ensure unhampered access to relevant information. Reportedly, the country that raised the strongest objection to the new nonaligned position was China, on which some of the human rights bodies had begun to focus attention. When the vote came, however, the United States alone failed to support the proposal.

During its first thirty years or so, the U.N. human rights program concentrated primarily on standard setting. There were only a few modest attempts to develop procedures for enforcing human rights standards. The agreements worked out at the spring session of ECOSOC offer a reasonable way of implementing these standards even as an effort is being made to diminish them. Continuing scrutiny, hard work, consensus-building, creative diplomacy, objectivity, and good documentation may help the entire human rights effort.

The important standard-setting work of the United Nations goes on, reaching into new areas: the rights of indigenous peoples, migrant workers and human rights defenders; treatment of detainees and minorities; mental health; domestic violence; and disappearances. But today, most human rights advocates agree, the major challenge is to strengthen the implementation and enforcement of the human rights standards developed so well over the years.

Disappearances

The 45th General Assembly will readdress the phenomenon of disappearances, whereby an individual is seized, often by persons in plainclothes and either in government service or protected by government agencies, and not seen or heard from again. The government denies any knowledge of these individuals or any responsibility for their whereabouts, and the practice has a chilling effect: eliminating citizens, terrorizing the population, and rendering the government unaccountable. It flouts all international guarantees of personal liberty and due process and causes great anxiety among relatives and friends. This practice is "a gruesome form of human rights violation which . . . continue[s] to warrant the unstinting attention of the international community," according to the tenth anniversary report of the **Working Group on Disappearances** issued in January 1990 [E/CN.4/1990/13, para. 338]. The Working Group was the first of the specialized theme mechanisms set up by the Commission on Human Rights and the first to begin to intervene with governments for information on behalf of individual victims and their families.

In 1989 the General Assembly declared its continuing concern about the practice of forced or involuntary disappearances [A/Res/44/160]. As in the past, it expressed its anguish at the human suffering of the families of the disappeared and appealed to governments to take steps to protect them from intimidation or ill treatment. This emphasis on intimidation of victims and witnesses reiterated a key concern of the Working Group, whose Chairman, Ivan Tosevski of Yugoslavia, pointed out at the 1990 commission that the harassment of witnesses and relatives was directed mainly at women, who were already victims of a loss and were very vulnerable. Both the General Assembly and the commission [Res. 1990/30] have encouraged governments to respond more expeditiously to the Working Group's inquiries and, where appropriate, to invite a visit to the country to help clarify the fate of alleged victims.

Pursuing a strictly **nonaccusatory approach** aimed at finding out what happened to the victim rather than assigning blame for the act, the Working Group has examined disappearances throughout the world. In its ten years of operation it has asked some 41 governments to explain more than 19,000 cases of disappearances. According to Tosevski, the group had examined more than 50,000 reported cases, taking action on 19,000. In its current report the group repeats earlier statistics to the effect that while only 7 to 8 percent of all disappearance cases it has adopted have been formally clarified, the rate rises to 25 percent when it comes to cases that have been submitted promptly and taken up within three months of the actual disappearance.

According to the new report considered at the spring 1989 commission session, the group received data in 1989 on 2,700 disappearances (down from 4,200 in 1988), of which some 1,650 (or 61 percent, down from 82 percent in 1988) were sent to governments for explanations. However, 721 of the disappearances reported actually occurred in 1989 rather than in earlier years, almost twice the number for 1988 (392). In view of the speed with which the group transmits information, more of these cases may be clarified promptly than in the past. Of the 1989 caseload, the countries with the largest number of new reported disappearances were Peru (465), Iran (191), Sri Lanka (102), Iraq (65), India (59, including persons in Sri Lanka under Indian military occupation), Guatemala (54), and the Philippines (51).

The group has sent special delegations to Cyprus and Mexico (1982), Bolivia (1984), Peru (1985 and 1986), Guatemala (1987), and Colombia (1988) at the country's invitation. Such visits not only increase awareness about the group in the country they visit but help obtain official responses that begin to clarify cases. In 1989 the Working Group asked five governments with numerous unresolved disappearance cases to invite a visit: El Salvador, Iran, Iraq, the Philippines, and Sri Lanka. A planned late-1989 visit to the Philippines was postponed when a military coup attempt shook the government. The group reports it has now received oral invitations from El Salvador and Sri Lanka.

These statistics reveal that far from an isolated phenomenon confined to the Latin American region, disappearances are a **worldwide phenomenon**, with four of the six largest caseloads now coming from Asian countries.

During a private meeting of Western delegations at the 1990 session of the Commission on Human Rights, the United States reportedly called for an end to the Working Group [Iain Guest, *The Guardian*, 2/26/89] on the grounds that the phenomenon had diminished, the countries most affected were now democracies, and the cost of the five-member, regionally balanced Working Group is greater than an individual rapporteur, which the United States says it favors in a restructured human rights setup. The U.S. proposal, rejected promptly, became widely known, angering human rights nongovernmental organizations and Western delegations, who saw it as an unrealistic and ill-timed initiative that could undermine the group's work, its mandate's renewal, and the individual case orientation of the theme mechanisms. Whereas Tosevski asked for a four-year mandate renewal, the commission renewed it for two years [Res 1990/30]. ECOSOC, as part of a package of agreements on enlargement and strengthening of the commission, agreed that such mandates would be renewed for three years beginning in 1992.

Beyond the matter of cost, key future issues are whether the Working Group will devise more effective means of action on cases. Responding to a nongovernmental organization (NGO) suggestion, it began in 1989 to transmit follow-up requests on urgent cases to governments twice a year rather than once. Responding to government criticism, it offered governments an opportunity to respond in writing to NGO allegations received by the group and included in its reports. But other issues remain, including proposals that names and other case information be made public after a specified, prolonged period of noncooperation by a government.

Many NGOs, while working closely with the Working Group, have criticized it for overcautiousness in its acceptance of cases, demanding factual details that may not be readily available in time to save a disappeared person's life. Some argue the group should transmit to governments more of the cases sent to it by victims' families and private organizations. And the specific cases are not made public or mentioned (except in anonymous, numerical figures) in the report, a practice seen as shielding governments. Some NGOs have urged the Working Group to take the initiative by developing a model clarification form for governments to follow in their responses and a model list of specific government measures needed to investigate cases of disappearances transmitted by the group. Others have noted the urgent need for the group to follow up on its earlier visits and recommendations so that a visit leads to improvements and clarifications regarding disappearances. The group has said it plans to strengthen its follow-up procedures.

The Working Group has helped to improve the drafting of a declaration by the U.N. Subcommission on Prevention of Discrimination and Protection of Minorities that would detail various government obligations to put an end to disappearances and bring perpetrators to justice. In so doing, it has offered a definition of disappearances and proposed ways to prevent their occurrence. The group has been highly critical of government efforts to give impunity to perpetrators of disappearances because such action tends to encourage rather than prevent further disappearances and related abuses. In keeping with its nonaccusatory approach, however, it does not actively work to bring about prosecutions or identify perpetrators.

Torture

On the 15th anniversary of the U.N. **Declaration against Torture**, the Under-Secretary-General for Human Rights, Jan Martenson, described torture as "one of the most deplorable of all human rights violations" and said that ending it was among the highest priorities [E/CN.4/1990/SR 23, para. 36]. Although U.N. efforts in this field have been substantial, its achievements to date—as the U.N. **Special Rapporteur on Torture**, Peter Kooijmans of the Netherlands, noted in his annual report to the Commission on Human Rights [E/CN.4/1990/17]—have been mainly legal and institutional, awaiting translation into actual practice.

Torture has been formally criminalized. The United Nations adopted a binding 1984 treaty, the **Convention against Torture**, monitored by the new Committee against Torture, which has held four sessions. In addition, in an effort to stop torture in practice, an ad hoc theme mechanism of the Commission on Human Rights, the Special Rapporteur on Torture, takes action on emergency reports of torture cases worldwide and examines the current situation and future prevention of torture in other countries, visiting some at their request. The United Nations has also established a **Voluntary Fund for the Victims of Torture.**

The General Assembly has adopted relatively pro forma resolutions on the convention and torture of children in South Africa and Namibia in recent years and will address the topic again in 1990. The Special Rapporteur comes under the scrutiny of the Commission on Human Rights and, unlike the other three theme mechanisms of the commission, has not been the subject of a General Assembly resolution.

The Convention against Torture, which came into force in June 1987 with 20 states parties, had been ratified by 45 states by September 1, 1989, and was signed by 25 others, including the United States, whose Senate held hearings on the convention during 1990. The states parties must submit reports on their compliance with the convention, which the committee reviews in public session.

The committee, the convention's only implementational mechanism, is similar to those under other U.N. human rights treaties. It met for the third and fourth times in November 1989 and April 1990.

The meetings have already begun to indicate that the **Committee against Torture (CAT)** may develop stricter enforcement procedures than those of other treaty supervisory bodies. A thorough and detailed spring 1990 review of China's report, and its laws and practices on torture, led the committee to request a supplementary report by the end of 1990 to fill in the numerous blanks in the picture presented by that country. Earlier a review of Egypt brought forth a demand for detailed records of court proceedings in cases of alleged torturers. In its first individual case proceeding, the committee spoke forcefully against both the practice of torture and the decision to offer impunity to perpetrators of gross human rights violations in Argentina (although it rejected the complaint on technical grounds of timing). Additionally, it has been reported that the CAT began to take steps to look into torture under the Article 20 procedure, reportedly in Turkey. It has already established a streamlined procedure that gives responsibility for detailed questioning of country representatives to individual committee members.

Under Article 20 of the convention, the expert members of the committee can, on their own initiative, look into charges that torture is being systematically practiced in a state party and may carry out **on-site visits** if the country agrees. Unfortunately, this tough provision of the convention may be bypassed under Article 28 if a country specifically enters a reservation stating that it is not bound by it.

This convention, unlike other human rights treaties, requires that states parties pay independently for *all* expenses of the committee—its meetings, documents, and staff. The uncertainty of cash flow, the experience of other treaty bodies with a pay-as-you-go provision, and financial problems that curtailed committee meeting time during the first year have led the committee to ask the General Assembly to **assure the committee's finances** from the regular U.N. budget or make other financial arrangements, such as additional financing. The General Assembly has been unresponsive on this point. However, the 1989 General Assembly resolution [44/144], like resolutions of the Commission on Human Rights,

> stresses the importance of strict adherence by State Parties to the obligations under the Convention regarding the financing of the Committee against Torture, thus enabling it to carry out in an effective and efficient manner all the functions entrusted to it . . . [and] appeals to all States parties not to take any measures that might impair the financing of all the functions of the Committee under the Convention, so as to ensure the long-term viability of the Convention as an essential mechanism for overseeing the effective implementation of the provisions of the Convention.

An East German reservation—still not withdrawn despite earlier promises of the previous government and the changes of 1989–1990—that it will not pay for expenses in conjunction with any committee on-site visits under Article 20 has raised additional financial obstacles. A number of West European countries have submitted formal objections to the East

German reservation. During the debate at the commission in 1990, several countries called for Chile, the German Democratic Republic, and other countries that had attached onerous reservations to the convention to withdraw them, particularly in view of the changed governments in those countries. Hungary has already done so.

As the U.N. human rights bodies are seized with the problem of rationalizing the reporting systems of the treaty committees, the commission stressed the need for early attention to the development of an effective reporting system and attention to and coordination with the other treaty bodies.

The **Special Rapporteur on Torture** intervenes in emergency cases of torture in an attempt to stop it and asks governments to clarify other detailed allegations concerning torture. He has recommended an array of international and national measures designed to diminish the practice of torture.

In his 1990 annual report to the commission [E/CN.4/1990/17 and Add. 1], Professor Kooijmans detailed a number of important new findings. First, he noted that he had received more allegations of torture than before, which he attributed to greater awareness of the urgent procedure rather than to any increase in torture worldwide. In the continuing effort to obtain better data, he expressed appreciation to an NGO effort to produce a standardized form for allegations from NGOs. He also noted that a bureaucratic-methodological factor may inhibit one or another theme mechanism from receiving an incoming allegation addressed to him.

The Rapporteur's report described his **urgent communications** in 1989 on some 51 cases to 26 countries, among them Burma, China, Saudi Arabia, and the United Arab Emirates. He reported that about half replied. The report further described 48 countries with which the Rapporteur conducted correspondence about individual cases and situations involving torture; details are noted in the official report.

While the Rapporteur expressed courteous appreciation for the large proportion of replies from governments, he explained that when they say the charges are groundless, he "would appreciate it if he were informed on what basis such a conclusion had been drawn." A number of Western governments reiterated the need for fuller information during the general debate at the commission, explaining that otherwise the denial amounted to little more than a "not-guilty" plea without further explanation.

The Rapporteur also presented findings and recommendations from his visits to Guatemala, Honduras, and Zaire in 1989–1990 and from his follow-up correspondence with the governments of Turkey and South Korea, which he visited in 1988–1989. The Rapporteur stated that the primary purpose of his visits are consultative and preventative—not accusatory or investigative; an invitation for him to visit is not, he stressed, an admission of torture. Like so many other experts presenting evidence to the 1990 commission, Kooijmans indicated a profoundly deteriorated situation in Guatemala and stressed the linkage of all basic human rights violations there, not singling out torture in the panoply of problems.

He welcomed an invitation to visit the Philippines during the coming year and then mentioned that he is also available to go to other countries to investigate conditions regarding specific case allegations. No country has invited him for those purposes.

The Rapporteur thoughtfully reflected in his report on the ways to eliminate torture and its interrelatedness with other human rights violations. He presented a rather lengthy analysis of how compliance with the 1988 Body of Principles for the Protection of All Persons under Any Form of Detention or Imprisonment "would make torture during detention or imprisonment virtually impossible."

The 1990 Commission on Human Rights summed up the outlaw nature of torture in Resolution 1990/34, noting that it is "aware that torture constitutes a criminal obliteration of the human personality which can never be justified under any circumstances by any ideology or by any overriding interest, and convinced that a society that tolerates torture can never claim to respect human rights."

The commission stressed the need for a system of periodic visits by independent experts to places of detention—an idea proposed in 1980 by Costa Rica as a possible optional protocol and then shelved. The new European Convention on Torture has a provision along these lines.

Despite consultations between them, the Rapporteur's relationship to the Committee against Torture has been a source of differences. Some Soviet-bloc countries, preferring mechanisms established under binding treaties to those set up by the commission on an ad hoc basis, have in the past tried to define the Rapporteur's role quite narrowly and to limit it to non–states parties. This view did not carry much support. At the 1990 session of the commission, the Soviet delegation—despite perestroika, a softened tone, and acknowledgment that there was not yet universal ratification of the CAT treaty—spoke again of the need to avoid duplication between the committee and the Rapporteur, suggesting a need to look forward and plan for a way to avoid future duplication.

Among the Rapporteur's **recommendations on ending torture** was the need to send independent experts to examine places of detention, to provide detainees with prompt access to a lawyer and a medical examination, to outlaw incommunicado detention, and to establish a national body to receive complaints of torture. He spoke of the need to utilize U.N. advisory services programs to educate and improve behavior by police, law enforcement, and other officials. The Rapporteur's two-year mandate was renewed by the commission for two years.

The 43rd General Assembly also adopted a resolution expressing its outrage at the **detention, torture, and inhumane treatment of children in South Africa and Namibia.** The Special Rapporteur noted an increase in reports of torture against children, which he called "mind-boggling," particularly because cases occurred precisely at the time the United Nations was adopting, unanimously, the new Convention of the Rights of the Child.

The General Assembly is expected to adopt another routine resolution encouraging the work of the Voluntary Fund for Victims of Torture. Among other points, in 1989 it asked the Secretary-General to prepare and disseminate informational materials about the Voluntary Fund to help make its work better known and to generate contributions.

Summary and Arbitrary Executions

The General Assembly uses harsh terms to condemn the practice of summary or arbitrary executions. Since 1982 the topic has been addressed in the report of Amos Wako of Kenya, who is **Special Rapporteur on Summary or Arbitrary Executions,** another theme mechanism of the Commission on Human Rights.

In 1989 the General Assembly once again strongly condemned the large number of summary or arbitrary executions in the world, demanded an end to the practice, appealed urgently to governments to take effective action to combat it, and requested the Special Rapporteur to respond to information on imminent summary or arbitrary executions and to promote exchange of information between governments and the NGOs that present "reliable information" to him [A/Res/44/159]. The Commission on Human Rights appealed in similar but somewhat toned-down terms, although it omitted any encouragement of diplomatic efforts to bring NGO informants together with government representatives.

In 1989, ECOSOC adopted new international standards: **Principles on the Effective Prevention and Investigation of Extra-Legal, Arbitrary and Summary Executions.** In his 1990 report to the Commission on Human Rights, Special Rapporteur Wako praised the principles as "a milestone for his mandate" and encouraged governments to bring their national laws into conformity with the new principles. He indicated that this consensus on international standards would ease his job; he planned to refer to them without reservation and press governments to follow them: "Any Government's practice that fails to reach the standards set out in the principles may be regarded as an indication of the Government's responsibility, even if no government officials are found to be directly involved in the acts of summary or arbitrary execution" [E/CN.4/1990/22 and Add. 1].

In his annual reports since 1982, Wako has continually expanded the scope of his concern, which now includes imminent as well as actual deaths, cases with the death penalty that lack legal safeguards, and other suspicious deaths. In the past, he identified as falling within his mandate actual or imminent execution, either without trial or with trial that lacks the due process safeguards for defendants assured under the omnibus International Covenant on Civil and Political Rights; and deaths as a result of torture, force used by police, military, or other government institutions, and assault by individual or paramilitary groups under official control, as well as those by similar bodies that oppose the government or are outside its control. In his 1990 report he expanded his concern to include death threats, including those by police, military, or other governmental or quasi-governmental forces, as well as individuals or paramilitary groups under official control or acting with official connivance. He added the latter category after noting that a large proportion of victims killed in summary or arbitrary extrajudicial killings have first received death threats. In his report, Wako stressed the need for governments to be responsible for providing protection to persons who receive death threats.

Wako made a special point of addressing one large target group of death threats: **human rights defenders**, who, he explained, "often end up as victims of summary or arbitrary executions." Urging better national and international measures to protect them, he noted that "the integrity and well-being of the entire community of a country depend very much on their uncompromising struggle." Curiously, he did not draw attention to an ongoing effort, in the Commission on Human Rights, to draft international standards outlining the rights of people and groups of human rights defenders to promote, protect, and claim their human rights. That effort, before a commission working group, is nearing completion of a first draft.

Most of the Rapporteur's report consisted of details, including names and dates, about cases he brought to the attention of governments and the replies, if any. In 1989 the number of cases reported to him had grown to some 1,500 communications—possibly, he speculated, because his mandate is better known worldwide.

In 1989, Wako contacted 48 governments, 2 more than in 1988 and about twice the number contacted in 1987. Of these, 25 received emergency cables (15 responded); 36 received letters with requests for information (12 replied). These figures are somewhat better than in the past but still reflect the Rapporteur's **continuing difficulty in getting government cooperation.** Some of the countries contacted are those rarely discussed in U.N. human rights bodies, among them China (killings in the Beijing crackdown and in Tibet), India (deaths following arrest, unacknowledged detention, and torture in the Punjab in conditions of political violence, and deaths following torture in police custody in Bihar), Saudi Arabia (death after torture and summary beheadings of Kuwaiti nationals accused of bombings), the Soviet Union (killings in Tbilisi, Georgia), and Yugoslavia (killings of ethnic Albanians in Kosovo, including elementary schoolchildren shot at from a helicopter by security forces). The other countries contacted were Angola, Argentina, Bahrain, Bangladesh, Benin, Brazil, Bulgaria, Burundi, Cameroon, Chad, Chile, Colombia, Yemen, El Salvador, Ethiopia, Guatemala, Guyana, Haiti, Honduras, Indonesia, Iran, Iraq, Israel, Malawi, Maldives, Mauritania, Mexico, Nicaragua, Pakistan, Panama, Peru, the Philippines, Romania, Somalia, South Africa, Sri Lanka, Sudan, Suriname, Turkey, Myanmar, the United States, and Venezuela.

The Rapporteur did not evaluate or comment upon the responses. He did not indicate—nor do most of the governments—whether government practices that may have led to some of the incidents were ended or subjected to remedial action; he did note the **cases where an execution was postponed, reviewed, or stayed**—a very small category, drawing attention to the serious need to strengthen and improve the effectiveness of the Rapporteur's urgent appeals.

Government responses have ranged from about 25 percent of the countries contacted (in 1985) to 75 percent (in 1986), with recent years falling between 40 and 60 percent. Reactions vary: silence (e.g., Iran and Libya), denial of the event itself or of the fact that the execution in question was summary or arbitrary (such respondents commonly challenge the Rapporteur's truthfulness and objectivity), counteraccusations against the victims (e.g., Latin American governments have accused opposition groups of violent tactics and killings), admission of the action but with a justification, promises to investigate and punish those responsible, a request for more information, or even, in some instances, an invitation for the Rapporteur to visit. Some have mentioned the creation of national commissions on human rights as well.

Sensitive to the need to do more to offset the continuance of summary and arbitrary executions, the Rapporteur has previously suggested undertaking more on-site visits and maintaining greater cooperation with other international organizations. His on-site visits have been to Suriname in 1984, 1986, and 1989, to Uganda in 1986, and to Colombia in 1989 [described in Add. 1], all at the government's invitation. (An earlier invitation to Guatemala, in 1983, was not pursued due to other limitations.) Little information is available on follow-up measures once a government has replied; we do not know whether the Rapporteur continues a dialogue, questions the government version of the facts, develops any personal contacts, or maintains continued pressure regarding the practices in question. Similarly, in the few cases (according to the reports, fewer than a dozen to date) where executions have been stayed because of the Rapporteur's appeals, it is not known whether the Rapporteur maintains a continued interest in the proceedings of the case.

Other responses by the Rapporteur included a request for clarification of international standards, improved government compliance with standards and U.N. provision of advisory services to advance this, a call for a reduction of domestic and international conflicts that contribute to summary and arbitrary executions, and calls for more coordinated action by international organizations and for regional initiatives.

A lengthy report on the Rapporteur's visit to Colombia put forth country-specific recommendations: the disbanding of all paramilitary organizations, dismissal of armed forces and police personnel known to have links to drug traffickers, a judge and witness protection plan, and a national campaign for human rights.

Like other theme mechanisms, the practice of **nonresponse by governments** has come in for special criticism. In his speech to the 1990 commission, the Rapporteur identified five countries that had replied not at all for two consecutive years—Chad, Haiti, Malawi, Somalia, and South Africa—and he added the Sudan to this list. In the debate at the commission, several countries addressed and responded to allegations in the Rapporteur's report: the Philippines, Brazil, Colombia, and Saudi Arabia.

In his recommendations the Rapporteur spoke of the advisory services program and offered a thoughtful list of criteria that should be applied before the program's resources are used. The list is a more detailed guide than any yet produced for the program.

Religious Intolerance

The 45th General Assembly will consider measures to end religious intolerance, a matter now studied by another of the Human Rights Commission's theme Rapporteurs, Angelo Vidal d'Almeida Ribeiro of Portugal.

Religious freedom has been a sensitive topic at the United Nations over the years because the Soviet Union and its allies had proclaimed atheism as national policy and sought to inhibit religion while still other states proclaimed an official state religion and lacked tolerance for persons professing other faiths. Soviet-bloc policies have been changing rapidly, but other impediments, including the policies and beliefs of Islamic governments, for example, which do not acknowledge religious sects formed after Islam or the right to change one's religion from Islam, continue to make the topic sensitive.

The **Special Rapporteur on Religious Intolerance**, established in 1985 by the Commission on Human Rights and extended since then by consensus, was renewed by the commission in 1990 along with other commission-appointed rapporteurs for two years and extended by ECOSOC for three. Ribeiro's reports have addressed individual country situations and contain excerpts from his correspondence with the governments involved and their replies, if any. His **response rate** is considerably higher than that of other theme rapporteurs, although many of the replies are nonsubstantive, merely citing legal provisions. Like the Rapporteur on executions, Ribeiro does not comment on the replies or offer country-specific recommendations for alleviating infringements on religious freedoms.

In the January 1990 report [E/CN.4/1990/46], Ribeiro states that he contacted 29 governments in 1989 (up from 23 in 1988), of which 18 replied (compared to 15 in 1988). Unlike 1988, he did not single out the names of countries that had refused to reply for a period of years.

Among the countries (and religious minorities) cited in the January 1990 report that rarely appear in a U.N. report were Saudi Arabia (for refusing to permit a half-million Christian immigrants to worship or construct churches); China (for persecuting Tibetan monks and nuns and the Buddhist religion, as well as for attacks on Catholic believers); Egypt (for seizing and closing numerous Coptic churches and reportedly denying building permits); Greece (for prosecuting some 2,000 non–Greek Orthodox persons who proselytize their religions); Iran (for discrimination against Baha'is and the pressure of "forced Islamization" directed particularly against Armenian Christians); Nepal (for discriminatory measures and arrests of Christians); Nicaragua (for harassment of institutions of the official Catholic church); Pakistan (for demolition of Ahmadi mosques, arrests, and other harassment of Ahmadis); Spain and Italy (for legal proceedings directed against the Church of Scientology); and Zaire, Burundi, Ethiopia, and Indonesia (for reported banning and harassment of Jehovah's Witnesses).

Ribeiro's report seemed more muted than in the past. He did mention, and express disapproval of, the Iranian "death sentence" against British author **Salman Rushdie**, whose book offended many Muslims. But he did so in classic U.N. diplomatic style: without mentioning the name of the country involved or of Rushdie [para. 104]. (In contrast, Amos Wako mentioned both by name in his report's discussion of Iran.) Later, in a clear reference to Saudi Arabia (also not named), Ribeiro expressed concern about "difficulties created by certain States in regard to the religious practices of foreigners who hold religious beliefs different from those held by the majority of the nationals of those states." His solution to the practice of restricting these persons not only from building churches but also from conducting private worship was classicly diplomatic: He called for reciprocity on a state-to-state or bilateral basis for one's citizens in another country. This "let's work it out" approach, rather than a rights-oriented approach upholding the freedom of religion of all persons residing in the state, is preferred by Ribeiro; it has angered some NGOs, which point out that observance of international human rights guarantees is not a matter for diplomatic or humanitarian negotiations on reciprocity but in fact a binding international legal obligation.

The report observed that infringements on religious freedom usually result in **infringements of other human rights**—for example, an individual's freedom of movement and expression—as well as in extrajudicial killings in clashes with other religious groups or even with government security forces. It went on to praise the **improvements in the Soviet Union** in the past year—all improvements in practice—but made no mention of the delay in adopting promised new laws governing religion.

By consensus, the 44th General Assembly largely reiterated its concerns on religious intolerance over the past several years. It supported efforts to continue measures to implement the **Declaration on the Elimination of All Forms of Intolerance based on Religion or Belief**, the principal instrument in this area, and expressed some caution on initiatives to begin drafting a **new binding instrument on religion**. It also emphasized the continuing role of nongovernmental organizations, including religious ones, and urged states to provide adequate constitutional and legal guarantees of freedom of thought, conscience, religion, and belief, including effective remedies for intolerance or discrimination. It encouraged better education and again invited the Secretary-General to disseminate the declaration widely and in all official languages (something called for repeatedly since 1982 but not yet accomplished) and for states to distribute it in national languages.

The General Assembly continues to be cool to the idea of drafting a binding instrument on religious intolerance, which the commission has been considering and which the Rapporteur enthusiastically recommended again in his latest report. Indeed, the main point of reluctance on a convention is the worry that any new convention will further erode the standards stated in the Declaration on Religious Intolerance and other instruments.

At the commission, most countries were also cool to the matter of such a convention. Support came from India, Ethiopia, Hungary, the Rapporteur's own Portugal, and a number of NGO religious-based organizations. Other countries, including most of the Western group, as well as such diverse countries as Egypt, Venezuela, and Senegal, expressed either disapproval or the need for "careful consideration"—a code word for a go-slow approach. Most speakers at the Commission on Human Rights spoke favorably of the cautionary recommendation by Subcommission Special Rapporteur Theo van Boven of the Netherlands, who has studied existing standards on religion and proposed that any new instrument be an optional protocol to an existing treaty, with supervision by a consolidated treaty mechanism.

Notably the 1990 commission did *not* advance any supportive language regarding the movement toward a binding instrument: There was no endorsement of the van Boven report or of the Rapporteur's recommendation for the establishment of a working group to begin drafting a new treaty. Instead, like the General Assembly, it encouraged an array of education and advisory services measures to help implement the present declaration and called for improved national laws and remedies.

Country Situations

In recent years the General Assembly has moved beyond its earlier pattern of publicly addressing human rights abuses in only three countries: Chile, South Africa, and Israel. The 46th Commission on Human Rights appointed special rapporteurs or representatives to conduct studies on Afghanistan, El Salvador, and Iran and report their findings to the General Assembly, which has itself adopted resolutions on these countries. The commission has also appointed special country experts to report on conditions in Romania and Haiti, but these experts have not been asked to appear before the Assembly. Other countries, Albania and Cuba among them, have been the subject of resolutions, but no expert has been appointed to report on the human rights situation within their borders.

Some countries are considered at the Commission on Human Rights under the category of "advisory services," which were established to provide the sort of technical assistance that a developing country might need to implement the standards set in various international covenants on human rights. A government has only to request the services to be eligible for them, and some have managed to head-off a full-scale human rights inquiry by requesting them. At the 46th commission the countries considered under this category included Guatemala, Haiti, and Equatorial Guinea.

Iran. Since 1984 human rights conditions in Iran have been under scrutiny by a **Special Representative** of the Commission on Human Rights, Galindo Pohl of El Salvador, who also reports to the General Assembly. The 45th General Assembly will have before it another interim report by the Special Representative, who earlier in 1990 made his **first visit to Iran** to examine conditions there. The result of that visit—the first agreed to by the Iranian government for *any* outside human rights organization or body since the 1978 revolution—was a weak and highly controversial report by Pohl to the Commission on Human Rights.

Behind-the-scenes negotiations at the 44th General Assembly had led to a nonsubstantive, noncritical resolution and, in exchange, the written invitation from Iran for the Special Representative's visit. (A second invitation has since been received.) Pohl's mission report, released in February 1990, was published too late for the commission to discuss it at any length. The commission adopted a mild substantive resolution that, like the report, was considerably weaker than any that had come before.

In the mission report [E/CN.4/1990/24], the Special Representative abandoned his past conclusion that the evidence, taken together, appeared convincing and merited further international monitoring. Instead Pohl seemed to give the benefit of the doubt to Iranian government statements and the assurances made to him. He uncharacteristically ruled out an array of charges by the **Mujahedin** resistance group on the basis of only four cases that he himself examined in Iran. However, his carefully composed description of the **witness testimonies** also mentions the tumult accompanying his visit and a few revealing and poignant details, such as when a government witness who was testifying that there was no torture in Iranian jails wrote him a note stating that "he had been forced to state the above and that many ex-prisoners had been induced by the authorities to make similar statements under threat of execution if they denounced their real experiences in prison" [para. 196]. He drew attention to reports received subsequently that witnesses who spoke to him had suffered reprisals and possibly disappeared [para. 171]. But these were almost hidden points in a larger analysis that never assessed or commented on such factors or drew any specific conclusions about continuing violations. For his part, the Representative did state that the February 1990 report should be considered together with, and as part of, his November 1989 interim report to the General Assembly, which had been even stronger than past ones.

Pohl stressed that the government still needed to provide "circumstantiated" detailed replies to the many allegations of abuses he had presented to them over the years. Moreover, noting the huge demand by witnesses to present evidence to him during the trip, he urged that a second visit be scheduled and that the subject remain before the commission.

The commission praised the Iranian government for permitting the trip and inviting Pohl for a **second visit**, for favorably receiving Pohl's recommendations (which it repeated), and for such clemency measures as it had taken. The resolution mentioned Pohl's condemnation of terrorism "in all its forms" and his decision to "rule out" (without specific proof otherwise) allegations that the drug traffickers put to death were in fact political prisoners.

Charges were later made by the Mujahedin that what Pohl saw had been carefully doctored to present the best possible impression. They claimed that thousands of political prisoners were transferred out of Tehran immediately prior to the delegation's arrival, with many kept in railroad cars out of town until the delegation left, and that guards posed as prisoners to trick the delegation. They discredited his presentation of the

Iranian position that there had been no public executions in Iran for five months, drawing attention to public hangings and beheadings reported by the Iranian press in January and February, even as the Representative was visiting the country. Later they called the Pohl report "manipulated, biased, and devoid of credibility" [UPI, 2/27/90] and attacked Pohl for allegedly making a behind-the-scenes deal that some in the news media linked to the prospect of a release of Western hostages in Lebanon. At a Geneva news conference, Pohl denied these accusations.

Other critics have suggested that the U.N. report placed the desire for continued direct contacts and investigations above the issue of reporting the truth at this time. The question remains as to what the Representative will be able to accomplish on his second trip.

The seriousness and dangerous nature of the whole matter is underscored by a later development. In late April, **Kazemi Rajavi**, the Geneva representative of the resistance group that had been so active in challenging the U.N. report, was shot in the head and killed in Coppet, a small village east of Geneva. It was the fifth political assassination during the year in which Iranian government agents were suspected to have had a hand [UPI, 4/24/90]. *The Washington Post* [4/27/90] quoted opposition spokesmen as charging that "Iran's ambassador to the UN in Geneva told Rajavi in late February, in the presence of witnesses, that he would be liquidated," which the Iranian mission in Geneva labeled "a mere lie."

El Salvador. El Salvador's human rights conditions have been under scrutiny in the General Assembly and Commission on Human Rights since 1981. The 45th General Assembly will consider a report on El Salvador by the **Special Representative** of the Commission on Human Rights, José Antonio Pastor Ridruejo of Spain.

The killings of **six priests and two civilians** at the **University of Central America** by military personnel and the subsequent judicial investigation dominated much of the debate on the situation in El Salvador at the General Assembly and commission. The rebel Farabundo Martí National Liberation Front (FMLN) offensive in San Salvador and the government's aerial bombing of poor neighborhoods also drew attention to the increased spiral of violence in the country.

The deteriorating human rights situation in El Salvador in 1989–1990 is detailed in Pastor Ridruejo's new reports [A/44/671; and E/CN.4/1990/26]. The Representative attributed the decline to the intensification of the fighting and also to the fact that "the constitutional authorities of El Salvador had not been able to exercise sufficient control over the actions of the various State agencies" [E/CN.4/1990/SR.30/para. 72]. His reports described a wide array of abuses, including continuing "politically motivated **summary executions**" on a scale "comparable to . . . last year," **disappearances and abductions** (for which he finds allegations about death squads "plausible" but not definite), increased **political arrests**, and "a resurgence" of **torture**, which he claimed is "not widespread and does not represent a government policy," attributing its practice to individual officials. He detailed numerous **actions against trade unions and peasant organizations**, criticized a "highly unsatisfactory" **judicial system**, which despite some progress in 1989–1990 had not taken action in most cases, and outlined "harsh and distressing" **treatment of the civilian population**, as well as an adverse situation in economic and social rights because of the continuing civil war.

The Representative's findings were critical of both **members of the state apparatus**, whom he listed as responsible for most of the violations listed, and **FMLN guerrilla organizations**, which he cited for executions and abductions, explosions of contact mines, extortion of goods from peasants, and systematic attacks on the country's economic infrastructure. However, continuing his generally supportive past comments about the government, Pastor Ridruejo expressed the view that Alfredo Christiani, El Salvador's President, is "sincerely resolved to defend democracy and ensure respect for human rights" [E/CN.4/1990/SR.30, para. 72] and cited as proof the fact that persons responsible for the killing of Father Ignacio Ellacuria and other individuals have been brought before the courts. Fair and exemplary sentences for still others accused of death-squad-type summary executions would be "real proof" of the government's intention to reform and ensure respect for rule of law principles.

The 44th General Assembly's resolution on El Salvador [A/Res/44/165] was more pointed than the previous year's, which had moved away from human rights issues and concentrated on the peace process and the refugee problem. That 1988 resolution expressed general concern about the increased human rights violations in El Salvador and referred to non-observance of the humanitarian laws of war and to the unsatisfactory judicial system, largely ignoring the other major human rights violations detailed in Pastor Ridruejo's report.

In 1989, although the Latin American group developed its own draft resolution on El Salvador, there was strong pressure from the Western European-and-other group (WEOG) to introduce the human rights matters in the Pastor Ridruejo report and a response to the slaying of the six priests at the General Assembly session. As a result, the final resolution contained several preambular paragraphs that referred to the Representative's findings and related topics. The resolution itself condemned "the brutal assassination" of the priests and called for the government to fulfill its pledge to carry out an investigation and punishment and expressed deep concern over the persistence of and increase in "politically motivated serious violations" of executions, torture, and disappearances, as well as the "death squads," which operate with impunity. It urged the "extremely unsatisfactory" justice system to make a variety of reforms. Ten additional Western governments cosponsored the resolution after the revisions.

At the 1990 commission, the resolution on El Salvador (adopted without a vote) referred not only to the Pastor Ridruejo report but also to the reports of the Special Rapporteur on Torture and the Working Group on Disappearances and regretted the increased attacks and threats against religious leaders; political, trade union, and peasant organizations; and relatives of civil servants and army personnel. It called upon the legal system to find and punish those responsible for human rights violations, including the assassinations of leading government figures, as well as the murder of **Bishop Romero** in 1980, on whose case, they regretted, "no progress" had been made. Like the General Assembly resolution, it expressed concern over executions, torture, abductions, and disappearances; condemned "the murder" of the six priests; acknowledged that the government had brought several suspects in the case to court and expressed hope that the procedure would continue; regretted the continuance of death squads that function with impunity, called for reforms in the "unsatisfactory" judicial system; requested respect for humanitarian standards applicable to the civilian population, and, in a late addition, urged the government and the FMLN "in no circumstances to penalize **medical and health personnel** for carrying out their activities" to provide humanitarian and medical assistance to the war wounded or others in need.

After the commission adopted the resolution by consensus, the U.S. government explained it would have voted against the draft, if there had been a vote, because it did not appropriately recognize the Salvadoran government's good faith or criticize the support the FMLN receives from abroad. Moreover, the United States rejected the claim that "systematic" torture is practiced in the country, although the term is never used in the text.

By the time ECOSOC met, word had reached the foreign press that the investigation and prosecutions in the case of the six priests had stalled, perhaps for good, with key witnesses transferred abroad.

Chile. For the first time in over a decade the General Assembly will not be receiving a report on Chile from the Special Rapporteur of the Commission on Human Rights, Fernando Volio of Costa Rica. At its 1990 session the commission decided **"not to renew the mandate of the Special Rapporteur,** as from the time the Government-elect takes office" (March 1990), as a sign of good faith that the new, democratic Chilean government would take measures to restore the rule of law and human rights.

In fact, however, the decision was more than a sign of good faith. Many institutional and legal problems still remained, and it would not have been unusual for the United Nations to continue scrutiny of human rights as the new government began to address these problems. Letting countries off the hook once they install a democratic government had been criticized in the past as a poor practice that diminishes concern about rights violations.

But the reality behind the decision was that the Chilean government-elect of Patricio Aylwin reportedly refused to accept the continuance of the Special Rapporteur, arguing along lines reminiscent of the Pinochet government that it was a special procedure and sign of opprobrium. Western and Latin governments went along with this—some, such as Sweden, quite reluctantly.

Even the Rapporteur, known for taking every opportunity to praise the Chilean government, had proposed an alternative arrangement. In his last report to the commission, he stated [para. 27] that in the new circumstance, "the activities of a special rapporteur will not be necessary, although it might be desirable to have a new and specific form of international co-operation for the protection of human rights on the part of the United Nations."

In his two reports [A/44/635 and E/CN.4/1990/5], the Special Rapporteur had offered a lengthy list of achievements as well as problem spots. Among the **achievements** were the lifting of the states of siege and all emergency conditions, permission for the return of all Chileans to the country, the December elections, a law determining the elected Congress, an end to administrative banishment of important labor leaders, amendments to the code of penal procedure, the dissolution of the secret police (CNI), and the sentencing of four CNI agents for attacking demonstrators. But the Rapporteur noted that the Chilean government of General Pinochet had refused to cooperate with the United Nations since May 1989 (when Volio had temporarily resigned his post on grounds of ill health), reviving its earlier argumentation that the post is a "selective procedure" that discriminates against Chile.

Among the **continuing problems** Volio noted were the existence of torture, abuses by military courts, the lack of independence of the judiciary, and the lack of appropriate judicial measures against persons involved in some of the notorious cases of killing, disappearance, and burning over recent years.

In its resolution, the commission identified the following items as "still pending":

- Judicial and administrative identification and punishment of persons responsible for disappearances, torture, persecution, intimidation, and other crimes.
- A reform of military justice.
- A review of rules whereby "persons committing serious violation of human rights are granted impunity," likely to be a particularly sticky issue in the year ahead.

The commission reached a compromise that would permit some form of follow-up with the Chilean situation at the commission. It requested the new Chilean government to report on its follow-up to the various recommendations adopted by the United Nations at a **special meeting** at the 1991 commission session.

Afghanistan. The 45th General Assembly will receive another interim report from its **Special Rapporteur,** Felix Ermacora of Austria.

Although his January 1990 visit to Afghanistan and Pakistan took place a year after the withdrawal of Soviet troops, Ermacora reported to the commission [E/CN.4/1990/25] that he found the human rights situation in Afghanistan still troubling, with the number of refugees still very large, as are civilian casualties of the conflict. He called for a political solution to the war, dwelled at length on the problems of the **refugees from Afghanistan,** urged an increase in international assistance to them, which he noted had fallen off, and addressed possible international or cooperative solutions for improved **mine detection**—a problem he had long identified as an obstacle to their returning. He discussed **detention conditions,** setting the estimate of political prisoners at 3,000 and expressing concern over the broad definition of state security that Afghan authorities had used to incarcerate leading intellectuals and others, creating a **climate of insecurity.** Ermacora stressed the importance of fair **trial procedures** and noted that the regime's opponents were still tried before special security courts that do not offer international due process guarantees. He called for upgraded prison conditions, which he described as "deplorable," and for visits to prisoners—including those held by the rebels—by the International Committee of the Red Cross, recommending the use of U.N. advisory services to help change the situation. Ermacora called for the release of all political prisoners and detained soldiers, application of amnesty decrees to foreign detainees, transmission of the names of all political prisoners and detained soldiers to humanitarian organizations, and investigation of the fate of the disappeared. He also stressed the need for efforts to bring the refugees back home.

Both the 44th General Assembly and the 46th commission adopted resolutions that addressed the human rights and humanitarian concerns raised by the Special Rapporteur. As in the previous year, both resolutions were approved by consensus, with negotiations on acceptable language taking place behind the scenes.

The commission resolution, similar to that adopted by the General Assembly, expressed appreciation to the Special Rapporteur and welcomed Afghan government cooperation with him. It no longer spoke of "improvements" but stressed the need to work for a **political settlement.** It mentioned that some 3,000 political prisoners remained and called for the end of use of weapons against civilians. Going beyond the General Assembly's resolution, the commission called for protection of all prisoners from reprisals and violence, notably including "ill-treatment, torture and summary execution." It called for names of prisoners to be given to the ICRC and asked that all reports of disappearances be investigated. The resolution carefully avoided use of the Rapporteur's term *political prisoners*, but a review of the report makes it clear that most of his recommendations related to political prisoners and incarcerated Afghan soldiers. The commission's resolution, like the General Assembly's, called for due process guarantees along the lines recommended by the Rapporteur.

This year's resolution noted deep concern over increased "acts of terrorism against civilians" but did not attribute these or other such abuses to one side or the other, calling for "all parties" to observe humanitarian laws of war. However, it noted "with concern" the allegations of atrocities against Afghan soldiers.

South Africa. The 45th General Assembly, addressing South Africa's political and human rights situation following African National Congress leader **Nelson Mandela**'s release from prison after 27 years and his triumphant June address to the U.N., will be looking for further evidence of continued, significant changes in the Republic. The 46th Commission on Human Rights, meeting in February-March, recognized improvements in the human rights situation but continued its call for **mandatory sanctions** and was generally critical of those who still conduct economic or military trade with Pretoria. At the commission, as in the past, all the Western governments (save Sweden and Canada) and Japan voted against, or abstained from, the key resolutions on South Africa, calling such passages problematic; but they expressed special appreciation to the sponsors for generally employing the sort of moderate language that paves the way to consensus. Many governments that abstained or voted "no" indicated that they had come very close to subscribing to a consensus resolution. It remains to be seen whether the 45th General Assembly will in fact achieve it.

The 44th General Assembly discussed and in 1989 adopted twelve related resolutions [44/27 A to L] on the policies of **apartheid** in South Africa, ranging from expressions of "solidarity with the liberation struggle" to calls for "comprehensive and mandatory" economic, financial, and other sanctions against the South African government to criticism of relations between Israel and South Africa. Still other resolutions in this group affirm support for U.N. bodies concerned with apartheid (the Special Committee against Apartheid, the U.N. Trust Fund for South Africa, and the Commission against Apartheid in Sports).

As before, the Assembly's condemnation of the policy of apartheid and related human rights violations by the South African government aims for comprehensiveness. Its resolutions demand abolition of apartheid, the unconditional release of all political prisoners, and an end to arbitrary detention, the widespread use of torture against political opponents, discriminatory laws, censorship, and the bantustans; they call for freedom of association, black trade union rights, and an end to the harassment, intimidation, and arrest and maltreatment of black union leaders; and they ask for the return of political refugees and widespread sanctions. To this already extensive list the Third Committee and the commission have added a denunciation of the detention and torture of children.

In 1989 the United States voted against all but two General Assembly resolutions on South Africa. One of these was a routine item on the U.N. Trust Fund for South Africa. The other was a substantive resolution ("B"), adopted by the General Assembly without a vote, that made some **moderate demands** (many of them fulfilled since) that would help create a climate for negotiations to end apartheid: lifting the state of emergency, releasing Nelson Mandela and other political detainees, ending the ban on political organizations opposing apartheid, repealing press restrictions, withdrawing troops from black townships, and putting a stop to political trials and political executions. The 46th commission did not have a separate resolution containing only these universally accepted demands, and as a result only Sweden among the Western countries voted for the commission's principal resolution on human rights in South Africa [1990/26].

One of the striking differences at the 46th commission was the **absence of criticism of certain Western governments by name**—something that has become more common in General Assembly resolutions in recent years, with the United States, United Kingdom, Israel, and Japan coming in for special criticism because of ongoing trade with South Africa. The 44th General Assembly itself had dropped all negative references to the United States and United Kingdom, although it singled out the Federal Republic of Germany for criticism, citing its "emer[gence] as the leading trading partner of South Africa." Israel came in for sharp criticism for military collaboration with South Africa, the Federal Republic of Germany was criticized for actions by two of its corporations that were "supplying blueprints for the manufacture of submarines" and other matériel, and Chile was "deplored" for purchases of South African military hardware.

A new development at the 46th commission were the votes by the Soviet Union and other East European members (Bulgaria, Hungary, and the Ukraine) against the paragraphs calling for mandatory sanctions.

Israel and the Occupied Territories. At the 45th General Assembly, human rights in the territories occupied by Israel after the 1967 war will be discussed in the Special Political Committee in company with other issues relating to the "Palestine question," rather than in the Third Committee, where most human rights issues are debated and acted upon.

A variety of political and human rights topics are covered in many of the resolutions on the Israeli-occupied territories, but those addressing the traditional human rights issues are detailed in the Report of the **Special Committee to Investigate Israeli Practices Affecting the Human Rights of the Population of the Occupied Territories**—redesignated "the **Palestinian People and Other Arabs of the Occupied Territories**" in 1989. This name change by the 44th General Assembly was one indication of a move throughout the year to gain recognition of Palestinian statehood by U.N. member states. Another indicator was the reference in a 1990 Commission on Human Rights resolution [1990/2] to Palestine's "accession" to the four Geneva conventions. This drew a separate vote in which Western-bloc states opposed the reference and some nonaligned member countries (Peru and Mexico) made a special point of saying that their vote for the overall resolution did not necessarily signify recognition of the independent state of Palestine.

The special committee's three members represent the governments of Sri Lanka, Senegal, and Yugoslavia. Its annual lengthy report to the General Assembly concludes that the situation has been marked "by a **dangerous level of violence and repression which has constantly escalated**" since the "Intifada" uprising began in December 1987.

The report discerns an increase in the "frequency and intensity" of clashes between civilians and the Israeli army, border police, paratroopers, and settlers, noting that many deaths have resulted. According to its findings, which largely mirror those of the prior year, daily confrontations have resulted in "a climate of terror, violence and humiliation"; further deterioration in the military justice system and legal rights of the accused; "increasing recourse to . . . collective reprisals, such as the demolition of houses on a very large scale; the imposition of prolonged curfews or harsh economic sanctions"; and a "noticeable increase in the number of deportations," detainees, and measures against news media, as well as "prolonged closures" of educational institutions [see statement by H.E. Daya Perera to Special Committee, 11/20/89].

The committee, which relies upon oral testimony, written reports (mainly from Israeli, Arab, or Western newspapers), and information submitted by governments, has not been permitted to conduct **on-site investigations** in the Occupied Territories. The report details, topic by topic, each reported killing, wounding, or other action affecting the right to a fair trial, treatment of civilians, and such freedoms as those of movement, worship, expression, association, and education.

Instead of a set of actionable, well-thought-out and detailed recommendations, as is commonly provided by the independent expert reports prepared for the Commission on Human Rights, the committee's final proposals focus on the overall political situation. Although the committee calls for "urgent measures to ensure . . . protection of . . . basic rights," it states that civilian human rights in the Occupied Territories can be protected only after a "comprehensive, just, and lasting settlement of the Arab-Israeli conflict acceptable to all concerned." Until then, the committee offers the same four general measures that "could contribute . . . to the restoration of human rights" it has proposed in the past: Israel's full application of the **Fourth Geneva Convention** on the protection of civilians in time of war; its full cooperation with the International Committee of the Red Cross (ICRC) to help protect detained persons; the support of U.N. member states for the ICRC; and member states' support of U.N. Relief and Works Agency (UNRWA) activities in the Occupied Territories.

The Assembly, in considering the report, again passed a resolution containing seven separate resolutions (48A to G). Of these, "A" was the most comprehensive and detailed, addressed most topics on the traditional human rights agenda, and, as in the past, garnered by far the strongest opposition (107-2-41). In the main, the resolution repeats the language of the 1988 General Assembly resolution. It continues to declare that Israel's "grave breaches" of the Geneva Convention "are war crimes and an affront to humanity."

At the 1990 Commission on Human Rights, the sponsors of resolutions on the situation in the Occupied Territories largely followed the Assembly's lead. What is notable is the fact that they employed more moderate language than is usual at Geneva in an effort to obtain a broader consensus. For example, the references to "war crimes" that had in the past kept the United States, the United Kingdom, and other European countries from joining the consensus was now absent from the principal human rights resolution [1990/2 "A"], although a previously objectionable description of Israeli prisons as "concentration camps" remained. And a reference to Israeli actions as a "gross violation of human rights and an offence against the peace and security of mankind" was dropped from the main human rights resolution, although it was newly inserted in a resolution that was considered under the agenda item on self-determination [1990/6], causing the Western countries to abstain. As a result of the generally more moderate language, the **Western group**, including the United Kingdom but not the United States, now voted in favor of several of the Commission's human rights resolutions critical of Israel.

A new issue that will undoubtedly be addressed at the 45th General Assembly concerns "recent suggestions" that **Soviet Jews entering Israel** "may be settled in the occupied territories." A Western-sponsored commission resolution [1990/1] called on Israel to refrain from such practice, prefacing the moderate text with a clear affirmation of the right to leave. The United States alone abstained from voting. The issue has since been raised at the Security Council and can be expected to be pursued elsewhere.

The U.S. government cast a negative vote on all but one resolution on the Occupied Territories; and on this one [1990/1] it abstained. Its statements following the voting reiterated concern about the politicization of these topics at the commission and drew specific attention to the sponsors' lack of balance, as evidenced in the refusal to refer to Security Council Resolutions 242 and 338 and the need for negotiations between the parties.

Romania. Despite the December 1989 revolution that overthrew dictator Nicolae Ceaucescu of Romania, the Commission on Human Rights has renewed for a second year the mandate of its **Special Rapporteur on Romania**, Joseph Voyame of Switzerland [1990/50]. In contrast with the Ceaucescu government's complete noncooperation, the new government permitted the Rapporteur to visit even as the commission was already in session. It further agreed to an extension of the mandate to aid in its **transition to democracy** and help it address the issues that were noted in the Rapporteur's mission report. The Swedish government, original sponsor of the special mechanism for Romania, mentioned this cooperation favorably, stating that the new Romanian government's attitude "should help eliminate the stigma surrounding the system of Special Rapporteurs in the eyes of many governments" [E/CN.4/1990/SR.37, para. 69].

Hungary's Foreign Minister reminded the commission that the fall of Romania's dictatorship did not automatically "terminate . . . the previous practice of flagrant injustice" against the Hungarian minority, whose individual and collective rights the Foreign Minister still sought to safeguard.

Voyame's initial report [E/CN.4/1990/28], completed just as the Timosoara and Bucharest public protests were beginning, was a thorough right-by-right examination of repressive conditions in Romania, concluding with a recommendation that all laws and regulations in the country be brought into line with international instruments.

The supplement [Add. 1] spoke of "welcome improvement" and of various legal and administrative provisions that had already been repealed. It concluded that human rights were not yet fully restored, citing cases of physical violence, death threats, and widespread fear of the former Securitate, or secret police; and that for **ethnic minorities** there were persistent problems. The commission, following Voyame's proposals, recommended continued study of conditions in Romania and possible use of the Voluntary Fund for Advisory Services to help improve Romania's national institutions to protect human rights.

During the commission's debate the Romanian representative spoke of the abandonment of the past government's policy of "rigid and obstructive attitudes" and a new "desire for frank cooperation" with the commission. He observed that this was the first time **a government emerging from a revolution had agreed to cooperate with a special rapporteur from a prior regime** (in marked contrast to Chile, for example). Noting that fundamental freedoms had been restored *de jure* in Romania, he stated that there were still *de facto* problems resulting from the past and the fragility of the new social structure.

Guatemala. On Guatemala, the **Expert**, Hector Gros Espiell (who has announced his intention to retire), presented a very pessimistic analysis—his strongest words to date [E/CN.4/1990/45 and Add. 1]. Explaining that "**events have not justified the relative and cautious optimism** felt in 1987 and 1988," he pointed to a government that "lacked the firm and unrelenting determination to carry out a human rights policy, has "no possibility" of acting effectively today, and has done "virtually nothing . . . to investigate and punish earlier human rights violations." The acts that he considered beyond "effective government control" actually increased in number, Gros Espiell said, citing ongoing deaths and disappearances along with "habitual discrimination and exploitation" of the indigenous population. These patterns of abuse have been exacerbated by a "**contempt for pluralism.**"

In the addendum to his report, Gros Espiell formally endorsed the more specific and targeted recommendations of **two expert "advisors"** sent to Guatemala to offer advisory services. The two, Alejandro Gonzalez and Julio Maier, examined the functioning of particular Guatemalan agencies, among them police, investigations, the prosecutors, and the courts, and offered concrete recommendations on how to reform, restructure, and activate these agencies in ways that might improve human rights conditions. Gonzalez recommended establishing a unified political crimes investigation unit; Maier called for a transformation of the system of administering criminal justice. They were much more detailed and direct in their observations and conclusions than has been the Expert over the years.

Whether their reports or his pending retirement was responsible, Gros Espiell's final conclusions employed starker language than ever before. He spoke of an "insurmountable gulf between law and reality" [para. 76], of a government that "lacks the ability, power or authority" to ensure human rights and is "unable to punish violations": "It lives in fear, a prisoner of forces which it cannot control" [para. 79]. Eschewing any possibility of significant improvement in the short term, he nonetheless concluded that more international assistance and cooperative aid are needed to fund activities along the lines of those that have already been provided through the U.N. advisory services program—among them, courses for judges and police and armed forces officials as well as other educational programs in human rights; and specialized assistance for the Procurator for Human Rights.

The Swedish government entered the 1990 session of the commission advocating appointment of a special rapporteur or representative for Guatemala under agenda item 12, **"gross violations"** [see E/CN.4/1990/SR.37, para. 70]. It went so far as to gather a group of Western cosponsors, including commission members Canada, Belgium, and Spain, and to table an alternate resolution on this.

But the Latin American group, which had been coordinating the drafting of the Guatemala resolution for several years, sought a more traditional resolution under the advisory services item and no rapporteur. Following negotiations, the Latin group agreed to take on some of the language of the Swedish text and some of the issues of concern in return for a Swedish agreement to drop its initiative. The resolution [1990/80], which was adopted by consensus, "deeply deplores" the many human rights violations in Guatemala, expresses "profound concern at the resurgence of the so-called death squads," and calls upon the Guatemalan government "to initiate or intensify . . . investigations" aimed at bringing to justice those responsible for disappearances, torture, murder and extra-legal executions" and "to promote any measures necessary to identify and punish the members of death squads." The resolution strengthens the mandate of the independent expert by asking him "to examine the human rights situation in Guatemala" as well as to continue advisory assistance.

Finally, the resolution leaves open the question of the agenda item under which the report will be discussed next year—advisory services or gross violations—making this dependent on the report itself. A fight over the agenda thus can be expected at the next session. Behind the scenes, and before the General Assembly meets, there will be some maneuvering about the appointment of the new Expert.

Haiti. Gros Espiell's conclusions about the benefits of a continuing United Nations advisory role in Guatemala contrast sharply with another Expert's conclusions about its benefits for Haiti. Philippe Texier of France, who presents a dismal picture of the Haitian human rights situation, asks a question that gets to the heart of policy surrounding the advisory services program: "Ought one to go on offering advisory services to a Government which does not want them?" [para. 104 and para. 107(d)]. Texier, who made only one trip to Haiti, in contrast to the many undertaken to Guatemala under advisory services, has detailed a substantial range of violations and analyzes the **structural obstacles to improvement**, such as an ineffective judicial system, the militarization of rural areas, nonseparation of the army and military, and the impunity of those responsible for the massacres of 1987 and 1988 [see para. 106(e)]. He asks the commission to consider appointing a special rapporteur to monitor the situation and report to the commission—unless the government itself "is prepared to accept genuine advisory services."

Haiti had been under discussion in the **"1503" confidential procedure,** but that status was dropped following adoption of a **public resolution** critical of Haiti. The commission's resolution—voted upon under the "advisory services" item at the request of the Latin group—in fact calls for an "**independent expert**" who will examine the situation and report next year under item 12, "**gross violations.**"

The commission's **advisory services** to Guatemala and Haiti illustrate the problem of mixing scrutiny of violations with the advisory services program. In both cases, the countries had been reviewed under fact-finding/item 12 procedures and, owing to changes in the government and hopes for improvement in human rights, were "promoted" to item 22, advisory services, with provision for expert advisors. Advisory services programs—which lack guidelines and receive no scrutiny—create serious problems when used to "reward" countries with records of egregious rights violations because there has been a change of government or when used to avoid monitoring human rights practices under the gross violations item.

Nongovernmental organizations and a number of governments are concerned that advisory services must not become a substitute for the investigative and reporting functions of the Commission on Human Rights under item 12 of the agenda.

Cuba. Even before the 1990 Commission on Human Rights session got under way, the United States government was engaged in a public duel over Cuba with the U.N. Secretary-General. The argument started over whether Pérez de Cuéllar would make public new information he had collected on rights conditions in Cuba during 1989, as the 1989 commission had authorized.

Reportedly, the Secretary-General reversed his December 1989 oral assurances to U.S. Vice President Dan Quayle that the data would be made public upon the request of any member government. His office explained that the "legislative history of the Commission decision" on Cuba prevented such action, as the earlier vote had specifically rejected a reporting mechanism.

The Secretary-General informed the commission at its first substantive meeting that he had collected the information and would await a request from the full commission. It never came. In fact, the Secretary-General's position may have helped to mobilize the U.S. delegation to concentrate even harder on obtaining a **resolution on the Cuba question**—something it had never been able to do. The commission adopted Resolution 1990/48 by a vote of 19–14–10. Among those supplying this margin were Eastern-bloc governments Bulgaria and Hungary (nonmembers Poland and Czechoslovakia had actually cosponsored the resolution), and the Latin American governments (save Panama and Cuba) which abstained. Some diplomats noted that the Latin governments could do this more easily this year because they had already shown their anti-American credentials by voting for the Cuban-led resolution criticizing the U.S. for its invasion of Panama.

The mild resolution called on the Cuban government to honor the guarantee it had made to the 1988 U.N. mission team: that persons who attempted to provide information on rights conditions would not be subjected to reprisals, detention, or other negative consequences. Requesting the Cubans to provide a response to the many unanswered questions detailed in the report of the mission team, it asked the U.N. Secretary-General to provide the results of his ongoing contacts to the commission at its 1991 session.

The issue of **reprisals against persons who provided testimony** to the U.N. mission had become a strong point on the United States side, and the Cubans did little to allay Washington's concern. In fact, during the days before the vote was to take place, mobs were sent to harass a few Cuban dissidents who were trying to hold a human rights meeting.

The Reagan administration had made condemnation of Cuba its top—some would say only—priority at the commission. Several years of intense diplomatic and verbal pyrotechnics on the subject brought about a ten-day **U.N. investigatory mission to Cuba** in 1988. Cuba invited the delegation as a last-ditch measure when the commission seemed ready to pass a condemnatory resolution.

Most delegations agreed that U.N. scrutiny had caused Castro to clean up his act somewhat by improving prison conditions, releasing several hundred prisoners, and changing some laws. Despite this, by a 17–17 vote in 1989, the commission rejected strong language calling for a specific follow-up report and maintenance of contacts "with the Cuban people." Instead, it called for continued Secretary-General contacts with the Cuban government and stated that "these contacts and their results will be taken up by the Secretary-General in an appropriate manner." It was over the interpretation of this weaker language that the Bush administration and the Secretary-General were at odds at the year's end.

Many Western delegates had argued that the U.S. delegation, headed by Cuban poet and former political prisoner Armando Valladeres, overemphasized claims against Cuba. In any event, 1989-90 saw significant regression in the Cuban rights situation.

At the 1990 commission, a combination of focused U.S. pressure, the active diplomacy of U.S. Ambassador to the U.N. in Geneva Morris Abram, changes in the Communist bloc, stepped-up Cuban harassment of human rights activists, and excessive protestations by the Cubans (including their complicated and to all reports annoying procedural maneuvers on the Panama resolution) led to the surprise success of the U.S.-sponsored resolution.

Since then, Cuba has rejected the resolution, calling it "null and void," and continued to tighten restrictions at home. Havana, which is host to the Eighth U.N. Congress on the Prevention of Crime and the Treatment of Offenders (August 27–September 7, 1990), had promised that nongovernmental organizations could participate fully in the work of the congress. It remains to be seen whether the meeting or those who attend can help to ease conditions in Cuba in any way.

Panama. The **United States invasion of Panama** was the subject of a critical commission resolution [1990/10] that "deplored the foreign military intervention," demanded its "cessation," and demanded as well full respect for the Torrijos-Carter treaties on the Panama Canal. It was spearheaded by Cuba under the self-determination agenda item. The resolution, similar in form to (but milder in language than) the one adopted by the General Assembly [A/Res/44/240], was the focus of considerable attention as the Cuban delegation demanded roll call votes on numerous paragraphs. These won, if by votes as close as 10–9 with 19 abstentions (the abstentions outnumbering the "yes" or "no" tallies in each case). Many delegates later complained that the Cubans were wasting the commission's time by pursuing all these votes.

The U.S. delegation proposed sweeping amendments that would have changed the thrust of the entire resolution—by bringing up the withdrawal of U.S. troops; the May 1989 elections, whose results were ignored by the Noriega government; and the fact that the present Panamanian government was the very one elected in the May voting. After offering these amendments and explaining that a resolution might discuss the situation in Panama *following* the invasion, U.S. Ambassador Morris Abram withdrew all of them. The Panamanian delegate in Geneva, a former chairman of the Panamanian Human Rights Committee during General Noriega's rule, noted that "in 10 years of military dictatorship in Panama, the Cuban government had never once spoken out in condemnation of the many violations of human rights committed in that country" [E/CN.4/1990/SR 32]. Most Western countries stated that the topic properly belonged in the General Assembly or Security Council.

Cyprus. The subject of human rights in Cyprus is purportedly given priority at the Commission on Human Rights under the agenda item "gross violations." In fact, it receives no such attention. What debate there is on the subject is fairly sterile and repetitive, directed mainly at the need to reach a "just and lasting" **political settlement** in order to improve human rights on the island. The main focus of attention continues to be the **Security Council** and the negotiations undertaken by the **Secretary-General**. These fell apart in early 1990, after a period of some optimism. A key issue has been whether Cyprus will become a single nation again or be permanently partitioned, with the Greeks and the nonaligned favoring the former.

In considering human rights on Cyprus, a key issue is finding what happened to 1,618 "disappeared" Greek Cypriots and up to 600 Turkish Cypriots. A three-person **Committee on Missing Persons** was established by the Secretary-General, composed of a delegate from the International Committee of the Red Cross, a Greek Cypriot, and a Turkish Cypriot. Each year the Secretary-General reports that scores of meetings by the three have taken place, both formal and informal, but to date not a single missing person has been accounted for. The committee's restricted mandate and the fact that interested parties serve on it are largely responsible for its lack of success. Some NGOs have called for a restructuring of the committee or for other U.N. bodies, such as the Disappearances Working Group, to look into the question of the missing, but there is apparently little political will to do anything but wait for the Secretary-General's negotiations to succeed.

The commission has also focused on restrictions of **freedom of movement** in Cyprus, limiting family contacts between Greek Cypriots in the north of the island and their relatives in the south and between Turkish Cypriots in the south and their relatives in the north. In 1990 the commission again took a decision to postpone debate on the subject.

Albania. Between 1984 and 1988 the case of Albania came before the commission under the **"1503" confidential procedure**. In 1988, however, the commission decided that the country's noncooperation and nonappearance at the closed sessions merited more serious action: It voted to make all the prior confidential complaints public—and to make all future consideration of human rights abuses in Albania a matter for **public scrutiny**, beginning with the 1989 session.

The commission's decision to make the Albanian documentation public was reversed by ECOSOC, in large part due to the defection of some of the West European countries that had helped bring the original complaint. Greece, Italy, West Germany, and France now voted against making the documentation public, reportedly because the Albanians had begun to "open up."

Responding to the ECOSOC reversal, the 1989 commission adopted by a wide margin a Portugal-sponsored public resolution on Albania that offered the history of U.N. attention to human rights in Albania, omitting reference to the ECOSOC reversal.

In 1990 the 46th commission adopted a resolution that noted the surprise **Albanian invitation to the U.N. Secretary-General to visit** this isolated country and reiterated the U.N.'s history of concern to reverse Albania's noncooperation. For the first time, the resolution (adopted by an overwhelming margin of 27–3–12) actually referred to "violations of human rights," mentioning "especially freedom of thought, conscience and religion, the right to leave the country, and the right to a fair trial with all guarantees . . ." [1990/49].

When the Secretary-General visited Tirana in mid-May 1990, Albania had just announced that it was changing its laws to permit, among other things, the right to seek a passport and was ending its ban on religious literature. Reportedly, it is also considering reestablishing the right to engage a lawyer, which had been abolished in 1967.

China. Until the June 1989 **Beijing massacre**, the human rights practices of China, one of the five permanent members of the Security Council, had been curiously exempt from criticism at the U.N. (with the odd mention of repression in Tibet). Now speeches and information critical of China began to flow.

The first major test of this changed climate of criticism came in August 1989 at the U.N. **Subcommission on Prevention of Discrimination and Protection of Minorities**, a subsidiary expert body of the Commission on Human Rights. There a bland resolution was put forward and voted on in secret ballot, carrying by a vote of 15–9, and becoming the **first resolution criticizing a permanent member of the Security Council for human rights abuses at home**. The resolution, bitterly denounced by the Chinese government, called for transmitting information about "the events in China and their impact in the domain of human rights" to the commission when it met in the spring. With that document supplied by the Secretary-General [E/CN.4/1990/52] before them and a bitter Chinese rebuttal [E/CN.4/1990/55], the commission members went on to craft another bland draft resolution [E/CN.4/1990/L. 47], one noting the debate at the subcommission and the Secretary-General's document, welcoming the release of some prisoners, encouraging further actions along those lines, and calling for the transmittal of additional information to the commission in 1992. Even this mild text could not succeed.

The decision of the 46th Commission on Human Rights to "take no action" on the resolution about human rights in China came in a close final vote, 17–15–11. The Soviet Union and the Ukraine (which has a vote in the commission this year) voted with China, as did Yugoslavia and Cuba, but two East European countries, Hungary and Bulgaria, showed surprising independence in voting with the Western bloc to criticize the Chinese. The African countries that were heavily lobbied by the expanded Chinese delegation split between China and abstentions, with the sole exception of Swaziland, which voted against the Chinese. The major reason for the vote's failure was an abstention on the procedural motion by Argentina, Brazil, Colombia, Mexico, Peru, and Venezuela—all democracies that human rights groups had seen as crucial to any victory. The same is true for the Philippines, which also abstained.

Despite this defeat at the commission, the 1990 session saw the first official U.N. document from the Secretary-General [E/CN.4/1990/52] containing detailed information about the specific nature of repression in China during and after the June massacre. It brought the first substantive debate at the U.N. Commission on Human Rights about repression in China, and it was a full one, including eyewitness testimony from **Beijing student leader Wuer Kaixi**, expert commentaries on Chinese rights violations by NGOs, a written statement critical of China signed by twenty-three NGOs at the commission session, and substantial critical oral remarks by a wide array of countries (including many that later voted to take no action or abstained to permit passage of the resolution).

Chinese initiatives at the commission to intimidate witnesses and NGOs were firmly rebuffed by commission officers. And delegates to the commission expressed unusual agreement, in private, about the facts: The extent of the repression and other violations of human rights were widely acknowledged. The few arguments in support of China were political in nature ("They are our friends," "They send us economic aid," or "They are bringing political pressure on our government") or sought to exploit anti-Western sentiment. Governments did not accept the Chinese propaganda that the June massacre and its aftermath were a justifiable "quelling."

The government of China had to apply enormous political pressure and expend much goodwill to muster the slim majority of 17 votes (versus 15) that blocked consideration of the substantive motion. The Chinese delegation was one of the largest at the commission; its members appeared everywhere to listen in on private discussions, intimidate witnesses, or lobby actively for support. The Chinese Foreign Minister even went to Geneva to give a press conference, purportedly on an unrelated matter, and Chinese efforts to avoid criticism reached a fever pitch in Geneva and in country capitals elsewhere in the world.

On February 27, 1990, the governing body of the **International Labour Organisation (ILO)** in Geneva endorsed the findings of an expert committee that had been extremely critical of China for its treatment of workers who had supported the pro-democracy movement and had formed independent unions. And in April, the **Committee against Torture** gave the Chinese government's report an in-depth review, concluding that it was so sketchy on the facts as to warrant a supplementary report by the end of 1990.

While it cannot be expected that a specific measure on China will come before the 45th General Assembly, it seems clear that the subject will not disappear from U.N. human rights bodies.

Iraq. For several years, the human rights situation in Iraq has been a subject of debate and attempted resolutions. In 1990, Iraq escaped being the subject of a critical resolution when it got a positive decision on a no-action motion. In summer 1989 the U.N. Subcommission on the Prevention of Discrimination and Protection of Minorities also set aside a motion critical of Iraq after it received a surprise invitation for individuals to visit Iraq to observe the situation first-hand under the auspices of a supposed nongovernmental Iraqi group. An attempt had begun at the commission to turn the trip into an official U.N. mission, replete with translators and other officials. This was foiled when the no-action motion was adopted.

"1503" Confidential Scrutiny

At the 1990 session of the Commission on Human Rights, the following countries succeeded in ending confidential scrutiny of their "gross pattern of violations" of human rights: Brunei, Paraguay, and Haiti (the latter because it was now cited in a public resolution). Only Burma and Somalia remained to be reviewed again next year. Thus, for the first time in a decade, no Latin American country was the subject of continuing confidential scrutiny at the commission.

The "1503" confidential country procedure has been criticized by some NGOs and others who believe these private proceedings, intended to produce frank and open exchanges, have served rather to shield governments from scrutiny.

Reportedly, the commission's confidential scrutiny of **Burma** has led it to appoint a special representative. If the landslide opposition victory in free elections in May 1990 is honored, many of the commission's concerns may diminish. By mid-June, **opposition leader Aung San Suu Kyi** remained under house arrest and could not participate in transition planning. The military government claimed it needed substantial time to give effect to the election results.

Human Rights Treaties

The standards of the Universal Declaration were given binding form in two overarching human rights treaties adopted in 1966: the **International**

Covenant on Civil and Political Rights and the **International Covenant on Economic, Social, and Cultural Rights.** These, along with several other human rights treaties adopted by the United Nations—addressing **racial discrimination, gender discrimination,** and **torture**—are overseen by the **special committees of experts** charged with monitoring compliance. The committees examine progress reports officially submitted by the countries that become party to the treaties. Committee members raise questions with the country's representatives and, in this way, countries that might otherwise avoid any scrutiny of their human rights records come under formal U.N. review in public sessions.

More than half the members of the United Nations are party to the two covenants, with still more states signatory to the race and/or gender discrimination treaties.

The two top-priority issues of concern at the General Assembly regarding the independent treaty supervisory bodies have been their **financing** and the **improvement of their reporting systems.**

To improve a rather bulky system involving six treaty bodies, all with the burden of reviewing reports and some receiving individual communications, the 44th General Assembly approved a second **meeting of treaty chairpersons** (scheduled for September 1990), welcomed (and the commission later endorsed the findings of) an independent expert's **study of long-term approaches to the treaty bodies,** and moved ahead on some of the expert's recommendations. These include plans for the computerization of reporting and the development of a consolidated first portion of all reports. The report of independent expert Philip Alston, Rapporteur of the Committee on Economic, Social and Cultural Rights [A/44/668], is probably the most thoughtful and thorough study of the mechanics, problems, and future needs of the human rights treaty system to date. It has set the stage for numerous actions and recommendations for improvement in the functioning of the treaty committees and their ability to examine the issues they are charged with overseeing.

In response to a request by the 44th Assembly, the Secretariat concluded that all the treaty bodies need additional staffing to carry out their responsibilities effectively and that all require a means of assuring that financial arrangements do not hinder their actual work. The difficulties encountered by the **Committee on the Elimination of Racial Discrimination (CERD),** which is financed by the states parties to the treaty alone, are particularly pronounced. The commission endorsed the Secretariat's suggestion of a contingency reserve plan for CERD [E/CN.4/1990/67, para. 10] consisting of voluntary contributions of up to $200,000 to offset financial uncertainties caused by the late payments by states parties, which have led to the cancellation of some CERD sessions. While the General Assembly has not previously been receptive to new financial arrangements other than those specified in the treaties themselves, it is possible that the ongoing crisis of CERD will bring about a change of heart at the 45th Assembly.

Recent resolutions concerning the treaty bodies have encouraged these bodies to comment on the recommendations made at the meeting of chairpersons and those contained in the Alston report. Each treaty body (except the Committee on Economic, Social and Cultural Rights, which was created by ECOSOC) is **independent**, reporting only to the meeting of its states parties, but all treaty bodies report to the General Assembly through the Economic and Social Council. Their annual reports will be prepared during summer 1990 and submitted to the Assembly with various suggestions and recommendations on ways to improve their functioning.

U.N. Advisory Services Program

The U.N. program of advisory services—a kind of **limited technical assistance for human rights**—has increasingly been a favored subject in the U.N. human rights program. Near the end of its resolutions on theme mechanisms, country situations, and reports to treaty committees, the General Assembly and the commission urged each body and expert to consider appropriate new advisory services.

The small budget for the United Nation's regular advisory services program has been substantially augmented by a **Voluntary Fund for Advisory Services** of the Commission on Human Rights, which has been used in a variety of ways, ranging from splashy international meetings around the globe to meetings aimed at training law enforcement officials; from the preparation of human rights publications to a two-year "technical cooperation" effort for Guatemala.

The objectives, scope, and content of the program have been addressed by the Secretary-General in several documents. The program, which has much potential but has been criticized for its lack of formal criteria and financial accountability, has been systematized slightly through the establishment of a **new unit** consisting of the Under-Secretary-General for Human Rights and his senior staff, but the central policy question remains unanswered: Under what circumstances should the United Nations provide advisory services to governments?

While none object to advisory services as a supplement to core U.N. human rights activities, some observers have expressed concern that the advisory services program will result in what one commentator has characterized as the "**gentrification**" of human rights, in which the United Nations responds to serious violations with an offer of cooperative assistance that is not supervised or reviewed according to any standard or criteria. At present, the Voluntary Fund, a Western-initiative, has received contributions solely from Western countries (with the exception of a pledge from Togo and some modest NGO donations). The success of the program will depend on how funds and projects are handled. NGOs believe that a defined procedure, guidelines, and scrutiny by independent experts other than the Secretariat acting alone are needed to utilize the program effectively.

Public Information

In 1988 the Assembly launched a new **World Public Information Campaign in Human Rights.**

Since **Jan Martenson** assumed the post of Director of the Human Rights Center in Geneva with the title of Under-Secretary-General, he has made public information matters a high priority, arguing that the United Nations could do much more to publicize the standards it has already adopted and the good work it accomplishes. Accordingly, the United Nations has begun to produce an attractive array of basic publications on human rights and has begun to move toward printing—or reprinting—many basic instruments in special pamphlet format and taking other measures to advance awareness of human rights through public media. Significant problems remain, among them: the continuing bureaucratic struggle between the **Geneva-based Centre for Human Rights** (the substantive experts) and the **New York-based Department of Public Information** (DPI—the promotional experts) as to who has primary responsibility for the campaign and its substantive content; the lack of clear-cut targets and of accountability; and the merely descriptive nature of much of the audio-visual material, particularly radio programs, which reproduce U.N. debates or resolutions but fail to explain the nature of rights guarantees or their denial.

Despite problems in focus and coherence, the project has begun to address "the right to know" in a far more serious fashion than at any time in recent memory.

The General Assembly has continued to call for information materials on human rights that are "clear and accessible," tailored to regional and national requirements and circumstances, with specific target audiences in mind, and disseminated in national and local languages and in sufficient volume. It has called for effective use of mass media to reach wider audiences, particularly children and the disadvantaged. It has acknowledged the efforts of DPI and the Centre for Human Rights to computerize their facilities, to expand audio-visual activities, and to update texts, increase stocks, and extend language versions of human rights materials—especially basic instruments—and has encouraged more such efforts, making use of regional, national, and local institutions and U.N. Information Centres. It has also called for a variety of follow-up promotional efforts by member states and has urged them to include human rights matters in educational curricula.

But the Commission on Human Rights, reviewing documents it had requested about the budget and financing of the campaign, has yet to receive the kind of detailed information that would permit genuine scrutiny and helpful evaluation.

The World Public Information Campaign in Human Rights also lists certain training seminars and workshops, fellowships, and other matters that incorporate aspects of the advisory services program. Certainly some of the technical assistance-type activities recommended by theme and country rapporteurs fall into the category of "public information." For this reason, both programs should be watched carefully to see how they can work together to reinforce the efforts of the United Nations in implementing human rights.

2. Refugees

At a spring 1989 meeting, the U.S. Ambassador to Hungary, Mark Palmer, told a group of journalists to keep an eye on Hungary's treatment of refugees. Budapest, he said, had just signed onto several U.N. treaties covering refugees' rights, obligating Hungary to protect all émigrés fleeing persecution. Palmer predicted East Germans would soon begin slipping across the border to seek shelter. If Hungary chose to live up to its obligations, a major Soviet-bloc row might ensue.

Summer and autumn newspaper reports and television broadcasts showed busloads and trainloads of ecstatic East Germans fleeing their repressive homeland for the democratic West. It is hard to remember a year in which refugees themselves helped deliver such a final blow to a totalitarian regime; it is hard to recall a time when the entire Western world drew such inspiration from those fleeing communism.

But like all else over the past year, the excitement and promise of events in Europe threaten to draw attention and resources away from developing world problems. While tens of thousands of Eastern Europeans have found homes in Germany or elsewhere, an estimated 15 million refugees linger in desperation in camps around the world—6 million more than only six years ago [National Geographic News Service, 1/17/90]. The United Nations estimates another 15 million people may be internally displaced within their own countries by hunger or civil strife, many beyond the reach of international aid [A/44/520].

As numbers have risen, shelter and aid have not kept pace. The **United Nations High Commissioner for Refugees' (UNHCR)** budget has grown only 25 percent over the past five years—half of that needed to care for the new migrants under the agency's protection [*The New York Times*, 3/18/90]. The U.S. share of contributions has fallen over the past five years from 27 to 22 percent [ibid.]. The agency estimates its 1990 needs at $700 million but so far expects no more than $550 million from donor nations [ibid.].

One problem facing the U.N. and other efforts to protect refugees has been the narrow interpretation of **who constitutes a refugee**, as defined by U.N. and other treaties. The Universal Declaration of Human Rights, considered binding on all states, "affirms a full range of civil, political, economic and social rights for all persons, citizens and refugees alike. It also significantly provides the right to seek and enjoy asylum, the right to freedom of movement, and the right to a nationality" [Refugee Policy Group, 1/90]. Other pacts, such as the International Covenant on Civil and Political Rights, cover all people within a nation's territory and prohibit expulsion of aliens or limitations on movement.

But other pacts that spell out refugee rights define protected refugees more narrowly. The 1950 Statute of the UNHCR and the 1951 Convention Relating to the Status of Refugees prohibit forced return of refugees and state they must be treated almost as well as citizens. Refugees must be

Table IV-1
Asylum Seekers in Western Europe, the United States, and Canada

	Applicants	Backlog	Costs* $ billion	Acceptance rate %	Proportion that stays %
1983	90,000	60,000	0.5	40	90
1985	200,000	100,000	2	35	90
1987	240,000	360,000	3	25	90
1989+	450,000++	400,000	5	20	90
1991**	550,000	500,000	6	15	90

*Includes social assistance for those awaiting verdict **Forecast + Estimates
++ Exlcudes East Germans, Bulgarian Turks, Soviet Jews, and other Soviet emigres.

SOURCE: UNHCR

accorded free movement, ownership of property, legal rights, access to education, work, and other human rights. The instruments define refugees as people with a well-founded fear of persecution based on racial, religious, national, social, or political grounds. This definition covers some—but not all—émigrés fleeing civil strife, war, or poverty related to political persecution or ethnic conflict. It applies to individuals who fear persecution on personal grounds but leaves out the millions who know they will probably die or suffer if they return to countries torn by war or civil conflict.

The General Assembly adopted the Declaration on Territorial Asylum in 1967. It seeks to bar states from rejecting asylum seekers at the nation's frontiers and would bar the return of asylum seekers to countries in which they would be persecuted. But like all other Assembly resolutions, it is nonbinding. Efforts to draft a binding convention collapsed in 1977.

Many of the problems facing refugees stem from disagreement over these definitions of who deserves asylum. Politically it has been a good year for tens of thousands of anticommunist, generally educated Warsaw Pact refugees whose flight has vindicated years of Western criticism of Moscow and its satellites. But it has been a terrible year for more simple masses fleeing persecution and war, or merely life-threatening poverty, in the developing world. Countries continue to show a preference for refugees fleeing the host nation's enemies as well as for migrants with good skills and education. Welcoming countries also tend to favor exiles supported by powerful domestic groups. How to define a refugee—as opposed to someone merely seeking economic opportunity—continues to be an issue, one that some governments use as a fig leaf to cover their choice of which refugees to admit and which to reject.

On December 12, 1989, the British government began a secret operation to repatriate forcibly up to 44,000 of the 55,000 Vietnamese exiles who have flooded Hong Kong over the past few years [*The New York Times*, 12/12/89]. A document drafted by the region's first-asylum countries for an International Conference on Indo-Chinese Refugees earlier in 1989 had established a process for screening Indochinese boat people to distinguish political refugees from economic migrants, but the United States and Vietnam rejected the notion of forced repatriation for those denied refugee status. In the summer of 1990, as the refugee/migrant waves continued and Washington and Hanoi stood their ground vis-à-vis forced repatriation, the countries of first asylum threatened to refuse landing rights to all new arrivals. It was to avoid formalizing this lack of consensus, say observers, that both sides requested the UNHCR to postpone indefinitely a conference scheduled for mid-July [*The New York Times*, 7/12/90].

U.S. refugee policies—intended to protect those in political danger—reveal similar contradictions. Washington usually accepts those fleeing governments it opposes or refugees who bring skills and education with them. Of 125,000 annual openings for refugees, the lion's share goes to Soviet-bloc and other exiles fleeing communism. The United States rejects 97 percent of asylum requests from friendly El Salvador, though 60,000 civilians have been killed there in the past decade. Only six of 20,000 Haitian boat people intercepted through October 1989 were admitted. The United States accepts 1,000 refugees from Marxist Ethiopia, and a handful more from the rest of the continent, though Africa houses nearly one-third of the world's refugees [*Newsweek*, 10/9/89].

Other examples of ambiguous refugee policies abound. There are 320,000 Cambodian refugees in Thailand. Most live as virtual prisoners with no freedom of movement in camps along the Thai-Cambodian border, deprived of rights accorded them under various refugee pacts. UNHCR has little direct access to these camps; and many Cambodians have been pressed into military service by the brutal Khmer Rouge faction, which runs its camps like fiefdoms.

In late 1989, Arab countries mounted a major diplomatic effort to convince the Soviet Union and transit countries not to aid the flow of Soviet Jews to Israel, claiming they would colonize the occupied Arab territories—this despite the fact that only a few hundred so far have chosen to settle in the occupied lands.

Most countries have done little to aid tens of thousands of Kurds fleeing intense persecution and chemical bombardment in Iraq for fear of alienating the influential Baghdad regime or Turkey, a member of the North Atlantic Treaty Organization.

Eritrean migrants in Gulf states are often carted out to sea and dumped on islands off the Ethiopian coast, where conditions often lead to death [*The Economist*, 12/23/89]. Both Sudan and Ethiopia use food and aid as weapons against their own and refugee populations in their countries' civil wars.

The United Nations itself must negotiate these tricky political issues supporting refugee rights without aggravating major donors or countries sheltering exiles. Critics say it sometimes plays the political game too well. The High Commissioner for Refugees, Jean-Pierre Hocké, resigned on October 26, 1989, amid widespread charges that he undercut the agency's management and had misused hundreds of thousands of dollars for entertainment and travel [*The Washington Post*, 10/27/89]. But Hocké, a Swiss native, was also accused of catering to the interests of UNHCR's big donors at the expense of the interests of refugees.

In January 1988 he had ordered the burning of more than 130,000 copies of a UNHCR magazine containing an article critical of West Germany's refugee policies. Roger Winter, head of the U.S. Committee for Refugees, also charged that Hocké "took the low road on the function of protecting refugees," refusing to criticize governments when they deported

Table IV-2
Origin of Asylum Seekers

Countries of origin of asylum-seekers in Western Europe, the United States, and Canada

1983–88*

Iran	140,000	Czechoslovakia	29,000
Turkey	110,000	Chile	27,000
Poland	108,000	India	26,000
Sri Lanka	80,000	Pakistan	26,000
Ghana	45,000	Hungary	25,000
Lebanon	40,000	Zaire	24,000
Romania	31,000	Ethiopia	23,000
Yugoslavia	31,000	Iraq	15,000

*Excluding applications from Central Americans

Source: UNHCR

controversial exiles. Winter cited U.S. actions to keep Haitians out and Thai and Hong Kong policies of evicting Indochinese refugees, issues on which he said Hocké was "conspicuously silent."

The new High Commissioner, Thorvald Stoltenberg, has been a more vocal advocate of greater support for those under his protection. Complaining of budget constraints, he told *The New York Times* on March 18, "I can't fulfill my mandate—levels of care are falling, I have only half the resources per refugee today that we had in 1980."

The General Assembly, for its part, continues to pass dozens of resolutions each year calling attention to specific refugee issues and the needs of refugee groups around the world. On December 8, 1989, it adopted 11 resolutions on Palestinian refugees who fall under the mandate of the United Nations Relief and Works Agency (UNRWA). The resolutions appealed for more funding for UNRWA, demanded that Israel not resettle any refugees in the Occupied Territories, affirmed the need for scholarships and strengthened educational facilities, and in general sought to further the Palestinians' cause. While the resolutions may have been worthy, they reflect the fact that only refugees with vocal political supporters—in this case the Arab group—tend to get major political support in the General Assembly.

On December 15 the Assembly adopted by consensus a resolution supporting UNHCR. It called for all states to grant asylum in accordance with international law, noted the fact that many of those seeking asylum are held in detention or forced to serve in armed forces, and affirmed other UNHCR programs, including an emphasis on aiding refugees through development.

Another December 15 consensus resolution called for support for South African refugees. Other texts praised the International Conference on Indo-Chinese Refugees and the May 1989 Guatemala City conference on Central American refugees. Still other texts adopted that day by consensus called for aid to refugees and displaced persons in Malawi, Djibouti, the Sudan, Somalia, Chad, Ethiopia, and student refugees in southern Africa. These resolutions help draw attention to pressing refugee needs, but they do not always translate into sufficient resources or political will to solve refugee crises.

In the face of this ambivalent world attitude toward refugees, the United Nations has tried several strategies. Many refugees seek aid in already impoverished countries barely able to cope with their own peoples' needs. Malawi is home to about 720,000 exiles fleeing brutal civil war in Mozambique. Ethiopia, beleaguered by its own civil war, houses 705,000 refugees from Somalia and Sudan. Sudan shelters 690,000 Ethiopians, Chadians, Zaireans, and Ugandans. In this regard, several General Assembly resolutions in 1989 stressed the need to link aid to refugees to general development strategies, recognizing that only by aiding poor countries as a whole can one aid the strangers in their midst.

On another tack, the United Nations is attempting to develop **early warning systems** designed to predict when a large group of people may flood a country. This effort would allow agencies to meet exiles' needs quickly while laying the ground for their proper reception. In southern Africa, UNHCR has prepared emergency preparedness profiles for Malawi, Mozambique, Botswana, Lesotho, Swaziland, and Zimbabwe [A/44/520].

But at base, most refugees' decisions to flee their homelands stem from political and social crises in these homelands; only the ending of these crises will convince most to return home. Sometimes the United Nations tries to nudge refugees to return in the hope that this will help move a nation toward settling its conflicts. This has been the effort with 5 million Afghan refugees in Pakistan and Iran. Operation Salaam has mounted a major effort to prepare refugees for their return home and the rebuilding of their country, hoping this would goad Afghan belligerents toward a settlement of the nation's civil war. But critics say that few refugees have chosen to return, adding that the United Nations may be overstating its success in this area.

Only peace can convince exiles to go home. A settlement of the Nicaraguan civil war—if it sees the return of contra rebels under U.N. auspices, as called for under regional peace treaties—would prove this simple thesis. In the expectation of a successful conclusion to the peace process, the U.N. Secretary-General, the U.N. Development Programme, and UNHCR called an international meeting on Central American refugees and displaced persons, June 27–28—a follow-up to the May 1989 conference in Guatemala City. Their hope was to gather support for 59 projects to resettle, settle, or otherwise benefit Central America's 2 million refugees [U.N. press release C/27, 6/26/90].

Meanwhile, the situation for most refugees will remain delicate as long as resources are scarce and nations fail to address the gap between their stated humanitarian goals and actual policies.

3. The Information Issue

The 45th Session of the General Assembly is expected to adopt without a vote a draft resolution on information that represents a radical departure from established U.N. practice since the 1970s. The draft, adopted by consensus in an extended session of the **Committee on Information** (COI) in May 1990, drastically scales back plans to implement the highly controversial **New World Information and Communication Order** (NWICO), a 1977 proposal of the Nonaligned Movement designed to redress alleged imbalances in media coverage and infrastructure between the developed North and the developing South. The appearance in the draft of a single and rather oblique reference to "what in the United Nations and at various international forums has been termed 'a new world information and communication order'" [A/AC.199/1990/L.1/Add. 2] is considered a major victory for Western states, which have opposed NWICO as a scheme to muzzle free speech and impose government censorship; and for the first time since 1983, COI's recommendations could be passed on to the General Assembly without a vote.

Progress in this year's COI session had its origin in the approval of reforms in the Communications in the Service of Humanity program (Program IV) by both developed and developing countries at the November 1989 session of the Governing Council of the **U.N. Educational, Scientific and Cultural Organization** (UNESCO). Both Western concerns for guarantees on the free flow of information and requests for assistance from the South in developing national information infrastructures were taken into account in the program's New Strategy in the Field of Communications. The program and strategy call for an upgrading of UNESCO's ongoing efforts to assist the Third World through its International Program for the Development of Communication (IPDC), which began operation in 1982. As part of UNESCO's pragmatic, nonideological approach to solving communications problems, IPDC will become the "chief instrument for action in Program IV" and the "basic mechanism for the establishment of communications infrastructure in developing countries" [A/44/SPC/SR.15]. IPDC will also incorporate training programs for the staff responsible for operating and selecting appropriate communications technologies adapted to local conditions.

UNESCO's change in attitude came too late to affect debate in the 1989 COI session, and the committee, which makes all decisions by consensus, was unable to agree on recommendations for submission to the 44th General Assembly. Guarantees on free speech emanating from UNESCO's Governing Council were, however, included in the Group of 77's draft resolution on information, which traditionally forms the basis for debate in the General Assembly's Special Political Committee. Without a complete rejection of NWICO, this concession by the Nonaligned Movement was not enough to win approval of the draft by consensus, and the United States requested a roll call vote on the information draft in both the Special Political Committee and the General Assembly plenary. Israel joined the United States in opposition, with the Western states abstaining [A/Res/44/50].

As it has since the founding of COI in 1978, the United States objected to the inclusion of NWICO and the enumeration of specific directives to the U.N.'s **Department of Public Information** (DPI) in the General Assembly's annual information resolution. Washington has never supported U.N. resolutions that it says can be interpreted as an abridgement of free speech and has charged that the management of DPI "from the outside" leads to politicization and inefficiency. Washington has argued that DPI can be strengthened and Third World interests in the sphere of information respected only through a renewed commitment of the original General Assembly mandate for the department: "to promote to the greatest possible extent an informed understanding of the work and purposes of the U.N. among the peoples of the world" [U.S. Mission to the U.N. press release 143, 11/9/89].

Delegations in the Special Political Committee generally supported the recommendations on DPI reform contained in two highly critical reports by the U.N. **Joint Inspection Unit** (JIU), and the Secretary-General, in written comments, accepted the majority of them, with some pointed qualifications. While important, the recommendations were of a technical nature (eliminating the Division for Committee Liaison and Administrative Services, strengthening the Joint U.N. Information Committee, and eliminating the Distribution Division, for example) and were of much less interest than the Inspector's more general comments, to which the Secretary-General made no official reply.

The surprisingly personal and somewhat accusatory tone of the reports, drafted by Inspector Alain Gourdon of France, elicited a rather defensive response from both the Secretary-General and the Under-Secretary-General for Public Information, Thérèse Sévigny, who apparently resented allegations of noncooperation by DPI officials in the preparation of the reports. The Secretary-General referred repeatedly to "misunderstandings," "unsubstantiated allegations," and factual errors on the part of the Inspector and promised to draft clear guidelines for the preparation of future JIU reports.

In his first report, on the reorganization of DPI in accordance with Recommendation 37 of the **Group of 18** [A/44/433], the Inspector concluded forthrightly that "DPI's new administrative machinery seems no more efficient than the one it replaced. It satisfies no better than did the former one the acknowledged need for coordination and coherence, for rationalization and for simplification." He did defend Sévigny (referred to throughout the report as the "head of DPI") against charges of commercialism for suggesting that certain projects be financed through extrabudgetary resources and argued that appeals for extrabudgetary funds were not incompatible with the management of an international public service or with priorities laid down for U.N. public information activities. He likened the situation to the donation of uniforms for certain U.N. staff by the Italian textile company Benetton: "The fact that a well-known European firm is equipping the United Nations tour guides in exchange for some advertising concessions should not arouse indignation, which cannot be otherwise than somewhat artificial."

The Inspector also defended Sévigny's use of outside public relations consultants by drawing a distinction between press relations and self-promotion—skills possessed by current DPI staff members and the presentation of an image or message to the international community through more sophisticated means than those available in-house. But the apparent naiveté of Sévigny and other media professionals in the department "who thought it possible to carry out a reorganization of DPI without paying adequate attention to the administrative environment and political context of the United Nations system" came in for particular censure. No amount of media professionalism, the Inspector argued, could overcome differences of opinion between states that favored a restrictive interpretation of DPI's mandate and those that construe the department's role more broadly. This contradiction, he concluded, "would always influence the administrative practice of DPI and the administrative structure in which it operates."

Finally, while recognizing the inherent difficulties in implementing both Recommendation 37 on DPI reform and Recommendation 15, which called for an overall 15 percent reduction in U.N. personnel, the Inspector stated that structural reform was being weakened and "biased to some extent" by the mandated cuts and wondered whether the "increased number of senior positions did not take too much account of the posts held by certain senior officials and the need to adjust the organizational structure accordingly." In addition, the Under-Secretary-General "would seem to have complied only partly" with the recommendation to continue to recruit staff members at junior professional levels, and her proposals for staff cuts "tended to affect more the junior than the higher echelon posts."

The Inspector had kinder words for efforts to reorganize the system of **U.N. Information Centres** around the world, terming the DPI plan "very acceptable" [A/44/329]. He urged that a clearer distinction be made between types of audience and targets and between press intermediaries and final recipients or consumers; the use of United Nations Associations (UNAs) and UNESCO and U.N. clubs in the dissemination network; the closing of some centers and the expansion of the responsibilities of others; greater cooperation between DPI field offices and those of UNDP; improvements in the operation and management of the centers (such as the grouping of U.N. commemorations by the General Assembly); and the simplification of reports from centers to DPI headquarters and the Office for Research and the Collection of Information (ORCI).

In his comments on the JIU report [A/44/329/Add. 1], the Secretary-General found the de facto replacement of centers with local UNAs unworkable due to conflicting agendas and priorities and rejected the closing of some centers (especially the office in the capital of France, "a permanent member of the Security Council") as politically impossible. But he called increased DPI-UNDP cooperation "a solid recommendation" that would be considered after the expiration of the current informal arrangement in a year's time. The Secretary-General also agreed that media coverage of all U.N. commemorations was becoming increasingly difficult but cited his obligation to observe legislative mandates, and he warned against changing the frequency of DPI reports to ORCI, which are used to brief the Secretary-General on political developments in various regions.

UNESCO

Despite the approval of **Director-General Federico Mayor's** reform program by the Governing Council, the jettisoning of NWICO as an operative policy guide, and recommendations for U.S. reentry from numerous NGOs, including UNA-USA's American Panel on UNESCO, the **U.S. Department of State** concluded in April 1990 that "the time is not yet ripe to reopen the question of renewing United States membership in UNESCO." This announcement, contained in a report by the Secretary of State entitled *The Activities of UNESCO Since U.S. Withdrawal*, followed by a month the decision of the British government to delay for at least a year any move to rejoin the organization, pending the implementation of Mayor's announced reforms.

Drafted by the State Department's Bureau of International Organization Affairs under the direction of **Assistant Secretary of State John R. Bolton**, the report maintains that politicization, waste, and mismanagement continue to plague UNESCO as they did when the United States withdrew in 1984. Informed observers, including members of UNA's panel, have noted that the report is based on a highly selective reading of the recent changes in UNESCO, gathered from numerous unnamed sources, and that it gives disproportionate weight to the sensitive communications issue. (Though only 5 percent of UNESCO's budget, the information program fills 6 of the report's 43 pages.) While the report of the British Foreign Affairs Committee of the House of Commons stated that even those "who in the past have been highly critical of UNESCO's Communication Program . . . now see NWICO as being only a minor problem," the State Department chose to emphasize continuity over change, writing: "It is undeniable that the critical elements to which the United States so strongly objected in the past are still present."

In an Epilogue to its report, *A Forum in Restoration: International Intellectual Cooperation and America's Interests in UNESCO*, UNA-USA's American Panel on UNESCO pointed out that the organization's new medium-term plan affirms the "free flow of information" as a main policy goal 23 times, without subjecting it, as in the past, to any condition of "balance." For the first time, private and independent media are recognized as important channels of communication that deserve the support of governments and UNESCO itself. Freedom of the press also makes its first appearance as an objective that the organization should foster actively.

The other major source of "politicization" in UNESCO's activities, its support for the **Palestine Liberation Organization**, also received harsh treatment in the State Department report. Along with other specialized agencies, UNESCO received an application for membership from the "State of Palestine," and Mayor was successful in convincing the General Conference to delay its consideration of the application for two years, reportedly to encourage U.S. reentry. The State Department remained unconvinced and emphasized instead the new right of the Palestinian observer to submit requests for program assistance directly to the

Governing Council, not, as it had done, through the representative of the League of Arab States (also a nonmember).

On management and personnel issues, the report strongly criticizes one part of Mayor's restructuring plan that proposed the appointment of 44 staff members and outside consultants to senior executive positions, as well as the creation of about 20 new senior positions, at an estimated cost of $6.2 million over two years [*The New York Times*, 4/17/89]. Yet planned offsets, to be obtained through the freezing of existing vacancies, are not even mentioned by Washington. Neither is praise forthcoming for Mayor's major success in depoliticizing personnel policy by eschewing patronage appointments, returning hiring responsibility for program staff to program heads, and replacing all but one deputy director-general. Mayor also plans to decentralize administration—a major U.S. demand—by moving 21 professional staff out of headquarters and into the field, albeit in a haphazard way. Three assistant director-general positions are to be abolished, and new evaluation procedures are to be implemented for all short-term staff. Nevertheless, many view the sudden announcement of Mayor's managerial directives, issued in February and March 1990 without consultation with the executive board, as a major political blunder that has alienated staff and made managerial reform even harder.

Regarding "budgetary waste," in 1989 Mayor requested a modest 2.5 percent increase in spending after five years of no real budget growth, but the General Conference overrode his proposal and voted another zero-growth budget. Washington ignored UNESCO efforts at fiscal restraint and chose instead to cite the lack of progress in implementing a budgetary decision-making process that would give adequate weight to the views of major donors. Similar criticism is leveled at Mayor's decision to cut back but not entirely eliminate UNESCO's major programs in education, science, and culture. The State Department report calls on UNESCO to concentrate its activities "in a few key areas" but does not specify which areas or where program cuts should be made.

4. Health

During its 41st year in operation the World Health Organization (WHO), the U.N. specialized agency dedicated to solving and preventing major public health problems, recorded many successes but was not itself immune to controversy.

The year saw further progress in vaccinating the world's children against such childhood killers as polio, measles, whooping cough, pertussis, tetanus, and diphtheria under the agency's Expanded Programme on Immunization (EPI), begun in 1974 when less than 5 percent of children in the developing world had been immunized against these preventable diseases. By the end of 1989 the figure was 60 percent and climbing [*World Health*, 12/89]. An earlier global immunization campaign resulted in the eradication of smallpox in 1979. Additional progress has been made in saving the lives of millions of Third World infants and children affected by diarrheal diseases, and WHO has gone on to launch a new program aimed at preventing the noncommunicable diseases that are related to such lifestyle factors as smoking, drinking, and overindulgence in fatty meats [*World Chronicle*, Program 377, 1/23/90].

The controversy swirled in March 1990 when **Dr. Jonathan Mann**, Director of WHO's **Global Programme on AIDS (GPA)**, tendered his resignation, effective in June. Under Mann's leadership from its inception four years ago, the agency's AIDS effort has developed into its largest program. In an interview with *The New York Times* [3/16/90], Mann asserted that WHO Director-General Dr. Hiroshi Nakajima of Japan underestimates the importance of the war against AIDS. A number of observers have noted that Nakajima believes there is an overemphasis on AIDS, which kills far fewer each year than, for example, diarrhea and malaria; still others pointed out that most of the GPA's $109 million annual budget does not draw down WHO funds but is raised by the program itself [*New Scientist*, 3/24/90]. In late March, Nakajima announced the appointment of **Dr. Michael H. Merson**, Director of the Diarrhoeal Diseases Control Programme, as Acting Director of the GPA [press release, WHO/LUN 28, 3/21/90].

As of mid-1989, GPA was working with 155 countries, had supplied over $60 million in financial support to 127 countries, and had lent technical support through some 1,000 consultant and expert missions as its contribution to the planning and implementation of national AIDS prevention and control programs [*Development Forum*, 7–8/89]—this in addition to its efforts at establishing global AIDS policies and coordinating AIDS information networks. In April 1990, WHO put the cumulative worldwide total of officially reported cases of AIDS at 254,078, while noting that reporting is incomplete and that a more accurate figure is 600,000. It estimated that 3 million to 5 million are infected with the human immunodeficiency virus (HIV) that causes the disease [*The Wall Street Journal*, 5/7/90]. According to a recent WHO study, the number of those who are HIV infected may increase up to four times by the year 2000, with over 5 million new cases of AIDS developing during the 1990s. Concluding on a guardedly optimistic note, the study said that even without a vaccine, a continued strong and coordinated global program may prevent almost half of the projected future HIV infections [*Development Forum*, 7–8/89].

Romania is one of the countries benefiting from WHO's assistance. A team of experts from WHO, visiting the country in February 1990 at the government's invitation, found 600 children infected with the AIDS virus and 50 others with full-fledged AIDS—all as a result of **transfusions of untested blood** from a few infected patients or from the reuse of contaminated needles. Working together, WHO and Romania have devised an emergency course of action, involving training programs for technicians and physicians and the provision of diagnostic kits. At the same time, Mann announced a campaign to discover the extent of the AIDS epidemic in Eastern Europe [*The New York Times*, 2/8/90]. In the same month, WHO contributed prominently to the Special Session of the General Assembly to Consider the Question of International Co-operation against Illicit Production, Supply, Demand, Trafficking and Distribution of Narcotic Drugs, its research on ways to reduce demand for illicit drugs and on the **connection between drug abuse and the spread of AIDS** obviously of great use in the global war against both problems [press release, WHO/LUN 18, 2/20/90]. Late in 1989, WHO had been one of the organizers of a meeting of international experts to review the **epidemiological and demographic factors influencing the spread of AIDS**. The conclusion—that the future course of AIDS would be shaped by possible changes in sexual behavior, among other factors—was accompanied by a call for the collection of more information on the spread of the disease [U.N. press release, POP/403, 12/18/89].

WHO is also behind a number of symbolic actions aimed at increasing the awareness of AIDS—most recently, the U.N. Postal Administration's issuance of six stamps and a souvenir card on the subject [press release, WHO/LUN 26, 3/16/90] and the now annual proclamation of **AIDS Day**. The second such commemoration, on December 1, 1989, took as its theme "AIDS and Youth" [U.N. press release, SG/SM/4375, 11/30/89].

Among other WHO constituents are the approximately 1.3 billion people—over 20 percent of the world's population—who are seriously **sick or malnourished**—and the children in the developing world who have yet to be **inoculated against the six "killer diseases."** The final stages of this latter battle, involving the efforts of UNICEF, Rotary International, the U.S. Agency for International Development, and the Inter-American Development Bank, among others, are estimated to cost under $1 billion. "We are shooting to reach 80% or more of all children in the world—and that means all children, in the developing countries too—by the end of 1990," says Dr. Ralph Henderson, head of the **Expanded Programme on Immunization** and, since January 1990, Assistant Director-General in charge of such other major WHO programs as Tropical Diseases, Diarrhoeal Diseases, and Communicable Diseases [*World Health*, 12/89].

The eradication of **polio**, which now strikes about 208,000 children annually, is high on the list of childhood diseases against which WHO is concentrating its efforts; its aim is to rout the enemy by the year 2000. So far the program has enjoyed the greatest success in the Western Hemisphere. The Pan American Health Organization has reported that the number of confirmed polio cases declined by 85 percent between 1986 and 1989 and that polio in the Western Hemisphere is at the brink of extinction [press release, WHO/LUN 25, 3/15/90]. Assistant Director-General Henderson projects a polio-free Europe by 1995 [*World Health*, 12/89].

WHO's newly established Division of Control of Tropical Diseases will mount an attack on **malaria**, which claims some 2 million lives each year, relatively unchanged in 15 years, and in 1989 it inaugurated efforts to eliminate **guinea worm disease** (dracunculiasis), a water-borne parasitic ailment that affects 5 million to 10 million people each year in remote rural areas of developing countries [press release, WHO/LUN 21, 2/23/90]. WHO has also announced that it will set in place an international early warning system to increase the ability to detect outbreaks of **Legionnaires' disease**, a bacterial disease associated to date with hotels and conference centers in the industrialized world but "likely to emerge soon in the Third World as more and more developing countries urbanize and modernize" [press release, WHO/LUN 82, 12/8/89; WHO/LUN 29, 3/21/90].

WHO's estimate that **noncommunicable diseases** are the cause of 75 percent of the deaths in the developed world and of an increasing number of deaths in the Third World led to the January 1990 launching of **Inter-Health**, a program to "promote healthy living, as well as to advance the cause of tobacco-free societies" [press release, WHO/1, 1/8/90]. The third **World No-Tobacco Day** on May 31, 1990, focused on the danger of smoking to young people [press release, WHO/LUN 85, 12/15/89], amid evidence that 2.5 million will die of tobacco-related diseases in this year alone [WHO, *Tobacco Alert*, 1/90]. WHO Director-General Nakajima notes that the agency has increased its budget for tobacco and associated health work by 120 percent [press release, WHO/LUN 85].

In May 1990, heading off a potential controversy, WHO's governing body, **the World Health Assembly**, voted to defer indefinitely the **Palestine Liberation Organization's (PLO) application for membership** in the agency. In 1989 it had voted to defer for one year its consideration of the application, in which the PLO requested membership as the state of Palestine, upgrading its status from that of nonvoting observer. The **United States**—responsible for a quarter of the agency's $600 million biennial budget—had threatened to suspend all payments of dues to WHO or any other agency that admitted the PLO. It and other Western nations argued that the PLO did not meet the standard tests of statehood, such as clearly defined territory, and Washington argued further that such a move would undermine peace efforts in the Middle East by appearing to favor the Palestinian side at the expense of Israel [*The New York Times*, 4/30/89].

The World Health Assembly's May 1990 decision was adopted by consensus. The PLO "accepted" the resolution, reported *The New York Times* [5/11/90], because it "'reaffirms'" the 1989 resolution, which had supported the principle of full membership for the Palestinian people eventually.

5. Drug Abuse, Production, and Trafficking

Colombia's President Virgilio Barco received a standing ovation from the General Assembly in September when, fresh from the front lines of a high-casualty war against "narco-terrorists" in his own country, he called for a special General Assembly session to address the drug problem. A month later the Assembly agreed to that request [A/Res/44/16] and, fulfilling it speedily, held the special session February 20–23, 1990. For Under-Secretary-General Margaret Anstee, coordinator of all U.N. activities related to drug control, this was yet another indication that the drug question had reached politically high ground. At an estimated value of $500 billion, the international drug trade has surpassed the oil trade and is second only to the international trade in armaments [*London Financial Times*, 4/9/90]. An enormous—200 ton—shipment of cocaine recently seized in Los Angeles would have commanded a sum in excess of the gross national product of 100 individual U.N. member states, yet its interdiction affected the street price of cocaine in the United States not at all [ibid.]. The number of drug users worldwide has been estimated at 48 million [ST/ESA/213].

Even as U.N. member states were outlining a Global Programme of Action to be elaborated at the Special Session [A/RES/44/141], the U.N. organs that would be instrumental in coordinating those actions had been feeling the effects of shrinking operating budgets—and faced even greater difficulty in carrying out the first phases of battle plotted by the U.N.-sponsored **International Conference on Drug Abuse and Illicit Trafficking** in 1987. The same financing problem threatened to hinder implementation of the 1988 **U.N. Convention against Illicit Traffic in Narcotic Drugs and Psychotropic Substances**, now two ratifications short of the 20 required for its entry into force.

In January 1990 financial constraints cut short the 11th special session of the **Commission of Narcotic Drugs (CND)**—the 40-member functional commission of ECOSOC that is the main policymaking organ for international drug control—which failed to reach consensus on a series of antidrug measures to recommend to the General Assembly's Special Session, settling for a statement of general principles to guide the delegates' deliberations. (It did, however, agree to impose international controls on six "designer drugs" and four psychotropic substances identified by WHO as being abused or having the potential to be abused, according to guidelines set out by the 1971 **Convention on Psychotropic Substances** [E/1990/24].) In the case of the **Division of Narcotic Drugs (DND)**, the U.N. regular budget has been supplying only $730,000 of a $3.8 million operational budget, forcing this body—the United Nations's own cadre of professional and technical experts and the secretariat for CND—to spend precious time and resources in raising the difference. (One group of experts working under DND auspices is exploring the use of satellites to detect areas given over to the cultivation of illicit crops and to detect cases of deforestation that may be a result of drug-related pollution or cultivation [A/C.3/44/SR.29]).

It is the extrabudgetary resources obtained by the voluntary **U.N. Fund for Drug Abuse Control (UNFDAC)** that support special **technical assistance programs** aiding national efforts to address drug-related problems. In 1989, UNFDAC invested a budget of $62.5 million in 152 projects in 49 countries: 33 percent for reducing demand, 33 percent for reducing supply, and 25 percent for controlling the distribution of narcotic and psychotropic drugs produced for medical and scientific purposes. Despite all such activities, noted the **International Narcotics Control Board (INCB)** in its annual review of the world drug situation, the illicit production and use of drugs has increased, with an attendant escalation of violence [E/1990/16]. INCB—an independent body under U.N. auspices that assists governments in complying with the obligations outlined in the international drug conventions—called for greater attention to reducing the demand for illicit drugs and, at the same time, noted the **unavailability of opiates for medical and scientific use** [E/INCB/1989/1 and Supp.]. The **World Health Organization** (WHO), another combatant in the war on drugs, has been contributing to the research on ways to reduce demand as well as exploring the connection between drug abuse and the spread of AIDS [press release, WHO/LUN 18, 2/20/90].

The **Special Session to Consider the Question of International Cooperation against Illicit Production, Supply, Demand, Trafficking and Distribution of Narcotic Drugs and Psychotropic Substances**—the U.N.'s 17th Special Session—adopted, without a vote, both a declaration and the **Global Programme of Action** (GPA) [GA/8005] called for by the 44th General Assembly. This GPA establishes priorities among the activities outlined by the 1987 international conference and by the 1988 Convention against Illlicit Traffic in Narcotic Drugs and Psychotropic Substances, elaborating on them and giving **equal attention to trafficking, supply, and demand.** Wide acceptance of the importance of the last of the three distinguishes this document from previous ones, as does the recognition that efforts on one front must be matched by efforts on the others. Under-Secretary-General Anstee contrasted this new perspective with the old, noting that "previously, there had been a tendency to think that you could solve the [drug] problem simply by pulling up a few coca bushes in Latin America or poppy plants somewhere else in Asia and so forth" [*World Chronicle*, Program 368, 11/14/89].

Among the GPA's priorities in the demand category are education, research into the social causes underlying the drug problem, the collection of data on trends in drug abuse, the introduction of coursework on the "rational prescribing and use of narcotic drugs" in medical training institutions, and the development of national strategies "for the social reintegration, rehabilitation and treatment of drug abusers and drug-addicted offenders," with renewed emphasis on children.

Priorities in the supply category include "prompt identification, eradication, and substitution of illicit cultivation of narcotic plants" and a call to regional and governmental actors to aid in creating viable economic alternatives for supplier countries and ensuring these countries' commodities fair access to world markets. The traffic category exhorted member states to ratify the 1988 convention and, in anticipation, apply its measures regarding money laundering and extradition of offenders; and it stressed the need for further action to develop laws and procedures that expedite the seizure and forfeiture of "property and proceeds derived from, used in or intended for use in illicit drug trafficking."

The 17th Special Session's declaration expressed the conviction that the "international fight against illicit drug trafficking should be pursued in full conformity with the principles of non-interference in internal affairs," pledged to increase the scope and effectiveness of that international fight, and proclaimed the years **1991–2000 the United Nations Decade against Drug Abuse**. An earlier call in the General Assembly for a U.N. **drug czar** to coordinate international efforts in this area was being considered by a 15-member group of experts appointed by the Secretary-General, who will be reporting to the 45th General Assembly on its findings [SOC/NAR/560].

During its regular session the 44th Assembly joined the call for a special session and a Global Programme of Action to Combat Drug Abuse with a call for the speedy implementation of the 1988 Convention against Illicit Traffic in Narcotic Drugs and Psychotropic Substances [A/RES/44/140]—an important element of the GPA. Another resolution stressed the importance of international cooperation in combating drug traffic [44/142]. Yet another requested that the International Law Commission consider the establishment of an **international criminal court to try drug traffickers**, money launderers, and others involved in the international drug trade according to the principles established in the U.N. treaties on drug control [44/39]. (Past efforts to establish international tribunals with authority to prosecute individuals have foundered on the fear that such courts are likely to infringe on national sovereignty. This matter will likely be the subject of lengthy debate.)

In December 1989 the General Assembly passed without dissent, and opened for ratification, an international convention that establishes the criminality of mercenary activities in general and goes on to deplore the connection between mercenaries and drug traffickers [A/Res/44/34]. Drawing on the guidelines for extradition contained in this new **U.N. Convention against the Recruitment, Use, Financing and Training of Mercenaries,** the United Kingdom and Colombia have agreed that British nationals who aid drug armies in Colombia will be handed over to the United Kingdom for criminal prosecution.

6. Other Social Issues

Aging

Confronting a "graying" world population—in the year 2025 there are expected to be 1.2 billion elderly people, some 70 percent of whom will be living in developing regions—the General Assembly adopted an **International Plan of Action on Aging** in 1982 [A/Res/37/51]. Two of its primary goals are to ensure the elderly such basics as food, water, shelter, health protection, and education and to gain the elderly recognition of their humanitarian needs and human resource potential [E/1989/Inf/7]. The 44th General Assembly received the Secretary-General's report following the **Commission for Social Development's** second four-year review of the progress made in implementing the Plan of Action [A/44/420] and agreed to establish an ad hoc group in the Third (Social, Humanitarian, and Cultural) Committee to consider the review. Anticipating the plan's tenth anniversary in 1992, it suggested a variety of special activities [A/Res/44/67].

Stage 1 of the three-stage Plan of Action sought—and achieved to a considerable degree, said the first review in 1985—global awareness of the phenomenon of aging. With **stage 2**, currently under way, the aim is to develop an appropriate infrastructure at the national level to deal with the needs of an aging population (national committees for the elderly, governmental and nongovernmental; organizations of the elderly themselves; gerontological societies and training institutes). Here, progress has been slow, the Secretary-General advised the Commission for Social Development in a report prepared to assist the commission in its **Second Review and Appraisal of the implementation of the plan**. Among the evidence he cited—drawing on the replies to a questionnaire sent to U.N. member states, U.N. bodies, and various intergovernmental and nongovernmental organizations—is the fact that in 1985 there were 72 national coordinating committees for addressing problems of the elderly; in early 1989 there were just a dozen or so more (51 in developing countries and 33 in the developed) [E/1989/13].

The Secretary-General's report to the 44th General Assembly put a more optimistic spin on such statistics. Here it was noted that "as the traditional social support structures of family and community change and, on the whole, weaken, new structures are emerging. National machineries on aging now number 90. Gerontological societies are to be found in many regions and countries. Training institutes on aging are emerging" [A/44/420]. Whatever the emerging trend, the Secretary-General's report had concluded that the actual progress made in implementing the Plan of Action "in a few parts of the world" was "not sufficient to change the global assessment. . . . Far from anticipating the process of aging, [policies and programs] have not even kept pace with it" [E/1989/13].

In some cases, noted the Secretary-General, this situation reflects a lack of political will to deal with the problem; in others, there is a lack of funds for social programs in general. Among the Secretary-General's recommendations for aiding the development of national machineries on aging were bilateral and multilateral "research arrangements, particularly between developing and developed countries . . . to understand and respond better to global- and country-specific aging issues" [E/1989/13]. Singled out for new attention were the families of the elderly. The Secretary-General and the commission called for burden sharing to keep the elderly at home and out of expensive care facilities.

Stage 3 of the Plan of Action relates to the contribution of the elderly to the national development process—their human resource potential—and to bettering the economic lot of the elderly. It anticipates creating a "virtuous cycle" (to borrow from economics) as opposed to a vicious one: "As the elderly are enabled to be more active, self-reliant, self-determining and contributing members of society, they will become healthier and less isolated and economically dependent."

Indicative of the back-burner approach of most governments to the problem of aging is the paucity of funds contributed to the ten-year-old **U.N. Trust Fund for Aging**—a mere $1.5 million, most of it "in connection with the 1982 World Assembly on Aging" [E/1989/13]; in the first half of 1989, donations amounted to only $18,513 [A/Conf. 145/2]. The fund has disbursed most of its funds in small seed-money grants to several dozen regional and country-level projects and to a few interregional and global activities. In September 1989 the Secretary-General convened a meeting of eminent persons to develop an international fund-raising strategy for policies and programs on population aging. The meeting agreed on the urgency of establishing an **independent international foundation on aging** under the patronage of the United Nations and appointed a task force to work toward this goal [A/44/420/Add. 1].

The commission speculated that contributions to the trust fund might increase again in **1992, the tenth anniversary of the World Assembly on Aging and the Plan of Action**. The **44th General Assembly** urged governments to reach into their pockets and support a body that "is particularly well placed to act as a catalyst for resource mobilization," and it directed the 45th Assembly to review the commission's draft program of activities to mark the anniversary year [A/Res/44/67]. These activities, aimed "at celebrating aging as a significant phenomenon and achievement of the twentieth century" [E/1989/INF/7], will be coordinated by the **Centre for Social Development and Humanitarian Affairs of the U.N. Office at Vienna.** Additional points of the General Assembly's resolution on the subject of aging indicate, in the Assembly's phrase, "the gap between globally espoused standards and the real living conditions of the elderly." In a separate resolution, the Assembly requested the Commission on the Status of Women and other U.N.-related groups and agencies to pay particular heed to the situation of **elderly women** and their contribution to national development [A/Res/44/76]. The Secretary-General will apprise the 45th General Assembly of progress here.

Crime

The United Nations has organized the **Congress on the Prevention of Crime and the Treatment of Offenders** every five years since 1955, and various U.N. bodies, governments, and nongovernmental organizations began preparing for the eighth such "universal" forum—a ten-day event hosted by Cuba in late summer 1990—soon after the seventh was gaveled to a close. These crime congresses have taken the lead in formulating and implementing many of the U.N. declarations and agreements that offer standards, norms, and codes to guide lawmakers, law enforcers, and judiciaries throughout the world. The Seventh Congress, for example, meeting in Milan, trained the spotlight on a number of transboundary crimes that fall into the "space between the laws" [E/1988/20], among them international organized crime, terrorism, and the illicit trade in national art treasures. The **Milan Plan of Action** recommended a variety of legal reforms and improvements in criminal justice systems to close the loopholes.

Representatives of 129 U.N. member states helped to prepare for the Eighth Congress in the course of five interregional and regional meetings in 1988 and 1989. Draft recommendations and resolutions from these conferences were taken up by the **Committee on Crime Prevention and Control (CCPC)**, a 27-member standing body of experts answering to the Economic and Social Council (ECOSOC), which examined and shaped the drafts for submission to the congress. The Crime Prevention and Criminal Justice Branch of the Centre for Social Development and Humanitarian Affairs at the U.N. Office in Vienna acted as congress secretariat throughout the preparation period.

The 44th General Assembly, playing its role as town crier to the world, directed the attention of the international community to the August 27–September 7 event in Havana. The Third (Social, Humanitarian, and

Cultural) Committee's two draft resolutions drew from the Secretary-General's report "Crime Prevention and Criminal Justice" [A/44/400], which noted the danger of all forms of transnational criminality, "thriving at unprecedented levels and in ways previously unheard of," emphasized the necessity of worldwide participation in preparations for the congress, and expressed concern over severe resource constraints that threatened to jeopardize its success. These two resolutions—one on "International co-operation in combating organized crime" [44/71] and the other a catch-all, which, among other things, invited governments to provide information on the progress made in implementing the Milan Plan of Action [44/72]—passed the Assembly by consensus. The latter also requested the Secretary-General to submit to the 45th Assembly his views and recommendations on implementing the conclusions of the Eighth Congress.

Meeting for its 11th annual session in Vienna in February 1990, the CCPC, which is charged with developing practical policies for crime prevention and criminal justice and with monitoring the implementation of U.N. standards and norms, considered various measures, both national and international, to combat the sorts of transboundary offenses addressed in the Milan Plan. One of the resolutions it recommended for adoption in Havana calls for studies concerning the linkage of such crimes to corruption, for new legislation targeted at money laundering and organized fraud, and for heightened cooperation among nations in combating **organized crime**. In May, ECOSOC had urged the committee to give special attention to this issue, noting that organized crime has become increasingly "transnational in character, leading, in particular, to the spread of such negative phenomena as violence, terrorism, . . . illegal trade in narcotic drugs and, in general, undermining the development process, impairing the quality of life and threatening human rights and fundamental freedoms" [E/Res/1989/70].

The CCPC's proposal to combat **international terrorism**, contained in an annex, observes that existing international norms "might" not be sufficient to control all forms of terrorist violence and suggests attacking the problem on several new fronts, ranging from extradition to the creation of an international criminal court. The committee's draft model treaty against the illicit import and export of "**movable cultural property**" would require states to "confiscate and return such property taken without authorization" and to "introduce measures to prevent the acquisition by museums and similar institutions of such property," imposing sanctions on those responsible [U.N. press release, SOC/CP/31, 2/21/90].

Other agenda items for the crime congress are the CCPC's proposed rules for the protection of **juveniles** deprived of their liberty, affirming that detention should be the punishment of last resort and for the minimum period necessary. A related draft offering guidelines on the prevention of juvenile delinquency pays particular attention to children at social risk. The CCPC's draft U.N. "standard minimum rules for noncustodial measures of imprisonment" (dubbed the **Tokyo rules**) calls for appropriate actions to rationalize criminal justice policies from the standpoint of human rights. A draft offering basic principles for the use of force and firearms by law enforcement officials is yet another CCPC entry on the lengthy agenda of the crime congress [ibid.].

The overarching theme of the Havana congress is International Cooperation in Crime Prevention and Criminal Justice for the Twenty-first Century. Delegates will be offered a workshop on alternatives to imprisonment and another workshop on computerizing the criminal justice system.

Beyond the considerable problem of finances, the congress faces a **boycott by the United States**, which, as expressed by a U.S. Mission spokesman, considers it highly inappropriate to hold the meeting in a country that "flouts" international norms in the area of crime prevention and criminal justice [interview with *Issues Before the 45th General Assembly*].

The Disabled

Seven years into the **U.N. Decade of Disabled Persons** (1983–1992) and eight years after the passage of the **U.N. World Programme of Action Concerning Disabled Persons** (1982), most nations' efforts to rehabilitate and open up opportunities for the world's 500 million disabled have been limited in scope. In the Secretary-General's words, "The Decade . . . has not met the expectations of the international community nor, most important, those of disabled persons themselves" [A/44/406/Rev. 1].

Declining contributions to the **Voluntary Fund for the U.N. Decade of Disabled Persons**, managed by the U.N. Office at Vienna, continue to inhibit a broader effort. Since becoming operational in 1980, the Fund has provided over $2 million in seed money for 110 projects, but many others could not be financed at all. For the year and a half beginning January 1988, for example, it was able to honor only 25 out of 70 grant requests. With the Secretary-General's appointment of a **Special Representative to Promote the Decade**, there have been a number of fund-raising initiatives [A/44/406/Rev. 1].

Pointed to as a solid achievement of the decade is the new legislation in several countries—Canada, China, and Pakistan among them—designed to integrate disabled persons in such areas as education and employment. Some countries have begun offering allowances and income tax relief to the severely handicapped and their families, and some others—including Brazil, Botswana, and Cyprus—are now providing incentives to businesses that employ the disabled. Antigua and China now have special schools for the hearing impaired; in Portugal and Thailand there are newly published sign language dictionaries; and Ghana has an official sign language [A/44/406/Rev. 1].

Lending a hand in emergency situations, the Special Representative assessed the needs of Armenia's disabled population following the 1988 earthquake, and as chairman of the Committee on Assistance to Disabled Afghans, he oversaw the drafting of "guidelines and priorities" for such assistance by the bodies of the U.N. system [A/44/406/Rev. 1].

Coordinating and fostering the system-wide contribution to the Programme of Action is the **Centre for Social Development and Humanitarian Aid** of the U.N. Office at Vienna. The U.N. Secretariat's **Statistical Office** prepares the data on disability that will guide national programs. **Regional U.N. bodies**, such as the Economic and Social Commission for Western Asia, have prepared a number of studies and technical publications on the disabled, including a directory of specialized institutions. The **United Nations Children's Fund** (UNICEF) focuses on detecting and preventing childhood impairments; the **U.N. Educational, Scientific and Cultural Organization** (UNESCO) sponsors educational materials, seminars, and workshops that will benefit children with special needs; and the **World Health Organization** (WHO) helps to create community-based rehabilitation services, with the aim of establishing these services in half the countries of the world by 1995 [A/44/406/Rev. 1]. **Nongovernmental organizations** (NGOs) around the world are important to the success of the entire effort. The Special Representative keeps in regular contact with some 200 organizations of and for disabled persons, and he may—as at a meeting in Vienna in June 1989—call the group together for consultation.

The Secretary-General's report to the 44th General Assembly regarding Implementation of the World Programme of Action Concerning Disabled Persons and the United Nations Decade of Disabled Persons recommended a number of **priorities for governments**, among them the establishment of national mechanisms to aid the disabled and the strengthening of those already in place, the drafting and enactment of suitable legislation, the expansion of braille services, and the implementation of the Nairobi protocol of the so-called Florence agreement to allow, duty free, the international movement of all equipment and materials that disabled people require for their daily lives [A/44/406/Rev. 1]. The General Assembly, requesting a progress report on the Programme of Action and the Decade at its 45th Session, called attention to a strategy for promoting "the participation, training and employment of disabled persons" developed at an international meeting in Talinn, Estonia, in mid-August 1989 [A/Res/44/70].

The 45th Assembly will also be advised of the results of a feasibility study of alternate possibilities for marking the end of the Decade of Disabled Persons in 1992. One of the possibilities entertained at an experts' meeting in Finland in May 1990 was that of developing a strategy for action up to and beyond the year 2000 [A/44/406/Rev. 1]. The experts called for the convening of a ministerial-level world conference on disability in 1993.

The Homeless

During the **International Year of Shelter for the Homeless** 1987, when attention was drawn to homelessness as a worldwide phenomenon—a billion people without adequate housing and 100 million more with no shelter at all [A/44/8 Supp. 8]—the U.N.'s Nairobi-based **Centre for Human Settlements (HABITAT)** served as focal point for the drafting of a **Global Strategy for Shelter to the Year 2000.** In December 1988 the General Assembly gave its unanimous approval to the strategy [43/181], which was launched at U.N. Headquarters in February 1989. HABITAT was named coordinator of the U.N. system's shelter programs, and the intergovernmental **Commission on Human Settlements** was asked to review the progress made at the national level.

Four principles guide the strategy: private as well as public resources should be encouraged and allowed to work to best advantage; women, often the family breadwinner and head of household, should be involved in shelter programs and policymaking; the links between shelter and economic development are strong and abiding; and "sustainable development" must be a consideration in all matters relating to the building of shelters. Singled out for attention are the developing countries, where an estimated third to a half of all citizens are ill housed or without shelter [A/43/8, Add. 1].

In the **first stage** of the Global Strategy, 1989–1991, the focus is on formulating national shelter strategies, designing new institutional arrangements, and implementing national programs. In **stage 2,** 1992–1994, these new institutional arrangements are expected to be put into effect and existing national programs strengthened. In the **last stage,** 1995–2000, it is envisioned that national programs will go into high gear, and national institutions will be on the path to sustained progress [A/44/8 Supp. 8].

Meeting at its 12th (biannual) session in spring 1989, the commission adopted a set of guidelines drafted by HABITAT to aid governments in developing national shelter strategies and in assessing their performance, and it also suggested a timetable for national efforts [A/44/8 Supp. 8 annex]. The 44th General Assembly "not[ed] with satisfaction" the assistance rendered by various member states in helping other governments develop these strategies and "urge[d]" the organizations of the U.N. system to supply financial and technical support for implementing them [A/Res/44/173].

On **World Habitat Day** 1990—by tradition, the first Monday in October—U.N. member states will begin reporting to the commission on their progress in implementing the strategies. Every two years HABITAT will offer a "consolidated monitoring report," and the first such report will be reviewed by the commission at its 13th session in 1991.

The Status of Women

The five-year review of progress made in implementing the **Nairobi Forward-Looking Strategies for the Advancement of Women to the Year 2000** found some advances in the "area of *de jure* equality" but few in "*de facto* equality . . . in both developing and developed countries" and even a "trend to regression" in women's education, employment, and health in some parts of the developing world. This trend, described as a result of the Third World's debt problems, recession, and the austerity measures encouraged by multilateral and other lending institutions, is undermining some of the progress charted during the **U.N. Decade for Women, 1976–85** [E/1990/25]. The **Commission on the Status of Women**, the subsidiary of ECOSOC that carried out the midterm review at its 34th session, February 26–March 9, 1990, based its findings on a report prepared by the Secretary-General [E/CN.6/1990/7]. His report drew upon responses the Secretariat had received to a questionnaire sent to member states in 1988, and it went on to recommend remedial actions by governments. These draft findings and recommendations were reviewed by three expert groups that had gathered in Vienna in advance of the commission's February session [E/CN.6/1990/2, 3, 4].

The Nairobi document remains the springboard for U.N. efforts at improving the status of women throughout the world and in U.N. bodies themselves. Its three interrelated "priority themes," or goals—equality, development, and peace—seek to acknowledge and increase the role of women in the social, political, and economic life of their nations, and each recognizes as a first step the need to educate women as well as men to the importance of achieving this objective. Today, with the decrease in per capita expenditures in such sectors as education—a 60 percent decrease in Latin America from 1979 to 1983, for example—women are even less likely than at the start of the Decade to obtain the basic education that is a prerequisite to learning about their rights and exercising them. Indeed, under conditions of scarcity, girls are likely to be slighted in still other ways that affect their health and welfare. According to one study cited by the expert group on development, when immunization was free of charge, boys and girls were immunized at the same rate; when a fee was charged, the immunization of girls decreased by half [E/CN.6/1990/3]. And at a time when there is a rise in female-headed households, undereducated women will continue to have a lower earning capacity, perpetuating the cycle of poverty and traditional concepts of power.

The Commission on the Status of Women issued 24 recommendations for governments, among them setting up or continuing "campaigns for women's 'legal literacy'" by formal and informal educational means; establishing the machinery for putting legal equality into practice (including the creation of an ombudsman or similar system and mobilizing grass-roots groups to stimulate this process); promoting "the training of teachers on gender issues" and otherwise helping to "promote change in psychological, social and traditional practices that are the foundation of the *de facto* obstacles to women's progress"; increasing the involvement of women in economic and political decision making, with the aim of increasing the proportion of women in all leadership positions to at least 30 percent by 1995 and achieving equal representation by the year 2000; increasing "the number of women in paid employment"; ensuring that women have access to "education and training at all levels and in all fields"; taking "concrete measures to eliminate poverty"; and introducing "appropriate penalties for violence against women in the family, the work place and society" [E/1990/25]. These recommendations will be considered by ECOSOC, and the commission's findings on the implementation of the Forward-Looking Strategies will be reported to the 45th General Assembly by the Secretary-General [A/Res/44/77]. At the 44th Assembly's suggestion [ibid.], the commission agreed to hold a **world conference on women in 1995**. At that time it will be conducting its next review and appraisal of the progress made in implementing the strategies [E/1990/25].

The 44th Assembly also endorsed the calling of a high-level interregional **consultation on women in public life** in 1991, cautioning that it must be "financed within existing resources and voluntary and other contributions" [A/Res/44/77]. ECOSOC, looking forward to the 1992 U.N. Conference on Environment and Development during its spring 1990 meeting, recommended that governments consider giving special attention to "the issue of **women and the environment** to ensure that the experience and knowledge of women [are] fully taken into account" [U.N. press release, ECOSOC/5210, 4/30/90].

By June 1990, 102 states had ratified the 1979 **Convention on the Elimination of Discrimination against Women**, agreeing to submit a report on the situation of women in their own country within a year of ratification and to report at four-year intervals thereafter. To date, the **Committee on the Elimination of Discrimination against Women** (CEDAW)—the 23-member body of experts established to monitor implementation of the Convention—has received only 63 of the initial reports and 28 second periodic reports [A/45/38]. Its findings on each country situation, reported to the General Assembly through ECOSOC, are accompanied by general recommendations and suggestions.

Meeting at U.N. Headquarters in New York between January 22 and February 2, 1990, CEDAW considered seven initial reports and five second periodic reports; because of time constraints, it had the opportunity to discuss and approve only two of the general recommendations made by its working groups. One called on state parties to eradicate **the practice of female circumcision**, traditional in regions of North Africa and elsewhere on that continent, because of serious health and other consequences for women and children; the other called on states to intensify their efforts at increasing public awareness of the **risk of HIV infection and AIDS to women and children.**

The 44th General Assembly directed the Secretary-General to report annually on the status of the Convention and, in the same resolution, expressed its support for measures that will ensure CEDAW adequate funding and facilities to carry out its mandate [A/Res/44/73].

The 44th Assembly took special note of the work done by the two voluntarily funded U.N. organs concerned with women's issues: the **U.N. International Research and Training Institute for the Advancement of Women (INSTRAW)** [A/Res/44/60] and the **U.N. Development Fund for Women (UNIFEM)** [A/Res/44/803 and Corr. 1]. INSTRAW, described as "both an agent for sensitization on the role of women in the mainstream of development" and "a centre for specialized research, training and information" [E/1990/68], draws upon an extensive network of organizations inside and outside the United Nations in carrying out these roles. The INSTRAW board of trustees, applauding the institute's current efforts to supply "**statistics and indicators on women,** including women's role in the informal sector," noted that these are the first phase of a broad research program "on monitoring and evaluating **methodologies for development programs related to women,**" with emphasis on water supply and sanitation, new and renewable sources of energy, and environmental concerns. The board urged INSTRAW to "continue work on new methodological approaches in these fields" and to consider cosponsoring a **World Festival of Creative Women** to mark its tenth anniversary in 1990. It approved a program budget ceiling of $3,105,700 for 1990–1991 [E/1990/34]. A report by the U.N. Secretary-General on the work of INSTRAW will be presented to the 46th General Assembly in 1991 [A/Res/44/60].

UNIFEM, founded in 1976, saw its mandate expand in 1984 as it prepared to take up a role in implementing the Nairobi Forward-Looking Strategies. Donations to this voluntary fund have also expanded; for 1990 the total of voluntary contributions is expected to increase to $7.6 million, up 14 percent from the previous year. The 44th Assembly "emphasiz[ed]" the Fund's "catalytic role" not only within the U.N. system but also with governmental and nongovernmental organizations and financial institutions. It reaffirmed UNIFEM's concurrent "support for innovative and experimental activities directly benefiting women in line with national and regional priorities," and it "not[ed] the focused and proactive intervention of the Fund . . . through investments in tested and documented models and approaches for women and development." UNIFEM scheduled a review of its work and objectives for May 1990, and a report on the findings and on its recent activities in implementing the strategies will be submitted to the 45th General Assembly by the administrator of the U.N. Development Programme [A/Res/44/74].

The Nairobi Strategies had called upon the **U.N. Secretariat** to serve as a role model in matters affecting women. The goals set for the Secretariat and the progress to date are reviewed in a subsequent section, "Personnel and Staff Administration." The 45th General Assembly will have in hand the Secretary-General's outline of a program intended to improve the status of women in the Secretariat during the next five years [A/Res/44/75].

Youth

For the world's children it was the best of times and the worst of times. On November 20 the 44th General Assembly adopted by consensus and opened for ratification the **Convention on the Rights of the Child** [A/Res/44/25], after ten years of negotiations under the auspices of the United Nations Centre for Human Rights. To date, 97 countries have signed this document setting minimum standards for the survival, health, and education of children and offering protection against exploitation and abuse, and 13 states have gone on to ratify it (almost two-thirds of the number required for the convention to enter into force). Later in the year, the **United Nations Children's Fund (UNICEF)** reported that 42 countries, eight more than in 1988, had achieved the important goal of **immunizing** 80 percent of their nation's children by age 1. This rise in immunization coverage itself prevented an estimated 2 million infant and child deaths in the past year.

At the same time, **malnutrition** among children is on the rise, the death toll from **easily preventable illnesses** remains high, expenditures on such social services as **education and health care** have declined as many regions of the Third World slide deeper into poverty, the number of children who live in poverty has increased (even in the United States the figure has risen from 11 percent to 15 percent over the last decade), and AIDS is causing a new social and health problem among Africa's young [UNICEF Annual Report, *State of the World's Children 1990*].

UNICEF, active in 128 developing countries and territories in advancing the cause of universal child immunization, control of diarrheal diseases, and primary health care for mothers and their young, has announced the launching of some new programs to deal with growing crises [E/ICEF/1990/3]. One is in **Africa**, where increasing numbers of children are being orphaned—and their unborn brothers and sisters placed at risk—by the spread of **AIDS** in the heterosexual population. Among the grim statistics supplied by the agency, approximately 1 million women in Africa have been infected with the AIDS virus and are expected to die in the next ten years; they will transmit the virus to a quarter or more of their babies, who are expected to die before reaching the age of 5. Working within the framework of the World Health Organization's (WHO) **Global Programme on AIDS,** UNICEF will be lending its efforts to information, education, and communications campaigns; to training health care workers in AIDS prevention strategies; and to providing situation analyses to study the impact of the virus on women, children, and their families.

Explaining its decision to provide a new "**basic education thrust**" to its work, UNICEF cites a 25 percent decline in school spending over the last decade by 37 of the world's poorest countries and a decline in the number of primary school students in one out of five developing nations, and it notes the impetus provided by the March 1990 World Conference on Education for All. **Early childhood development** is a primary aim of these new programs, with an emphasis on the health and nutrition of children under the age of 3 and mental stimulation for 4 to 6 year olds. Using "nonformal channels of education," another aim is to "impart the knowledge and skills that will empower people to improve their well-being," making a special effort to bring girls and women into the education process and to address the needs of "disadvantaged and deprived population groups" [ibid.].

UNICEF will also be lending "transitional assistance"—described as "necessarily modest"—to the **Eastern European countries** undergoing political and economic change. The UNICEF secretariat is examining the impact of these changes on the social sector in these countries and particularly their effect on children's needs [U.N. press release, ICEF/1709, 4/18/90].

Soviet President Mikhail Gorbachev was among those who took up the cause of children at the 44th General Assembly, stating in an address during its opening days that "mankind can no longer put up with the fact that millions of children die every year at the close of the twentieth century" [*State of the World's Children 1990*]. This concern, and the vigorous efforts of UNICEF Executive Director James Grant, are behind the first **World Summit for Children**, which will bring heads of state to U.N. Headquarters between September 29 and 30, just after the start of the 45th Session. The summit's ad hoc planning committee is composed of representatives of WHO, the U.N. Educational, Scientific and Cultural Organization, the U.N. Population Fund, the World Bank, the International Labour Organisation, and the U.N. Development Programme, as well as 25 member states. "Only something as dramatic and unprecedented as a summit meeting of world leaders to discuss the subject of children could significantly upgrade the priority which the world will give its children," noted

UNICEF in describing this initiative. It hopes for a summit agreement on a plan for "doing the things," nationally and internationally, "we know can be done to save children's lives and protect their healthy growth and environment" [UNICEF handout, "The World Summit for Children: Questions & Answers"].

The 45th General Assembly will consider a report from the Secretary-General on the "Implementation of the Convention on the Rights of the Child" [A/Res/44/25]. Once the convention enters into force, a ten-member committee of experts will be examining the progress made by ratifying states, reporting to the General Assembly through ECOSOC every two years. In preparation for the 45th Session, ECOSOC will be considering a draft Programme of Action to mark the **tenth anniversary of International Youth Year**. The Secretary-General's report on "Policies and Programmes Involving Youth" at the 44th Session [A/44/387], while noting some momentum toward "integrating youth policy into national development planning," also noted that "the overriding goal of improving the global situation of youth remains elusive." Among the problems he cited were a "lack of consensus" on the meaning of "youth" in various societies; the inability, especially in the developing countries, to compile the statistical profile on youth that is required for policy formulation; and, inevitably, a lack of financial resources both nationally and for the U.N. programs that lend technical assistance to governments in this area.

V
Legal Issues

The general movement toward what Soviet Deputy Foreign Minister Vladimir F. Petrovsky called a "post-confrontational world" produced, in the words of the U.S. Representative to the United Nations, Thomas R. Pickering, "one of the most constructive and realistic" General Assembly sessions in memory [*The New York Times*, 12/20/89]. The reduced superpower tensions were reflected in a historic joint U.S.–Soviet Union resolution reaffirming basic Charter principles, constructive ideas in the Special Committee on the Charter and Strengthening the Role of the Organization, and breakthroughs on long-pending draft conventions on the status of the diplomatic courier and bag and against the recruitment, use, financing, and the training of mercenaries. Developments in economic law and in the International Court of Justice also made 1990 an appropriate first year for the newly proclaimed Decade of International Law.

1. The International Law Commission

The International Law Commission (ILC) was established in 1947 by General Assembly resolution [A/Res/174 (II)] and charged with the task of assisting the Assembly to "encourag[e] the progressive development of international law and its codification" in accordance with Article 13 (1) (a) of the U.N. Charter. The ILC consists of 34 individuals who serve on the ILC in their personal capacities, not as representatives of their governments. During the ILC's 41st session, held from May to July 1989, the commission discussed five ongoing projects: a Draft Code of Crimes against the Peace and Security of Mankind, draft articles relating to the international liability for injurious consequences arising out of acts not prohibited by international law, draft articles relating to jurisdictional immunities of states and their property, draft articles on the law of the nonnavigational uses of international watercourses, and preliminary draft articles relating to the second part of the topic on relations between states and international organizations. In addition, the ILC completed its draft Convention on the Status of the Diplomatic Courier and the Diplomatic Bag not Accompanied by Diplomatic Courier. [For a summary of the discussion held in the Sixth (Legal) Committee on the ILC's 41st session, see A/CN.4/L.443, 1/16/90].

The ILC submitted its **Draft Articles and Draft Optional Protocols One and Two on the Status of the Diplomatic Courier and Diplomatic Bag Not Accompanied by Diplomatic Courier** to the 44th General Assembly with a recommendation that it convene a conference to study the drafts and conclude a convention on the subject [Report of the ILC on the Work of its 41st Session, A/44/475, including the text of the proposed convention and protocols]. During the 44th Session, the General Assembly "took note" of the ILC's recommendation and decided to hold informal consultations on the draft articles and protocols and to include the topic on the agenda of the 45th General Assembly [A/Res/44/36]. The ILC's submission culminates a project begun in 1976. The purpose of the draft Convention and Protocols is to establish a "comprehensive and uniform regime for all kinds of couriers and bags employed by States for official communications" [ILC Commentary to Draft Convention, Report, A/44/475, 27]. The ILC's task was made more difficult by the need to consolidate, harmonize, and add specificity to rules now contained in four existing multilateral conventions—the 1961 Vienna Convention on Diplomatic Relations, the 1963 Vienna Convention on Consular Relations, the 1969 Convention on Special Missions, and the 1975 Vienna Convention on the Representation of States in Their Relations with International Organizations of a Universal Character—as well as attempt to balance the competing interests of sending and receiving states in view of instances in which diplomatic bags have been used for the illicit import or export of currency, drugs, and arms and even the transport of human beings.

The main draft Convention deals with couriers and bags, both diplomatic and consular, sent by states, including bags of a state's permanent mission to an international organization. Optional Protocol One deals with couriers and bags of special missions; Protocol Two reaches couriers and bags of international organizations. The ILC opted for optional protocols to avoid jeopardizing wider acceptability of the main Convention. The fundamental obligation imposed by the Convention, contained in Article 28, provides that the diplomatic bag is "inviolable wherever it may be; it shall not be opened or detained and shall be exempt from examination directly or through electronic or other technical devices." It also reaffirms that receiving and transit states have an obligation to permit the speedy transit of the diplomatic bag [Art. 27]. On the other hand, the Convention obliges sending states to respect the laws and regulations of the receiving and transit states and use the bag only for official purposes—duties that can be enforced through, for example, reciprocal denial of benefits or a declaration that the courier is persona non grata. The Convention and Protocols for the most part echo existing treaty law on point and attempt to balance the competing interests of sending versus receiving and transit states in traditional ways through provisions, for example, permitting inspection or search of the accommodation or personal baggage of a diplomatic courier where "serious grounds" exist for believing that the courier is trafficking in prohibited goods [Art. 20(2)] or limiting the courier's immunity from civil or criminal jurisdiction to acts performed in the exercise of his or her functions [Art. 18]. Where receiving or transit states have "serious reason" to believe that the consular bag privilege is being abused, they may request that the bag be opened, and if this request is refused, they can return it to its place of origin [Art. 28(2)].

The draft Convention goes beyond existing law—for example, specifying when the role of the diplomatic courier comes to an end as well as when the courier's privileges and immunities begin and end; providing for the inviolability (subject to certain exceptions) of the person or of the temporary accommodation of the diplomatic courier; and requiring that couriers have insurance coverage while driving. In the view of some members, however, the commission did not go far enough to develop the law to prevent abuse of the diplomatic bag privilege. These members would have liked, for example, an exception to permit inspection by electronic devices.

It is unclear whether the ILC's ambitious goals for widespread acceptance of its drafts or the convening of a plenipotentiary conference will be fulfilled. During discussion in the Sixth Committee, some states also expressed reservations about the expense in convening a conference on the subject or about the need for a new multilateral instrument given existing treaties. [See, e.g., comments by the United States, the United Kingdom, and Australia, Sixth Committee, 24th and 25th Meetings, A/C.6/44/SR. 24, 25.]

The ILC's efforts to draft a **Code of Crimes against the Peace and Security of Mankind** date to 1947 when the General Assembly directed the commission to formulate the principles of international law recognized by the Nuremberg Tribunal [A/Res/2/177 (II)]. Long delayed because of difficulties in reaching an agreed definition of aggression, the ILC's work on this topic resumed, at the direction of the General Assembly, in 1981 [A/Res/36/106]. Through 1988, the ILC had provisionally adopted 12 articles. At its current session, the ILC debated its Special Rapporteur's seventh report [A/CN.4/419] dealing with draft articles on war crimes, crimes against humanity, other inhumane acts, as well as other possible crimes, including apartheid, slavery, and forced labor. It is anticipated that if the effort succeeds, the enumerated "crimes" would be enforced either by national courts exercising universal jurisdiction over the accused individuals or, less likely, by an international criminal court.

The ILC provisionally adopted three additional definitions of "crimes against peace." First, it adopted a new proposed Article 13, the "threat of aggression consisting of declarations, communications, demonstrations of force or any other measures which would give good reason to the Government of a State to believe that aggression is being seriously contemplated against that State" [Report of the ILC on the Work of its 41st Session, A/44/10, p. 178]. As stated in its commentary, this new article is inspired by Article 2(4) of the U.N. Charter, several General Assembly resolutions, as well as the judgment of the International Court of Justice in the case concerning military and paramilitary activities in and against Nicaragua (*Nicaragua v. United States of America)* [(Merits), Judgment of 6/27/86, 1986 ICJ Reports 14]. The commentary confirms that the definition is meant to be capable of objective determination by an impartial third party but that, unlike aggression, the mere threat of aggression does not justify a resort to military force in self-defense. It also acknowledges that the new article is controversial, since some members doubted whether an objective determination of existence of a threat could be made, while others stated that the Security Council should be given a role in any such determination. Others complained that the definition of threat of aggression was insufficiently precise and raised serious questions. Would naval exercises, for example, qualify? [See, e.g., comments at the Sixth Committee by the Federal Republic of Germany, the Netherlands, the United Kingdom, and the United States, 28th–30th Meetings, A/C.6/44/SR. 28-30.]

Second, a new Article 14 deals with "intervention in the internal or external affairs" of a state by "undermining the free exercise" of its sovereign rights through "subversive or terrorist activities," organizing, assisting, or financing such activities, or supplying arms. This new article was inspired by the Nicaragua case, as well as the Declaration on Principles of International Law concerning Friendly Relations and Co-operation among States in accordance with the Charter of the United Nations [A/Res/2625(XXV)]. To the ILC, the key element of wrongful intervention is coercion, but there were unresolved differences among members as to whether the subversive or terrorist activities need be "armed" and whether the crime as defined needed to be qualified further to indicate a "serious" undermining of the free exercise of sovereign rights. As with Article 13, questions were raised as to lack of clarity; some countries might consider foreign contributions to a domestic political party, for example, to be subversive.

Finally, the ILC, drawing on several General Assembly resolutions as well as its own work on state responsibility, provisionally adopted Article 15, condemning the "establishment or maintenance by force of colonial domination or any other form of alien domination contrary to the rights of peoples to self-determination as enshrined in the Charter of the United

Nations." Some members argued that other forms of alien domination included "neocolonialism"—that is, the exploitation in violation of General Assembly Resolution 1803 (XVII) of December 14, 1962 (Permanent Sovereignty over Natural Resources), while others contended that the limitation to measures defined by use of force precluded such an interpretation.

The General Assembly, following a recommendation from the Sixth (Legal) Committee, adopted a resolution inviting the ILC to continue its work on the elaboration of the draft Code of Crimes against the Peace and Security of Mankind and including further consideration of the code as part of its provisional agenda for the 45th Session [A/Res/44/32]. As in 1988, the resolution also included a request that the Secretary-General continue to seek the views of member states as to whether it would be appropriate to extend the ILC's mandate to preparation of a statute to provide for international criminal jurisdiction for individuals. [For the Secretary-General's Report of four replies received from members on this point in 1989, see A/44/465, 8/28/89.] The United Kingdom, the United States, Israel, the Federal Republic of Germany, and France, in the Sixth Committee and on the floor of the Assembly, voted against the resolution, and an additional fourteen members abstained. The objections varied from claims that it was inappropriate for the General Assembly to put political pressure on the ILC, to arguments that the code merited no special priority, to the United States' position that it was inappropriate to consider the code separately from the report of the ILC [GA/L/2641, 11/21/89]. In a related development, the General Assembly, following an initiative by Trinidad and Tobago, specifically requested the ILC to address at its 1990 session the question of establishing an **international criminal court** with jurisdiction over persons alleged to have committed acts in violation of the Code of Crimes against the Peace and Security of Mankind, "including persons engaged in illicit drug trafficking across national frontiers" [A/Res/44/39]. Since that resolution requests that the ILC report on this to the 45th General Assembly, the ILC's 1990 session may be largely devoted to this topic, already raised during the 1989 meetings of the Sixth Committee.

The ILC's general plan for its work on state responsibility, originally adopted in 1975, called for three parts: (1) the origin of international responsibility, (2) the content, forms, and degrees of international responsibility, and (3) the settlement of disputes and implementation. Part 1 was provisionally adopted in 1980. At its current session, the ILC considered only the preliminary report of a Special Rapporteur, Gaetano Arangio-Ruiz, who had been appointed in 1987. Ruiz would deal separately with the legal consequences of "delicts" and "crimes" in Part 2 of the topic, including the duty to cease doing the wrongful act, reparations, and other individual or collective sanctions. The ILC referred two of the Special Rapporteur's draft articles—on the duty to cease actions or omission that constitute an internationally wrongful act and on restitution in kind—to the Drafting Committee. The discussion during the session revealed disagreements among members about whether the new organizing scheme between "delicts" and "crimes" was workable, however [Report of the ILC, A/44/10, 194-195]. Given these disagreements, going to the basic schematic framework for further discussion of the topic, it remains doubtful that the ILC can fulfill its stated goal of completing a first reading of a complete set of draft articles on this subject by 1991.

The Commission's work on draft articles for a general convention on **International Liability for Injurious Consequences Arising Out of Acts Not Prohibited by International Law,** begun in 1978, is still at the conceptualization stage. Despite the drafting of initial draft articles on the subject, the ILC has yet to adopt any article. According to the newly revised draft Article 1, the topic seeks to provide international rules to govern activities carried out in one state that either "cause, or create an appreciable risk of causing, transboundary harm throughout the process" [Report of the ILC, A/44/10, 222]. In 1988 the ILC had referred to the Drafting Committee ten draft articles proposed by the Special Rapporteur. At that time, members had urged that the proposed convention extend to activities that both cause or create the risk of causing transboundary harm. At the current session, the commission revisited these articles, as revised by the Special Rapporteur, as well as his new proposals to oblige states to undertake assessment, provide warning for activities that cause or threaten to cause transboundary harm, and engage in consultations or fact finding with respect to such activities. [See Fifth Report of the Special Rapporteur, A/CN.4/423, 4/25/89]. Transboundary harm is now defined to include activities that are "appreciably detrimental to persons or objects, to the use or enjoyment of areas or to the environment, whether or not the States concerned have a common border" [Draft Art. 2]. States of origin of such harm have obligations under the proposed convention if they know or "had means of knowing" of the activity, and there is a presumption that such knowledge or means to acquire such knowledge exists. The Convention turns on the fundamental premise that the sovereign freedom of states "must be compatible with the protection of the rights emanating from the sovereignty of other States" and, accordingly, states of origin must "take appropriate measures to prevent or, where necessary, minimize the risk of transboundary harm" [Draft Arts. 6, 8]. Proposed Article 9 envisages reparations for "appreciable harm" caused by such activities.

At the 41st Session, ILC members had raised specific problems with the draft articles and discussed more schematic questions raised by the Special Rapporteur, including whether the Convention ought to consider activities involving extended harm or the risk of harm to many states, as well as liability for activities causing harm to the global commons"—that is, areas beyond the national jurisdiction of any state. The latter issue was no longer academic given current controversies on the impact of chlorofluorocarbons on the ozone layer. Although many members stated that the global commons issue could not be ignored, others expressed doubt about the manageability of the topic should it extend so far. As some members noted, discussion of the draft articles suggested the complexity of the subject, which required innovative borrowing of concepts from national tort law, as well as other ongoing ILC projects such as those on the law of nonnavigational uses of international watercourses, state responsibility, and crimes against peace and security. ILC members disagreed as to basic approach: whether to attempt to define "strict liability" for certain activities causing transboundary harm or whether to concentrate on prevention and impose liability for failure to take preventive measures [Report of the ILC, A/44/10, 237]. Others thought that both prevention and reparation were essential. At least one member wondered whether an umbrella convention was even necessary given the recent expansion of specific environmental conventions [ibid., 238].

The ILC did not as a whole support the draft articles proposed by the Special Rapporteur for a new Chapter 3 detailing rules for "Notification, Information and Warning" or providing for an "obligation to negotiate," and these were not referred to the Drafting Committee. The newly revised Articles 1–9, part of Chapters 1 and 2, relating to the scope of the proposed Convention, were referred to the Drafting Committee. At the ILC's 42nd session in 1990, the ILC will discuss the Special Rapporteur's Sixth Report [A/CN.4/428].

The topic **Jurisdictional Immunities of States and Their Property**, on the ILC's agenda also since 1978, remains stalemated over the status of the absolute versus restrictive theory of sovereign immunity in international law. ILC members from industrialized states continue to favor restricting sovereign immunity where states act in their economic capacity (acta jure gestionis), while those from some socialist states and some developing countries still contend that the absolute theory of state immunity, drawing no distinction for acts done in a state's sovereign capacity (acta jure imperii), governs. This fundamental disagreement continues to prevent progress on adoption of the entire set of draft articles on the subject, which had been adopted by the ILC in 1986. At its current session, the commission considered the Special Rapporteur's latest report and decided to refer draft articles 1–11 *bis*, including provisions on scope, definitions, state immunity regarding commercial contracts, and segregated state property, to the Drafting Committee, relying on the Rapporteur's expressed hope that in the absence of a consensus on the general issue, the only pragmatic way to proceed was to concentrate and seek agreement on individual articles dealing with distinct types of state activities. One hopeful sign of possible progress came from the Soviet Union and Poland, which reported on legal reforms within their respective countries granting state enterprises the right to administer and dispose of segregated national-owned property, granting these enterprises independent legal status, and providing that the state was not responsible for the obligations of state enterprises. The ILC is expected to attempt to complete the second or final reading of draft articles on point during its 1990 session.

At its 1989 session, the commission also considered the first part of its Special Rapporteur's latest report on an umbrella agreement on the **Law of the Navigational Uses of International Watercourses,** a topic on the ILC's agenda since 1971. Through 1988 the commission had provisionally adopted 21 articles on point and is scheduled to complete the first reading of the complete set of draft articles by 1991. At its 1989 session the ILC devoted only limited time to the topic and decided to refer two additional articles, to be contained in a separate chapter on water-related hazards, dangers, and emergency situations, to the Drafting Committee. Draft Article 22 provides that watercourse states must

> co-operate on an equitable basis in order to prevent or, as the case may be, mitigate water-related hazards, harmful conditions and other adverse effects such as floods, ice conditions, drainage problems, flow obstructions, siltation, erosion, salt-water intrusion, drought and desertification.

It provides that these states must exchange relevant information, engage in consultations, and prepare studies of the efficacy of measures taken. It also includes an obligation on such states to

> take all measures necessary to ensure that activities under their jurisdiction or control that affect an international watercourse are so conducted as not to cause water-related hazards, harmful conditions and other adverse effects that result in appreciable harm to other watercourse States. [Report of the ILC, A/44/10, 340]

Proposed Article 23 extends a similar obligation, on an expedited basis, in the case of a more sudden "water-related danger or emergency situation," including both natural situations and those resulting from human activities, such as toxic chemical spills. The new articles, which overlap to some extent with the ILC's consideration of "international liability for injurious consequences arising out of acts not prohibited by international law," were inspired in part by provisions in the U.N. Convention on the Law of the Sea [U.N. publication, Sales No. E.83.v.5]. Although some members suggested specific clarifications, most expressed support for the general thrust of both proposed articles.

The final topic on the ILC's agenda, the second half of the topic relating to **Relations between States and International Organizations,** received scant attention during the 1989 session. The ILC's study of the first half of the topic had resulted in a diplomatic conference to adopt the 1975 Vienna Convention on the Representation of States in Their Relations with International Organizations. At that conference, the ILC's multilateral convention, dealing with the privileges and immunities of missions to intergovernmental organizations, was adopted by a vote of 57–1, but with 15 abstentions, including the abstentions of many states that are hosts to international organizations. As is suggested by the vote, many states believed that the Convention disregarded the concerns of host states and was unbalanced. Perhaps in reaction, the ILC has repeatedly urged "great prudence" with regard to the second part of this topic, which would cover the privileges and immunities of international organizations, their property and premises, as well as officials, experts, and other affiliated persons. In recent years the ILC has only intermittently taken up this topic, and at its current session it was unable to study the Special Rapporteur's latest report, including 11 draft articles covering general provisions, legal personality and property, funds, and assets. The Rapporteur's report was merely introduced in order to facilitate work at the ILC's next session.

2. Peace and Security

On November 15, 1989, the General Assembly adopted by consensus the **first resolution jointly sponsored by the United States and the Soviet Union.** That resolution was a reaffirmation of basic Charter principles and urged all states to

> respect the principles of sovereign equality, political independence and territorial integrity of States and nonintervention in internal affairs, refrain from the threat or use of force inconsistent with the Charter, settle disputes peacefully, adhere to the principles of equal rights and self-determination of peoples, respect for human rights and fundamental freedoms, co-operation among States, and comply in good faith with their obligations assumed in accordance with the Charter [A/Res/44/21].

As described by U.S. Assistant Secretary of State John Bolton, the resolution symbolized a "new spirit of constructive cooperation" [U.N. Radio, Perspective, 11/8/89, quoting Bolton Press Conference of 11/3/89]. According to Vladimir Petrovsky, Soviet Deputy Foreign Minister, the resolution epitomized his country's "new foreign policy thinking; we do not separate our national interest from the interest of the international community and the United Nations takes a very important line in formulating these approaches to dealing with the interdependent world today" [ibid.].

As it has done every year since 1982, the General Assembly again passed a resolution urging all states to observe and promote the Manila Declaration on the Peaceful Settlement of International Disputes [A/Res/37/10; current resolution A/Res/44/31]. The resolution, as in the past, requests that the Secretary-General submit to the 45th Assembly a report on the implementation of the Manila Declaration and decides to make the question of **peaceful settlement of disputes** a separate agenda item at the 45th Session, to be considered in conjunction with the Report of the Special Committee on the Charter of the U.N. and on the Strengthening of the Role of the Organization. Western industrialized states, which had, in the Sixth Committee, sought unsuccessfully to remove both of these operative provisions and replace them with a clause permitting examination of the issue in the "framework of the United Nations Decade of International Law," abstained, as they have done in the past.

The General Assembly also adopted by consensus a lengthy resolution on **"strengthening of security and cooperation in the Mediterranean region"** [A/Res/44/125]. Among other things, that resolution expresses concern about "persistent tensions" in parts of the Mediterranean region and the "consequent threat to peace," reaffirms the Declaration on Principles of International Law Concerning Friendly Relations and Co-operation among States in accordance with the Charter of the United Nations [A/Res/2625(XXV), annex], as well as the Mediterranean chapter of the Final Act of the Conference on Security and Co-operation in Europe [Helsinki, 8/1/75], encourages further efforts to reduce tension and armaments, and calls upon the Secretary-General to submit a report based on replies received from members on the topic. The resolution puts "security and co-operation in the Mediterranean region" on the agenda for the 45th Session.

3. Terrorism

The Secretary-General filed a report [A/44/456, 8/25/89; A/44/456/Add. 1, 10/10/89] in response to the General Assembly's 1987 request that he seek the views of members as to ways to combat terrorism and as to the convening of an international conference on the subject [A/Res/42/159]. The replies received and contained in the report did not indicate a consensus in favor of convening a conference, especially since the resolution containing that proposal had suggested that one of the main purposes of such a conference would be to define terrorism and to differentiate it from the struggle of peoples for national liberation. Western industrialized states and Israel were opposed to any suggestion that individualized acts of violence might be justified in some cases; other states, such as Saudi Arabia and Syria, supported the idea. Instead, as was stated by the reply from Spain, on behalf of the European Economic Community, Western countries urged continued attention to multilateral conventions to prevent specific acts of terrorism, like those adopted under the auspices of the International Civil Aviation Organization (ICAO), as opposed to vaguer approaches to define terrorism generally.

The resulting resolution [A/Res/44/29], on **measures to prevent international terrorism**, does not call for an international conference but merely reiterates the request for a further report by the Secretary-General on the attitude of members to the convening of a future conference and continues the item as part of the provisional agenda for the 46th Session. Significantly, the resolution includes a detailed identification of relevant multilateral conventions on terrorism, singles out for praise recent efforts by the International Maritime Organization and ICAO, and notes the ongoing work of ICAO on devising an international regime for the detection of plastic or sheet explosives. Although the resolution again "unequivocally condemns . . . as criminal and not justifiable, all acts, methods and practices of terrorism wherever and by whomever committed," it again includes a paragraph stating that this is without prejudice to the rights of self-determination, freedom, and independence contained in the Charter.

In a related development, the President of the Council of ICAO advised the Secretary-General that in response to Security Council Resolution 635 [6/14/89], ICAO directed its Legal Committee to prepare "with the highest and overriding importance" a new legal instrument on the **marking of plastic or sheet explosives for detectability** [Note by Secretary General, Annex, A/44/398, 7/18/89].

On November 22, 1989, the U.S. Senate gave its advice and consent to ratification to the **Protocol for the Suppression of Unlawful Acts of Violence at Airports Serving International Civil Aviation,** done at Montreal in February 24, 1988 [27 ILM 627 (1988); in force as of 8/6/89] (which supplements the 1971 Convention for the Suppression of Unlawful Acts against the Safety of Civil Aviation), as well as the **Convention for the Suppression of Unlawful Acts against the Safety of Maritime Navigation and Protocol for the Suppression of Unlawful Acts against the Safety of Fixed Platforms Located on the Continental Shelf,** done at Rome at an international conference organized by the International Maritime Organization (IMO) on March 10, 1988 [27 ILM 668 (1988)].

4. Mercenaries

The General Assembly, acting by consensus and completing an effort begun in 1980 when it established an Ad Hoc Committee to draft an international convention on point, adopted and opened for signature and ratification the **International Convention against the Recruitment, Use, Financing and Training of Mercenaries** [A/Res/44/34; Convention contained in annex thereto and at 29 ILM 89 (1990)]. The Convention, the product of what the United States called "intense negotiations," reflected a series of compromises, particularly between industrialized and Third World states, that led many states to express reservations about particular provisions despite joining consensus for adoption. [See, e.g., Report of the Ad Hoc Committee, contained in Sixth Committee, 42nd and 44th Meetings, A/C.6/44/Sr.42, 11–12/89; see also Report of the Ad Hoc Committee on the Drafting of an International Convention against the Recruitment, Use, Financing and Training of Mercenaries, A/44/43].

Like recent terrorism conventions, the final Convention establishes universal jurisdiction to prosecute or extradite offenders. Among the most controversial provisions was the central definition of *mercenary*. For purposes of "armed conflicts," the definition adopted parallels that contained in the Geneva Protocols of 1949. Mercenaries in "other situation(s)" are now defined as persons "specifically recruited locally or abroad in order to fight in an armed conflict" or "for the purpose of participating in a concerted act of violence aimed at (i) overthrowing a Government or otherwise undermining the constitutional order of a State; or (ii) undermining the territorial integrity of a State." Although this definition represents a broadening of the concept, it does not encompass all situations involving mercenaries, since it is limited by other requirements—for example, that the person be motivated "by the desire for private gain" where the person is recruited to fight in armed conflict, or "significant private gain" in other instances. Perhaps most controversial, in the light of opposition by many Third World states such as Vietnam and Mongolia to such a limitation, is a requirement that "mercenaries" under the Convention be "neither a national . . . nor a resident of the State" against which the action is directed. [See definitions section, Art. 1.] The Convention makes it an offense to recruit, use, finance, or train mercenaries [Art. 2]; participate directly in hostilities or in a concerted act of violence under the Convention [Art. 3]; or attempt to commit the offenses defined or be the "accomplice of a person" who commits or attempts the offenses [Art. 4]. In addition, state parties are prohibited from recruiting, using, financing, or training mercenaries and agree to make the offenses defined in the Convention "punishable by appropriate penalties which take into account the grave nature of those offenses" [Art. 5]. The Convention obliges state parties to establish jurisdiction, coordinate preventive measures, cooperate in exchanging relevant information, and either submit cases to competent authorities for criminal proceedings or extradite alleged offenders [Arts. 6–12]. The Convention secures alleged offenders specific rights under both the Convention and national law and provides that "applicable norms of international law should be taken into account" [Arts. 10–11]. The Convention provides that state parties include the defined offenses as extraditable offenses in any existing or future extradition treaty [Art. 15]. Disputes as to the interpretation or application of the Convention are to be handled by arbitration, with residual jurisdiction in the ICJ should parties be unable to agree on the organization of arbitration [Art. 17]. The Convention, which is open for signature until December 31, 1990, enters into force when 22 states have ratified it [Arts. 18–19].

The prospects for ratification by individual U.N. members remain unclear, despite the consensus affirmation by the General Assembly. Colombia, for example, although it supported the Convention because it had noted that mercenaries "were working together with drug traffickers," questioned the decision to focus only on foreigner mercenaries and suggested that there was no legal right for third states to finance, train, use, or recruit nationals of the state against which violence is directed. (In this connection, the Convention's savings clause, at Article 16, providing that the Convention was without prejudice to the rules relating to international responsibility of states, armed conflict, and international humanitarian law, is significant.) The Netherlands, presumably echoing other Western states, expressed "strong reservations" as to the propriety of universal jurisdiction in this context, noting that this was likely to be ineffective and that it blurs the fundamental distinction between national and international responsibility for criminal prosecution. [See Report of the Ad Hoc Committee, heard at Sixth Committee, 44th Meeting, A/C.6/44/Sr.44, 5–6.]

As in previous years, the General Assembly passed a resolution on the **use of mercenaries as a means to violate human rights and to impede the exercise of the right of people to self-determination**, specifically condemning South Africa for "its use of groups of armed mercenaries against national liberation movements and for the destabilization of the Governments of southern African States," as well as denouncing "any State that persists in the recruitment, or permits or tolerates the recruitment, of mercenaries and provides facilities to them for launching armed aggression against other States" [A/Res/44/81]. As in the past, most industrialized states, as well as several Latin American states, either voted against the resolution or abstained. The resolution was adopted in the light of the report of the Special Rapporteur of the Commission on Human Rights, who had been requested to examine the issue [Report, A/44/526, annex].

5. Effectiveness of the Organization

The **Special Committee on the Charter of the United Nations and on the Strengthening of the Role of the Organization,** established in 1975 [A/Res/30/3499 (XXX)], is, at the request of the General Assembly, working on three interrelated projects: (1) the maintenance of international peace and security in order to strengthen the role of the United Nations, in particular the role of U.N. fact-finding activities; (2) the peaceful settlement of disputes between states, including a draft handbook on point; and (3) rationalization of existing U.N. procedures [See A/Res/44/37].

At its sessions in 1989 and 1990, the committee discussed **proposals on fact finding to assist the maintenance of international peace and security** that had been submitted by Belgium, the Federal Republic of Germany, Italy, Japan, New Zealand, and Spain [A/AC.182/L.60], by Czechoslovakia and the German Democratic Republic [A/AC.182/L.62], and broader proposals made by the Soviet Union [L/2608, 2/16/90; A/44/585, 10/2/89]. The committee's final report, to be presented to the 45th General Assembly, takes into account these various proposals and recommends that the United Nations, in its peacekeeping function, consider undertaking fact-finding activities, defined as "any activity designed to ascertain facts which the competent United Nations organs need to exercise effectively their functions," in order to have full knowledge of all the relevant facts in situations that pose a threat to the peace [A/AC.182/1990/CRP.3 and Add. 1–4 (on order)].

Also at its 1989 and 1990 sessions, the committee discussed various versions of a working paper on **rationalization of existing U.N. procedures** submitted by France and the United Kingdom [contained in Report of the Special Committee on the Charter of the United Nations and on the Strengthening of the Role of the Organization, A/44/33, pp. 33–42], including revisions submitted by the Soviet Union, and in its final report recommended, among other things, that before the end of each Assembly session, the General Committee consider drawing up its observations on the organization of the work of the session in order to facilitate the work of future Assembly sessions [A/AC.182/1990/CRP.3, Add. 1-4 (on order)]. At its 1989 meeting the committee took note of the Secretary-General's progress report on the **draft handbook on the peaceful settlement of disputes between states** [A/AC.182/L.61], which reviewed a further portion of the handbook, dealing with arbitration, which had been prepared by the Secretariat [A/44/33, 48–49]. According to the U.N. legal counsel, who introduced the report at the special committee, only the chapter on "procedures envisaged in the Charter of the United Nations" remained to be completed [L/2610, 2/22/90].

The General Assembly adopted by consensus the special committee's proposal concerning **resort to a commission of good offices, mediation, or**

conciliation within the United Nations, which had been initially submitted by Romania [General Assembly decision on report of the Sixth Committee, 44/415, 12/4/89; annex contains relevant document]. That document contains guidance for states that wish to resort to U.N. good offices, mediation, or conciliation mechanisms. It provides for a commission of good offices, mediation, or conciliation to be established for each case either through the agreement of parties to a dispute or, with their agreement, on the basis of the recommendation of the Security Council, the General Assembly, or following the parties' contacts with the Secretary-General. The commission will be made up of three states, not nationals of the parties to the dispute, that are chosen by the parties or, with their agreement, designated by the President of the Security Council, the President of the General Assembly, or the Secretary-General. In its good offices function the commission would "seek to bring the parties to enter immediately into direct negotiations for the settlement of the dispute, or to resume such negotiations or to resort to another means of peaceful settlement." In its mediation role, it would "offer the parties proposals which it deems adequate for facilitating the negotiations." If the affected states so choose, it can act as a conciliator, either on the legal basis to which the parties agree or, if such a basis is not obtained, on the basis of the Charter and international law. Costs of the procedure would be borne by the parties to the dispute.

With many of its ongoing tasks either completed or near completion, some members are considering the future direction of the work of the special committee. Some guidance on this may have been provided at the 1990 session of the special committee, when the Soviet Union submitted a working paper, "New Issues for Consideration." Among those identified were (1) ways of expanding cooperation between the United Nations and regional organizations; (2) broadening the peacemaking efforts of the Secretary-General, by, for example, regular reports about developments in any area of conflict or increased resort to use of Article 99 of the Charter (which enables the Secretary-General to bring matters that threaten peace to the attention of the Security Council); (3) the elaboration of a draft general instrument on peaceful settlement of disputes; and (4) implementation of Charter norms through provisional measures or other enforcement actions [A/AC.182/L.65, 2/23/90].

6. International Organizations and Host Country Relations

As in years past, the General Assembly took note of the report of the Secretary-General regarding the **Respect for the Privileges and Immunities of Officials of the United Nations and the Specialized Agencies and Related**

Organizations, including reports of one abduction and killing and high numbers of new cases of arrest and detention, and called upon all states to respect the privileges and immunities of all U.N. officials [A/Res/44/186; report at A/C.5/44/11]. That resolution, adopted by consensus, also urges states that are holding international organization officials under arrest to enable the Secretary-General or the executive head of the organization concerned to exercise the right of functional protection recognized in applicable international instruments. It calls upon the Secretary-General to continue to serve as the focal point for promoting and observing the privileges and immunities of these officials. The Secretary-General also filed with the Assembly, as requested by Resolution 43/167, a report on members' views relating to **consideration of effective measures to strengthen the protection, security, and safety of diplomatic and consular missions and representatives,** including representatives to and officials of international organizations [A/INF/44/5]. This matter is on the provisional agenda for the 45th Session of the Assembly.

The **Committee on Relations with the Host Country,** established in 1971 to deal with the security of missions and the safety of their personnel, apart from perennial complaints relating to acceleration of immigration and customs procedures, use of motor vehicles and parking, and the possibility of establishing a commissary at the U.N. headquarters to assist diplomatic personnel and staff, dealt with one major contentious issue in 1989: the ongoing controversy relating to U.S. travel restrictions on members of missions and U.N. personnel from certain member states. [See *Issues Before the 44th General Assembly of the United Nations,* p. 209.]

This year discussion focused on U.S. restrictions on all U.N. employees assigned to New York City (including those temporarily assigned) who are nationals of the People's Republic of China and their dependents. According to the U.S.'s Note Verbale, those persons wishing to travel beyond a 25-mile radius of Columbus Circle must submit advance written notification for all nonofficial travel [Note Verbale, 1/19/89, ST/IC/89/10, annex I]. China, the U.N. legal counsel, and the Secretary-General characterized these measures as discriminatory and counter to the essential character of the international civil service and urged revocation [Report of the Committee on Relations with the Host Country, A/44/26, 5–7; Secretary-General's Note Verbale, 1/20/89, ST/IC/89/10, annex II]. Other states, including the Soviet Union, echoed these comments and characterized the travel restrictions, including older ones applicable to socialist states generally, as the principal outstanding problem in terms of host country relations [Report, A/44/26, 6]. The United States responded, as it had in the past, that the restrictions were justified on the ground of national security and that since they did not affect official travel, they were consistent with U.S. obligations to the United Nations [ibid]. Unable to resolve members' inconsistent positions, the committee's report simply "takes note" of the positions of the affected states and the Secretary-General [A/44/26, 12]. The subsequent General Assembly resolution, adopted by consensus, only weakly urges the host country to "continue to take all measures necessary to prevent any interference with the functioning of missions" and expresses the hope that "outstanding problems raised" will be settled "in a spirit of co-operation and in accordance with international law" [A/Res/44/38].

In a reprise of the U.S. action of 1988 denying PLO leader Yasser Arafat a visa to address the General Assembly [see *Issues/44*, pp. 210–211], in May 1990 the United States indicated that it would **deny a visa to Arafat** again. This time Arafat was seeking entry to address the Security Council. To avoid a formal visa denial, the Security Council met in Geneva to discuss the possibility of sending a U.N. mission to investigate the treatment of Palestinians in the Israeli-occupied West Bank and Gaza Strip [*The New York Times*, 5/27/90].

The Secretary-General's report on the **Status of Contributions** as of December 31, 1989 [ST/Adm/Ser.B/325, 1/4/90], shows that the U.N.'s financial crisis continues and that an increasing number of members are flouting the legal duty to pay assessed contributions under Article 17 of the Charter. This report, required by the General Assembly's 1975 decision and intended to alert member states to the financial state of the organization, details (1) advances due the Working Capital Fund for 1988–1989; (2) member contributions to the regular budget; (3) contributions to the U.N. Emergency Force and the U.N. Disengagement Observer Force; (4) contributions to the U.N. Interim Force in Lebanon; (5) contributions to the U.N. Iran-Iraq Military Observer Group; (6) contributions to the U.N. Angola Verification Mission; (7) contributions to the U.N. Transition Assistance Group; (8) contributions by nonmembers; (9) the pattern of payments at year end, 1987–1989; and (10) the pattern of payments at year end for selected groups of member states. According to this report, the number of states in arrears on their contributions to the regular budget has grown since 1987; 86 states owed over $461 million in arrears as of January 1, 1990. The United States, the leading debtor as well as the largest contributor, was shown as owing over $365 million of this amount as of January 1, 1990. The amount owed by the United States has grown since that time; to date, the U.S. Congress has authorized contributions of only $144 million against an assessment of $216 million for the U.S. share of the 1989 regular budget [*Washington Weekly Report*, 5/4/90]. The Bush administration has, however, pledged to pay its arrears to the Organization over the course of five years. The financial crisis of the United Nations, often noted by the Secretary-General [see, e.g., Report of the Secretary General on the Work of the Organization,

A/44/1, 12] and others, is made worse by the habit of some member states, notably the United States, of paying their annual assessments toward the end of the U.N. fiscal year as well as withholding selective portions of their contributions. (The 43rd General Assembly fixed the scale of assessments for apportionment of expenses, including the United States's 25 percent, for the period through 1991 in Resolution 43/223, affirming that capacity to pay remains the fundamental criterion.)

7. Economic Relations

As it has every year since 1979, the General Assembly passed, over the abstaining votes of the industrialized states, a resolution calling upon the Secretary-General to continue to seek members' views concerning the "most appropriate procedures to be adopted with regard to the consideration of the analytical study, as well as the **codification and progressive development of the principles and norms of international law relating to the new international economic order**" [A/Res/44/30]. (Pursuant to a request of the previous Assembly, the Secretary-General filed a report containing members' views in August 1989 [A/44/455, 8/21/89]. The resolution recaps the long history of this effort, including the adoption of the 1974 Declaration on the Programme of Action on the Establishment of a New International Economic Order [A/Res/3201 (S-VI), 3202 (S-VI)], the 1974 Charter of Economic Rights and Duties of States [A/Res/3281 (XXIX)], and the 1980 International Development Strategy for the Third United Nations Development Decade [A/Res/35/56], but puts off to the 46th Session of the Assembly a final decision by the Legal Committee on the appropriate forum for elaboration of the "codification and progressive development" of the relevant principles and norms of international law. The topic will be reviewed next at the 46th Session of the Assembly.

The General Assembly considered the report of the **United Nations Commission on International Trade Law** (UNCITRAL) on its 22nd session, May 16–June 2, 1989, reaffirming the mandate of that body as the "core legal body within the United Nations system in the field of international trade law, to coordinate legal activities in this field in order to avoid duplication of effort and to promote efficiency, consistency and coherence in the unification and harmonization of international trade law" [A/Res/44/33]. UNCITRAL, established in 1966 and with a membership now numbering 36 states elected by the Assembly, has prepared a variety of multilateral conventions, including most recently a Convention on International Bills of Exchange and International Promissory Notes [28 ILM 170 (1989); see *Issues/44*]., as well as organized a variety of seminars and symposia, especially in developing countries. (The Convention on International Bills of Exchange and International Promissory Notes, approved by the General Assembly in 1988, has been endorsed for U.S. signature and ratification by the American Bar Association, the State Department Advisory Committee on Private International Law, and the New York State Bar Association and is expected to be submitted to the U.S. Senate for its advice and consent to ratification.) UNCITRAL also keeps track of the status of its conventions and model laws (published in its **Yearbook on International Trade Law**).

UNCITRAL devoted the major part of its 1989 session to a review of comments on its **Convention on the Liability of Operators of Transport Terminals in International Trade.** In addition, it submitted the Convention and comments to a drafting group, reviewed the draft articles of the Convention as modified, and presented the Convention to the General Assembly with a recommendation that it convene an international conference of plenipotentiaries to conclude the Convention. The conference would finally settle particular aspects of the Convention and involve states that were not members of UNCITRAL [Report of UNCITRAL on the work of its 22nd session, A/44/17; convention attached as Annex I]. General Assembly Resolution 44/33 adopts this recommendation, calling for a conference in Vienna for April 1991. The draft Convention governs the liability of terminal operators for loss, damage, or delay of goods while these are entrusted to them, whether the action is founded in contract, tort, or otherwise, and includes limits to liability. It is a major addition to the regime governing liability for the international carriage of goods since existing rules do not cover loss while the goods are in terminals, despite statistics showing that the largest losses occur just at this point. Under the proposed Convention, attempts by terminal operators to limit their liability in derogation of the Convention would generally be ineffective. The Convention is formulated with the intent of the broadest possible acceptance by states and is meant to be compatible with legal regimes under existing conventions, including regimes governing liability for goods before and after carriage.

Although the Convention has been under discussion since 1983, one of the last issues to be discussed was the form of the instrument, with some members in favor of a model law rather than a multilateral convention on the grounds that the former was more amenable to change to take into account technological developments. A more widely held view, however, was that a convention was more conducive to achieving uniformity and to fill in gaps left by international transport conventions covering individual modes of transport. States that did not want to adhere to the Convention could still use the text as a model for national law [Report, A/44/17, 6].

Another project under consideration by UNCITRAL is a draft **Model Law on International Credit Transfers.** In 1986, UNCITRAL decided to begin work on model rules on electronic fund transfers and entrusted that work to its Working Group on International Payments. The Working Group and Secretariat have been drafting provisions whose scope is currently limited to credit transfers that are international in nature but would apply to all international credit transfers, electronic and paperbased, and to the entire transfer, not just the international leg (or the international payment order). Because of proposed changes in the U.S. Uniform Commercial Code, the United States may seek a two-track approach that would provide two distinct sets of rules: for customers seeking high-speed, low-cost, "best-efforts" services integrated with electronic clearing house procedures and for those seeking traditional bank transfer services. UNCITRAL's goal is to consider a full text by its 23rd session in 1991 [Report, A/44/17, 42].

A third UNCITRAL project is a **Model Procurement Law,** which has been entrusted since 1986 to the Working Group on the New International Economic Order. This law would assist both developed and developing countries in restructuring or improving the rules governing transactions involving governmental agency participation. These constitute a significant amount of the trade between Third World and developed countries. At the 1989 session, it was observed that UNCITRAL's work in this field requires coordination with ongoing efforts to enlarge the scope of the General Agreement on Tariffs and Trade Agreement on Government Procurement [ibid., 43]. At its February 1990 meeting the Working Group made progress toward consensus on basic concepts; its next meeting, in October, is expected to consider the issue of remedies. It is expected that several countries will propose that any model law include at least some services, as well as goods and construction.

A fourth UNCITRAL project has resulted from its consideration, in 1988, of a report by the Secretary-General on standby letters of credit and guarantees concluding that a greater degree of certainty and uniformity was desirable in this area [A/CN.9/301]. UNCITRAL asked its Working Group on International Contract Practices to review the International Chamber of Commerce's draft Uniform Rules for Guarantees and make recommendations to the commission. The Working Group ultimately recommended changes to the ICC: the ICC's Draft Rules have not been finalized to date. At its 1989 session, UNCITRAL reviewed the recommendation of the Working Group for a **Uniform Law on Guarantees and Stand-by Letters of Credit** and directed the Working Group to undertake this task [Report, A/44/17, 44–45]. At the Working Group's February 1990 meeting, the United States proposed that UNCITRAL attempt a bridge law providing for transnational implementation of documents valid under other legal systems, which would reflect current market practices and provide guidance for daily transactions (as opposed to juridical rules for dispute settlement).

Finally, at its 1989 session, UNCITRAL requested its secretariat to prepare for the next session of the commission draft chapters for a **Legal**

Guide on Drawing Up International Countertrade Contracts. This topic is regarded as controversial by some members of the commission because it suggests approval of this type of trade (involving trade in goods and not in negotiable instruments), which in the view of some states discourages free trade and price competition [Report, A/44/17, 46]. It is expected to be the main item on the agenda for UNCITRAL's 23rd session, June 18–July 6, 1990. The secretariat has now prepared seven of twelve proposed chapters of the guide.

In other developments concerning economic multilateral conventions, the 1980 U.N. Convention on Contracts for the International Sale of Goods gained several adherents, bringing the total number of states ratifying or acceding to 26; the 1974 U.N. Convention on the Limitation Period for the International Sale of Goods and its 1980 Protocol were endorsed by the U.S. Secretary of State's Advisory Committee on Private International Law and the American Bar Association and are expected to be submitted to the Senate shortly; the same holds true for two 1988 conventions, on International Financial Leasing and on International Factoring, prepared by the International Institute for the Unification of Private Law (UNIDROIT).

The **Multilateral Investment Guarantee Agency (MIGA)**, a development organization created under the auspices of the World Bank to encourage the flow of foreign direct investment to developing countries [see *Issues/44*, p. 214], released its form of equity guarantee contract, the Standard Contract of Guarantee, on January 25, 1989 [28 ILM 1233 (1989)]. The Standard Contract of Guarantee sets out the respective rights of MIGA and insured investors, based on MIGA's Convention [24 ILM 1598 (1985)] and Operational Regulations [27 ILM 1227 (1988)].

8. Space Law

The General Assembly by consensus endorsed the 1989 report of the Committee on the Peaceful Uses of Outer Space [A/44/20], including the report of the 28th (1989) session of the Legal Subcommittee, specifically endorsing the subcommittee's threefold agenda for its 1990 session: the elaboration of draft principles on (1) the use of nuclear power sources in outer space, (2) the definition and delimitation of outer space and the character and utilization of the geostationary orbit, and (3) the application of the principle that exploration and utilization should be carried out for the benefit of all states, especially developing countries [A/Res/44/46].

Regarding the **use of nuclear power sources in outer space**, at its 1990 session, a Working Group of the Legal Subcommittee continued its review of twelve Canadian draft principles on point [see *Issues/44*, p. 215]. The Working Group reached consensus on Principle 3 containing "guidelines and criteria for safe use," including general goals for radiation protection for states launching space objects using nuclear power sources and guidelines for the operation of nuclear reactors and radioisotope generators in space [see Report of the Legal Subcommittee on the Work of its 29th Session, A/AC.105/457]. The Working Group discussed but was unable to reach consensus on other proposed safety measures, including Principles 2 (requiring notification to the Secretary-General of the existence and generic classification of nuclear power sources), 4 (requiring thorough safety assessments prior to launch), 8 (affirming that states and international organizations bear responsibility for outer space activities involving the use of nuclear power sources), and 9 (affirming that states shall be internationally liable for damage caused). The Legal Subcommittee agreed to continue its discussions at an informal meeting of interested delegations in June 1990 as well as at its next session.

The Subcommittee Working Group's discussion of **the definition and delimitation of outer space** continued to be stalemated between the opposing positions of those, like the Soviet Union, advocating a clear distinction between the legal regimes for airspace and outer space and those, like the United States, insisting that the absence of a boundary has not led to practical problems and arbitrary demarcation lines are unnecessary [see *Issues/44*, pp. 215–16]. Despite the lack of progress, an attempt to drop the topic from the agenda was not successful.

There was similar lack of progress concerning the question of the **geostationary orbit**. Delegations reiterated well-established views on the point. On the one hand were those who believed the orbit was in danger of saturation and who believed that a sui generis legal regime, regulating equitable access to and rational utilization of the orbit, was necessary in order to secure the needs of developing countries. Others denied the need for a separate regime, arguing that the 1967 Treaty on Principles Governing the Activities of States in the Exploration and Use of Outer Space established that the orbit, as an integral part of outer space, was not subject to national appropriation and all states enjoyed equal rights in its utilization. These states continued to argue that the rational and equitable use of the orbit should be left to determination by the ITU [ibid., p. 216].

This division precluded agreement on general formulations discussed at previous sessions and led to disagreement over whether consideration of legal norms or principles was even appropriate in this context. This was clear in the exchange of views on the following statement: "The geostationary orbit is a limited natural resource and, therefore, its utilization should be rational and equitable and for the benefit of all mankind, taking into account the special needs of the developing countries and the geographical situation of particular countries." Although many states agreed with this proposition, others noted that technical progress in satellite communications, resulting in increases in satellite capacity and the number of satellites that could be accommodated within the geostationary orbit, made even this statement inaccurate. The subcommittee could not even agree on whether to request that the Secretariat prepare a report indicating the degree to which there was a convergence of views within the subcommittee. The future direction of this topic is unclear.

General Assembly Resolution 44/46 also endorsed the recommendations of the 26th session of the **Scientific and Technical Subcommittee** of the Committee on the Peaceful Uses of Outer Space. The agenda for the 27th session of the subcommittee, February 26–March 9, 1990, was extensive and reviewed issues relating to remote sensing of the earth, the use of nuclear power sources in outer space, space transportation systems, planetary exploration and astronomy, character and utilization of the geostationary orbit, life sciences (including space medicine), the geosphere-biosphere (global change), and activities connected with International Space Year (1992) [A/AC.105/456].

The subcommittee's special theme for 1990 was the **"use of space technology in terrestrial search and rescue and in disaster relief activities."** Its conclusion that there is a need to ensure nondiscriminatory access for developing countries to the information acquired through remote sensing of the earth by satellite, and its recommendations regarding technical approaches to reduce the risks associated with nuclear power sources in space, has obvious legal implications. These topics overlap with ongoing discussions in the Legal Subcommittee, as well as with the work of the 8th (1990) Session of the Working Group on the Use of Nuclear Power Sources in Outer Space. During its 1990 session, that Working Group noted that countries launching nuclear power sources (NPS) should conduct safety assessments of those systems and make those assessments publicly available. Although there was discussion as to the proper forum for guidance on radiological health issues, such as whether the International Atomic Energy Agency (IAEA) ought to develop such advice, the Working Group agreed on, among other things, "design goals for radiation protection" [A/AC.105/C.1/L.168].

For its 1991 session, the Scientific and Technical Subcommittee's special theme will concern **"applications of airborne and satellite remote sensing for prospecting mineral and ground water on agriculture."** Various training courses for participants from developing countries sponsored by the United Nations and the Food and Agriculture Organization (FAO) deal with this topic [see, e.g., Reports, A/AC.105/440, A/AC.105/442].

As in 1988, the General Assembly passed, 153–1 (United States), a resolution on the **prevention of an arms race in outer space** [A/Res/44/112]. The resolution welcomes the reestablishment of an Ad Hoc Committee on the Prevention of an Arms Race in Outer Space, which occurred during the 1989 session of the Conference on Disarmament; "reaffirms" that "general and complete disarmament under effective international control warrants that outer space shall be used exclusively for peaceful purposes and that it shall not become an arena for an arms race"; calls upon all states "to take immediate measures to prevent an arms race in outer space"; reiterates that the Conference on Disarmament is the "single multilateral disarmament negotiating forum" for this purpose and requests that the Conference reestablish an ad hoc committee for 1990 for further negotiations; and specifically urges the Soviet Union and the United States to pursue ongoing bilateral negotiations to prevent an outer space arms race and to advise the Conference on Disarmament of their progress. The item is continued on the agenda for the 45th Assembly.

9. International Court of Justice

As the President of the World Court reported to the Sixth Committee, the Court is in a period of relatively intense activity, with an unusual variety of cases submitted by parties belonging to all five continents [Comments of President Ruda at 7th Meeting of Sixth Committee, 9/29/89, A/C.6/44/Sr.7]. A summary of its recent judgments and the status of pending cases is provided here.

On May 17, 1989, Iran filed a case against the United States seeking compensation for the destruction of Iran Air Airbus A-300B, flight 655, and the killing of its 290 passengers and crew by two surface-to-air missiles launched by the USS *Vincennes* on July 3, 1988 (**Aerial incident of 3 July 1988, (Islamic Republic of Iran v. United States of America**). Iran's assertion of jurisdiction is grounded in Article 36(1) of the Court's statute and is based on multilateral treaties between the two states: the 1944 Chicago Convention on International Civil Aviation and the 1971 Montreal Convention for the Suppression of Unlawful Acts against the Safety of Civil Aviation. According to its application [28 ILM 842 (1989)], Iran is alleging that the United States violated, contrary to the findings of the Council of the International Civil Aviation Organization (ICAO) in its decision of December 1988 [28 ILM 898 (1989)], certain provisions of the Chicago Convention and the Montreal Convention. Although the United States has offered to pay, on an ex gratia basis and not on the basis of a legal duty, compensation directly to the bereaved families [see Testimony of U.S. Department of State Legal Adviser Abraham D. Sofaer before the Defense Policy Panel, House of Representatives Armed Services Committee, 8/4/88], Iran is seeking damages payable to the Islamic Republic, in the amount to be determined by the Court, "as measured by the injuries suffered by the Islamic Republic and the bereaved families as a result of these violations, including additional financial losses which Iran Air and the bereaved families have suffered for the disruption of their activities." The United States indicated to the Court that it intended to file preliminary objections to jurisdiction and admissibility prior to the filing of a memorial by Iran. By order dated December 13, 1989 [29 ILM 123 (1990)], the Court found that its rules permit the filing of a preliminary objection either before or after the filing of Iran's memorial (due June 12, 1990). The United States has until December 10, 1990, to file its countermemorial.

The World Court issued its judgment on the merits in the **Case Concerning Elettronica Sicula A.p.A (ELSI) (U.S. v. Italy)** on July 20, 1989 [1989 ICJ 15; 28 ILM 1109 (1989)]. That case, which had been brought by the United States in 1987, involved Italian government actions against ELSI, an Italian company owned by U.S. shareholders. ELSI had ceased operations and was in liquidation in 1968 when, amid Italian government pressure to keep the plant open, the Mayor of Palermo requisitioned ELSI's plant and assets and Italian employees occupied the plant. ELSI filed for bankruptcy, and an Italian government-owned holding company acquired ELSI. The U.S. shareholders received nothing after ELSI's secured creditors were paid. Although an Italian court later ruled that the requisition order had been illegal and awarded damages for loss of the use of the plant, it refused compensation for the alleged decrease in the value of the plant caused by the requisition. The United States, on behalf of the U.S. shareholders of the company, argued that the requisition and other Italian government actions permitted Italy to acquire the company for less than its fair market value. The United States argued that Italy had violated provisions in a bilateral U.S.-Italy 1948 Treaty of Friendship, Commerce and Navigation (FCN) since its actions, among other things, constituted an unlawful "expropriation" without payment of prompt, adequate, and effective compensation and included "arbitrary and discriminatory measures" in derogation of specific treaty rights. The majority of the five-member ICJ panel that heard the case ruled, Judge Stephen M. Schwebel of the United States dissenting, that the United States had not carried its factual burden. In effect, the Court ruled that the United States had not been able to prove that the Italian government actions, as opposed to ELSI's own preexisting precarious financial condition, were the cause of any resulting financial damage to ELSI's shareholders. It accordingly dismissed the claim against Italy and awarded no damages.

Although the case was decided on the basis of the factual evidence presented, the Court's 70-page majority judgment dealt with numerous interpretative issues under the U.S.-Italy FCN. In the view of Judge Schwebel, the Court largely sustained U.S. views of the FCN and construed the treaty

> in ways which sustain rather than constrain it as an important instrument for the protection of the rights of the nationals, corporations and associa-

tions of the United States in Italy and the rights of nationals, corporations and associations of Italy in the United States [1989 ICJ at 1 (Schwebel, J., dissenting)].

As the first World Court case to consider in detail principles of economic international law that reappear in numerous treaties around the world, the Court's judgment in *United States v. Italy* is likely to be of considerable precedential value.

Another decision of substantial importance was the Court's advisory opinion in **Applicability of Article VI, Section 22, of the Convention on the Privileges and Immunities of the United Nations** issued December 15, 1989 [1989 ICJ Reports 177; 29 ILM 98 (1990)]. In that case, the Economic and Social Council, exercising its power to make such a request for the first time, asked the Court for an advisory opinion under Article 96(2) of the Charter as to the applicability of the General Convention on the Privileges and Immunities of the United Nations to Dumitru Mazilu, a Romanian who had been appointed Special Rapporteur of the United Nations Subcommission on Prevention of Discrimination and Protection of Minorities. Mazilu had been asked to prepare a report on human rights and youth in his country but had not completed his task, and Romania had refused him a travel permit, claiming that he had been relieved of governmental duties due to illness. Romania had refused to permit the United Nations to contact Mazilu, and U.N. legal counsel argued that this interference violated Article 22 of the General Convention guaranteeing "experts" performing U.N. missions certain privileges and immunities, including immunity from personal arrest or detention. Romania argued that the Court had no jurisdiction to render even an advisory opinion since it had reserved on the Court's jurisdiction when it adhered to the General Convention. It further contended that Mazilu, as a Rapporteur with an "occasional" mission for the United Nations, could not be equated to experts and could enjoy any privileges and immunities only while engaged in the U.N. task and only in the "countries in which [he] perform[s] the mission and in countries of transit." The Court unanimously rejected these arguments by Romania, upholding its advisory jurisdiction and affirming that Mazilu was covered by Article 22 of the Convention.

Although as an advisory opinion the Court's decision is technically not legally binding under the Charter, the Court's ruling regarding jurisdiction and its affirmation of the U.N.'s rights are as likely to be accorded precedential weight as any of the Court's judgments and may influence states' behavior toward persons covered by international privileges and immunities. Certainly the decision is in line with the Court's ringing endorsement of the international regime protecting diplomats in the U.S. Diplomatic and Consular Staff in Tehran *(United States v. Iran)*.

On January 27, 1989, Judge ad hoc Michel Virally, chosen by Honduras to serve as a member of a five-judge chamber on the case concerning **land, island, and maritime frontier dispute (El Salvador/Honduras)**, died. On February 9, 1989, Honduras chose Santiago Torres Bernardez to replace him. By Special Agreement concluded in 1986, the two states had agreed to submit their dispute to three members of the regular Court and two judges chosen ad hoc by the parties. The time limits for memorials by both parties were extended, by joint request, and the parties met the new prescribed time limits. On November 17, 1989, Nicaragua filed in the Court's registry an application for permission to intervene in this case, contending that a decision on whether it could intervene could be made only by the full court and not the special five-judge chamber. On March 6, 1990, the full court ruled, 12–3, that it was "for the tribunal seised of a principal issue to deal also with any issue subsidiary thereto" and accordingly found that it was for the five-judge chamber to rule on Nicaragua's intervention request. El Salvador and Honduras had exchanged their replies in this case on January 12, 1990.

The **Border and Transborder Armed Actions (Nicaragua v. Honduras)** case, relating to Nicaraguan claims that its territorial sovereignty had not been respected by Honduras [see *Issues/44*, pp. 217–218], is still at the pleadings stage. It is not clear what effect, if any, the change in government in Nicaragua will have on this case or on the Court's pending consideration of Nicaragua's claims for reparations in the **case concerning military and paramilitary activities in and against Nicaragua (Nicaragua vs. United States)** [see ibid., p. 218]. As in past years, the General Assembly again passed, by a vote of 91–2 (United States and Israel), with 41 abstentions, a resolution calling for "full and immediate compliance with the Judgment" of the Court in the latter case, requesting that the Secretary-General keep the General Assembly informed of implementation and keeping the matter on the agenda for its 45th Session [A/Res/44/43]. The new Nicaraguan government has informed The Hague that it is studying the different matters it has pending before the Court, and the Court has postponed oral hearings on Nicaragua's claims for reparations in the *Nicaragua v. United States* case [Court Communiqué, 6/29/90].

On May 19, 1989, the Republic of Nauru instituted proceedings against Australia in respect of the rehabilitation of **certain phosphate lands in Nauru** mined under Australian administration prior to Nauruan independence. Nauru claimed that Australia had breached the trusteeship obligations it had accepted under Article 76 of the Charter and under the trusteeship agreement for Nauru, as well as provisions of general international law. Nauru requested restitution or "other appropriate reparation" as determined by the Court. By order dated July 18, 1989, the Court fixed April 20, 1990, for the filing of Nauru's memorial and January 21, 1991, for the countermemorial by Australia.

The case concerning **maritime delimitation in the area between Greenland and Jan Mayen (Denmark vs. Norway)** also remains at the pleadings stage. It concerns a dispute over fishing zones and continental shelf areas in the waters between the east coast of Greenland and Norway [see *Issues/44*, pp. 219–220]. Denmark's reply brief is due on February 1, 1991; Norway's rejoinder is due October 1, 1991.

On August 23, 1989, the Republic of Guinea-Bissau instituted proceedings against the Republic of Senegal, a case concerning an **arbitral award of July 31, 1989**. Guinea-Bissau based jurisdiction for the case on Article 36(2) of the statute of the Court. It contended that the two states were unable to reach agreement regarding the settlement of a dispute concerning maritime delimitation and had submitted that dispute to ad hoc arbitration by a three-member arbitration tribunal. Guinea-Bissau disputed the validity of the arbitral award rendered and sought a declaration that the award was null and void. By later request, Guinea-Bissau alleged that the Senegalese Navy had asserted its sovereignty over the disputed area and requested that the Court indicate provisional measures "in order to safeguard the rights of each of the Parties" providing that each shall abstain from taking any action pending the Court's decision. The Court heard oral arguments on the request for provisional measures on February 12, 1990, and rendered its decision dismissing Guinea-Bissau's request, 14–1, on March 2, 1990. In that order, the Court found that it had jurisdiction to consider the request for provisional measures under Article 36(2) but that Guinea-Bissau had not requested in its initial application on the merits that the Court pass on the respective rights of the parties to the disputed maritime area but had only requested consideration of the validity of the arbitral award. Under those circumstances, the respective rights of the parties to the area were not the subject of the merits of the case, and the Court had the power only to consider provisional measures relating to the merits. The Court will consider the merits—the question of the validity of the arbitral award—after the parties file their respective pleadings.

On November 1, 1989, the Secretary-General announced the creation of a **trust fund** "to make available financial assistance to States where necessary so as to enable them to use the Court for the settlement of their legal differences" [28 ILM 1589 (1989)]. Citing among his reasons for establishing the fund the role of peaceful dispute settlement for the maintenance of international peace and security reaffirmed repeatedly by the General Assembly in such documents as the Manila Declaration on the Peaceful Settlement of Disputes, the Secretary-General stated that the Court's judgments "represent the most authoritative pronouncement on international law" and that he had a special responsibility to promote judicial settlement through the Court. The Secretary-General contended that there were instances in which parties would turn to the Court or would want to implement its decisions but "cannot proceed because of the lack of legal expertise or funds." Accordingly, he announced the establishment of the fund under the Financial Regulations and Rules of the United Nations to provide financial assistance for expenses incurred in connection with "(i) a dispute submitted to the International Court of Justice by way of special agreement, or (ii) the execution of a Judgment of the Court resulting from such special agreement." He then invited states and other organizations to make voluntary contributions. Applications for grants would be examined by a three-member panel of experts.

According to the latest report of the ICJ to the General Assembly [A/44/4], fifty states have now made declarations (though many with reservations) and are now parties to the Court's "compulsory" jurisdiction as contemplated by Article 36(2) and (5) of the statute of the Court. On April 18, 1989, the General Assembly and the Security Council filled the vacancy left by the death of Judge Nagendra Singh and elected Raghunandan Swarup Pathak as a member of the Court with a term ending February 5, 1991. In other related developments, at the initiation of the Soviet Union, talks between it and the United States are continuing on measures to increase states' resort to the World Court, particularly by permanent members of the Security Council. Pursuant to its earlier statements for an expanded role for the Court, the Soviet Union, by letter dated February 28, 1989, formally informed the Secretary-General that it was withdrawing its reservations concerning the jurisdiction of the Court in respect of six multilateral conventions [*Issues/44*, p. 219].

10. Other Legal Developments

In order to promote acceptance, respect, and the "progressive development" of international law, and "encourage" the peaceful settlement of disputes as well as the teaching and study of international law, the General Assembly declared the period 1990–1999 as the **United Nations Decade of International Law** and requested the Secretary-General to seek the views of members as well as other organizations on appropriate actions to be taken during the decade, "including the possibility of holding a third international peace conference or other suitable international conference at the end of the Decade" and report back to the 45th Session of the General Assembly [A/Res/44/23]. In a related development, the General Assembly reviewed the Secretary-General's report on the implementation of the **United Nations Programme of Assistance in the Teaching, Study, Dissemination and Wider Appreciation of International Law** [*Issues/44*, p. 220], and approved his recommendations to provide a number of fellowships for this purpose at the request of the governments of developing countries [A/Res/44/28]. That resolution also requests a further report by the Secretary-General for consideration by the 46th Session of the Assembly.

Other legal developments, including those related to human rights (including the adoption of the Convention on the Rights of the Child), the environment, drug trafficking, arms control, and law of the sea are discussed elsewhere in this book.

VI
Finance and Administration

1. U.N. Finances

On December 31, 1989, member states owed the United Nations $260.7 million on their 1989 assessed contributions for the regular budget and $200.6 million for prior years, making a total shortfall of $461.2 million [ST/ADM/SER.B/325]. This figure compares with $83.4 million at the end of 1978, $257.8 million at the end of 1986, and $394.9 million at the end of 1988. Thus, during 1989 the body's regular budget deficit rose by nearly 17 percent. Because of this mounting financial gap, the Organization's working capital fund of $100 million has, on occasion, fallen dangerously low, and in recent biennia the General Assembly has had to allow unspent appropriated funds to be retained instead of being returned to governments, as called for under the rules. Yet despite the resort to such emergency measures, maintaining the necessary cash balance at year's end had become a preoccupying task even more than in past years.

In early December, the Secretary-General warned the Assembly:

> The spectre of the financial crisis continues to haunt the United Nations. Throughout 1989 the possibility of imminent bankruptcy, which the Organization has narrowly managed to avoid so far, has been a source of grave concern to me. As I write this, three weeks before the end of the year, the prospects are very grim indeed [A/44/857, para. 1].

He pointed out that insolvency had been forestalled only because expenditures had been lower than anticipated as a result of favorable currency fluctuations and because more posts than usual had been vacant. He added that the overall pattern of payments had been less encouraging in 1989 than in previous years. By early December 1989 only 72 member states, compared to 79 the year before, had paid in full, and 22, compared to 14 in 1988, had made no payments at all.

The picture he painted for 1990 was, if anything, bleaker still. Assuming that 1990's pattern of income and disbursements will parallel the 1989 experience, the United Nations might, according to the Secretary-General, avoid insolvency for most of the year but only by utilizing its reserves until they are exhausted to meet cash requirements. On the basis of his assumptions in December 1989, he predicted that "all reserves will be exhausted and cash depletion will occur in the last quarter of 1990" [A/44/857, para. 9]. As of the end of June 1990 the situation looks even more ominous. Unpaid contributions to the regular budget had reached $857 million, of which $431 million related to 1990 and $426 million to prior years. These figures should be compared to the total assessments of all governments of $827 million.

There was one bright spot in this otherwise gloomy assessment. Government indebtedness to the United Nations is divided into sums withheld on the basis of principle (because a government objects to the activities that they would fund) and assessments that it has simply not gotten around to paying. In U.N. parlance, the first category is known as the short-term deficit. The good news is that this part of the deficit—the most threatening because it is deliberate—continued to decline, dropping from $326 to $315 million during the course of 1989.

Despite the Secretary-General's fears, there seems to be **little sense of impending crisis** at U.N. Headquarters and instead a surprising confidence among staff and government representatives alike that the Organization will come through the crunch intact. There are two main reasons that this is the case. The first is that the financial "crisis" is now in its fifth year, and the inflow and outflow of funds now follow a well-established broader pattern that can be closely watched by governments. The critical times of the year, particularly December, when the Organization is likely to have cash flow problems, are by now well known and can be prepared for in advance. Some governments can easily—and when necessary do—advance their contributions to keep the United Nations financially afloat at those times. The second reason is that, unlike in the early stages of the crisis, the Organization can now point to a steady stream of achievements: the Iran-Iraq truce, the Soviet withdrawal from Afghanistan, the successful monitoring of elections in Namibia and Nicaragua, and its sponsorship of much-needed agreements on the protective ozone layer, to name the more obvious ones. No one any longer believes that it will be allowed to close down shop just because its largest contributor, the United States, has become overly casual in paying its dues.

Thus, gradually, the financial crisis has been turning into a financial high-wire act with a fairly reliable safety net in which the Secretariat has to juggle expenditures and payments to keep funds on hand at minimal levels, while governments watch to see which one of them will come forward with emergency funding (usually, in the form of advance payments of their assessments) when that is needed to prevent a default that no one wishes to see. The onus for this situation inevitably falls on the main contributor and the **main defaulter, the United States.** As of June 30, 1990, it owed $591.5 million for 1990 and previous years, or about 72 percent of all arrearages. And, increasingly, even friendly governments are finding it hard to believe that one of the pillars of the world economy cannot locate the funds to pay for its share of operations that have been approved by consensus.

Changes may be in the wind. Satisfied with the reforms made in U.N. decision-making procedures, the outgoing Reagan administration in early 1988 called for virtually full funding of the U.S. assessment for that year in its 1989–1990 budget proposals, and it proposed a plan for paying the substantial arrearages over a six-year period. But these proposals fell by the wayside as the Congress struggled to complete its action on that budget, and again only $144 million of the $216 million due, and no arrearages at all, could be paid by the end of the year. In February 1990 another payment of $14.3 million was sent in. All of this meant that U.S. indebtedness to the United Nations, far from declining, increased by $57 million in 1989.

Early in 1990 the **Bush administration** unveiled a new plan for full funding of calendar year 1990 assessments and for the payment of arrearages over a five-year period. This plan called for $695 million to be authorized and appropriated for the 46 international organizations of which the United States is a member, including $231.4 million for the U.N. regular budget. It suggested that arrearages be paid off over a period of five rather than six years and that the monies needed for this should all be appropriated in 1990 though dispersed on a yearly basis. These arrearages now amount to $464 million. The United Nations alone claims $351 million in such arrearages, though a small part of this sum involves charges for activities, such as those of the Division of Palestinian Rights, which the United States opposes as a matter of principle and refuses to pay.

The foregoing plan, which constitutes a somewhat daring gambit to sweep away almost all U.S. indebtedness to the United Nations and the specialized agencies in one fell swoop, now enjoys strong White House support. During recent testimony before the Senate Foreign Relations Committee, Secretary of State James Baker III described the budget request for international organizations as one of four funding initiatives "integral to our ability to protect American values and interests into the next decade." According to Baker,

> The President feels strongly that a carefully structured arrears initiative is essential to maintaining U.S. leadership in these multilateral organizations. Over the next decade, we expect an invigorated U.N. to make greater contributions to peacekeeping efforts, refugee resettlement, and transnational issues including narcotics, the environment and terrorism. To

> maintain our credibility and influence with these multilateral organizations as they address some of the greatest challenges of the next decade, the United States must live up to its solemn financial commitments [UNA-USA *Washington Weekly Report*, 2/2/90].

On another occasion, Baker, while acknowledging competing priorities for limited funds, pointed out that "these commitments that we make to multilateral organizations are commitments, solemn commitments of the United States, made by the executive branch in full consultation with Congress." He argued that these commitments should be kept lest we gain a reputation of being "the international deadbeat" [ibid., 3/9/90].

There is broadening congressional support for the President's plan. For example, Congressman Bill Frenzel (R–Minn.) said that "it does seem outrageous to me that the United States cannot pay for its legitimate share of the operation of international organizations. . . . I hope that the administration will hold firm on trying to clear up arrearages even if it takes a little more money." Congressman Lee Hamilton (D–Ind.) commended the administration's full funding request: "I know it's not an easy request for you to make, but you have requested [funding] to clear arrearages to the U.N. and other multilateral institutions. . . . I personally appreciate that request very much" [ibid, 2/23/90].

In a surprising development, on June 7 the House Appropriations Subcommittee on Commerce, Justice, and State recommended to the 57-member Appropriations Committee full payment of calendar year 1990 assessed contributions to international organizations as well as a 20 percent payment on accumulated arrearages in Fiscal Year 1991. Perhaps even more surprising, days later the full Committee approved the recommendation without much debate. Despite such support, however, the ultimate fate of the plans remains in doubt. Appropriations come within the Gramm-Rudman-Hollings strictures and have to pass later in 1990 through financially oriented committees less likely to focus on international duties and more likely to be weighing the competing claims of numerous pressure groups. Whether the outcome is favorable to full funding depends on whether the administration and members of Congress are ready to give America's international reputation and obligations under the U.N. Charter priority over other pressing concerns. This may well hinge on the effectiveness of the lobbying effort undertaken by the administration's congressional liaison officers, and Americans generally, on the eve of crucial votes. The movement of the main appropriation bills through the Congress will continue through the summer, and perhaps even into the autumn; we shall not know the outcome of President Bush's initiative for some time to come.

While awaiting the outcome in Washington, the United Nations has been obliged to prepare for a further deterioration in its financial situation.

For several years the Secretary-General has urged that the **working capital fund,** which has remained at the $100 million level since 1982, be substantially increased. He has pointed out that this fund is supposed to offset shortfalls not just in the regular budget but in the increasing number of peacekeeping operations as well. At its current level, the working capital fund now represents only 6 percent of the combined regular budget and peacekeeping appropriations for 1989, as against 10.7 percent as recently as 1985. In proposing that the fund be doubled in size, he explained that such an increase was not intended to compensate for large unpaid assessments such as the Organization now faced. It was, rather, required to provide the basis for the better financial management of the U.N. regular budget and peacekeeping activities.

In his report on the administrative and budgetary aspects of the financing of the latter activities [A/44/605], the Secretary-General explained his difficulties in connection with the start-up financing of new peacekeeping operations:

> The Organization needs a definite financing authorization immediately after there is a decision to establish a new peace-keeping operation. Funds are, however, needed to meet pre-implementation and other immediate costs, arising before the requisite financing action by the General Assembly and prior to the receipt of the assessed contributions. Experience shows that in cases of medium to major peace-keeping operations the amount of funding immediately required is in the order of $50 million to $100 million. . . . The present resources made available for unforeseen and extraordinary expenses are sufficient to permit only a relatively small observer-type peace-keeping operation to be initiated, and operated, until the usual financing procedures are completed.

The Secretary-General pointed out that often a situation calls for speedy action once a new peacekeeping force has been authorized. For example, in the case of Namibia the Assembly took the necessary action on March 1, 1989, with the target date for beginning operation just a month later. On such occasions, it is counterproductive to delay start-up action until governments have been notified of their assessments and can send in their payments.

While there appears to be broad support for a doubling of the fund to $200 million, there is much less agreement on how the increase should be financed. Paid-up members fear that almost any method would have the effect of switching more of the burden to their shoulders and remove some of the pressures on the United States and other countries in default of their obligations. The Secretary-General has offered four main options for financing the increase: (1) apportioning the amount of the increase among all member states as part of their assessments, (2) assessing the increase over several years rather than at one time, (3) financing the increase through voluntary contributions, and (4) crediting the fund with the unspent appropriations remaining at the end of each biennium rather than returning them to governments or allocating them to current expenditures.

The General Assembly's financial watchdog group, the **Advisory Committee on Administrative and Budgetary Questions** (ACABQ), chose not to endorse any of these proposals for increasing the size of the working capital fund. Instead it concluded that the analysis in the Secretary-General's reports on the financial situation did not "provide a sufficient basis for the Advisory Committee to formulate and submit definitive recommendations concerning increasing the level of the Working Capital Fund and modalities for financing such an increase." The committee therefore suggested that the Secretary-General's proposal be deferred to this year's Assembly and promised that it would take up the matter on a priority basis at its spring 1990 session [A/44/873, para. 12].

Hopeful that the United States would finally pay most of its arrears and anxious not to jeopardize the complex negotiations between the Bush administration and the Congress, most members of the General Assembly took a low-key approach when the Fifth Committee considered the difficult financial situation of the United Nations. This consideration was delayed until the closing days of the session, taking place on December 14 and 15, 1989, when only nine delegations chose to take the floor. Much of what they said focused on the Secretary-General's proposal to enlarge the working capital fund, with support being given to the Secretary-General's fourth option (and a version of that option that would put less burden on paid-up members) and on the ACABQ's proposal to postpone action until 1990. The representative of Brazil, speaking in this connection, said that no state should be made to suffer the consequences of another's failure to fulfill its obligations. The representative of Australia stated bluntly that if states wished to be members of the United Nations, they should accept their obligations to the Organization as willingly as they accept its services to them [A/C.5/44/SR.56, 57].

The representative of the United States acknowledged that the inability of his country to meet its full assessments in recent years was "a serious issue for his government." He also acknowledged that "substantial progress" had already been achieved in the U.N. budgetary and administrative reforms and said he hoped that that momentum would not be lost. He promised that his government "would make every effort to meet its financial commitments in the coming year and return to a pattern of full payment" [A/C.5/44/SR.57].

In the end, the Assembly adopted a rather mildly worded resolution in which it "reaffirmed its commitment to seek a comprehensive and generally acceptable solution to the financial problems of the U.N., based on the principle of collective financial responsibility of Member States and in strict compliance with the Charter of the U.N." It also concurred with the Advisory Committee's proposal to postpone action for one year on the doubling in size of the working capital fund [A/Res/44/195].

Paying its arrearages to the regular budgets of the United Nations, the specialized agencies, and other international entities is only one of the "four funding initiatives" Secretary Baker mentioned. Another has to do with the need to ensure the timely financing of the many U.N. peacekeeping operations. The assessments on governments required for this purpose have increased dramatically in the last year or so. And in a few cases, as with the Cypus forces, such financing depends on voluntary contributions or regular budget entries. The third category involves the development aid institutions, such as the United Nations Development Programme (UNDP), UNICEF, and the World Food Programme, that are almost wholly dependent on voluntary contributions by governments and private donations by individuals. The last category embraces the providers of development loans such as the World Bank and the regional development banks in Africa, Asia, and Latin America. All of these units and organizations, if they are to continue their work, require adequate funding, and all have been deeply affected by cuts in their U.S. funding.

Some of them have been even harder hit by the financial crisis than the United Nations itself. For example, on March 31, 1990, payments to support the United Nations Forces in Lebanon (UNIFIL) were outstanding to the tune of $343.1 million, or more than two years in arrears in terms of the $142 million annual budget. Also, the ninth replenishment of the World Bank's soft loan window, the International Development Association (IDA), has been delayed, mainly because the sums involved are quite large (the U.S. share for three years is $3.18 billion) and there must first be agreement on how much each government will contribute. As much as half of IDA's funding is earmarked for critically needed development projects and economic restructuring programs in sub-Saharan Africa, which the United Nations has declared a top-priority area.

Actually the overall picture on financing the U.N. peacekeeping activities is quite good. UNIFIL's financial problems are serious because many governments other than the United States are behind in their payments. These include Czechoslovakia, France, East Germany, Iran, Italy, Poland, South Africa, the Soviet Union, and the United Kingdom. The slowness of payments may in this case spring, partly at least, from wide skepticism about the viability of its mission. On the other hand, the payments for the United Nations Middle East forces (U.N. Emergency Force [UNEF] and U.N. Disengagement Observer Force [UNDOF]) are only about one year in arrears; those for the Iran-Iraq Military Observer Group, the Observer Group in Central America, and the Angola Verification Mission, less than one year; while the Transition Assistance Group in Namibia, launched just a year ago, is already largely paid for. The evidence would seem to show that when operations go well, most governments are ready to reimburse their costs fairly promptly.

More than half the funds provided internationally go toward the economic development of the Third World and are provided not as assessments but as voluntary contributions or sums negotiated among contributors as a package. Many developed countries prefer this method of financing because it enables them to determine the amounts that they can provide and to choose the entities they wish to support. At the same time, it permits large contributors sometimes to apply undue pressure on an organization to spend those sums in the ways they wish. However, few supporters of development assistance to the Third World want to abolish this method of financing, since it clearly maximizes the sums actually made available to countries in need of economic and technical assistance. A number of difficult issues arise from this method of financing activities, explained in the next section.

The United States contributes voluntarily to about 30 programs of various kinds. The chief among them are: (1) the UNDP ($108.5 million requested for FY 1991), which provides technical and preinvestment assistance on quite a large scale to all developing countries with most of its projects organized and administered by the specialized agencies, each within its area of specialization; (2) UNICEF ($50 million requested); (3) the International Atomic Energy Agency ($24 million requested); and (4) the United Nations Environment Programme (UNEP) ($10 million requested). In 1989 the Congress upped some of the previous requests—UNICEF by 93 percent and UNEP by 50 percent. Still, the amounts being made available, especially for UNDP, are substantially lower than they were several years ago. The ups and downs of U.S. contributions to these organizations, because they usually represent a considerable proportion of available funds, have made it harder to program their activities.

Finally, $1.7 billion has been requested for FY 1991 for the various multilateral development banks. In addition to the $1.1 billion for IDA, this sum includes $111 million for the World Bank proper and $40 million for its International Finance Corporation (which supports Third World private companies), $302 million for the Asian Development Bank, $116 million for the African Development Bank and Fund, and $104 million for the Inter-American Development Bank and affiliated entities. Of the $1.7 billion, about $279 million is to pay for arrearages, which the Bush administration also characterizes as "formal obligations that the United States must honor" [*Washington Weekly Report*, 3/2/90].

2. Program Planning

The preceding section focused on problems connected with raising funds needed for activities that member states have determined the United Nations should carry out. It also has to be decided which activities the Organization should attend to and how much money it should spend on each of them and on all of them together. In order to perform this function as responsibly and efficiently as possible, the General Assembly has long had two specialized bodies to assist it: the ACABQ and a 34-member **Committee for Program and Co-ordination** (CPC). The former deals mainly with the financial aspects and the latter mainly with the substantive aspects of activities that the Organization has been asked to undertake. The systematic planning and programming of what the United Nations will do and how much it will cost is conducted primarily by means of two instruments: a six-year medium-term plan, which is the principal policy directive, and a two-year program budget, which mandates exactly what it will do and how much it will spend in the process. The drafts of the plan and the program budget are prepared by the Secretary-General and his staff. These drafts are then reviewed by the ACABQ, the CPC, and the General Assembly's Fifth Committee before being adopted by the Assembly in plenary meeting.

In the mid-1980s there were numerous complaints that the plan was not properly reflecting goals, objectives, and policies that could be transformed into action through funding and the setting of priorities in the program budget. It was also widely held that that budget was nothing more than "the financial compilation of a number of decisions and recommendations taken by a large number of intergovernmental bodies and interpreted in the various departments of the Secretariat" [A/41/49]. It was, in fact, clear that the earlier system, which had evolved somewhat haphazardly since the early 1970s, stood in need of review and rationalization. In 1986 the General Assembly, acting on the advice of a team of intergovernmental experts that it had set up to carry out this task, established a new "planning, programming and budgeting process." This process involved a two-year cycle in which the steps required of the General Assembly, ACABQ, CPC, the Secretariat, and a large number of substantive bodies such as the Human Rights Commission were specified in detail for budget years—the years in which biennial budgets are adopted—and intervening off-budget years. Matters were so arranged that the medium-term plan is adopted or revised in those off-budget years, thus evening out the workload for everyone concerned. In addition to the plan, an outline of the program budget is drawn up in each off-year so that governments can offer advance guidance to the Secretary-General before he and his staff begin work on that crucial document.

It was hoped that these procedural improvements would pave the way for a higher level of operational effectiveness in U.N. program planning and thus meet the criticisms of the former apparatus. This new process has now gone through one complete cycle, and 1990 begins its second time around. While not without its glitches and confusions, the first cycle appears to have worked reasonably well. Moreover, for the first time in a number of years, a biennial program budget could be adopted without voting, that is, no member insisted on recording its negative vote or abstention [A/Res/44/202]. A major underlying reason for its acceptance among the usually critical main contributors is the fact that it provided for little or no real growth. At the same time, developing countries were pleased that the United States did not vote against sections of the budget that it opposed on policy grounds.

There seems to be wide acceptance of the need for a no-real-growth budget so long as the Organization's financial situation remains so precarious. According to the Secretariat's data, continuing or recurrent activities are scheduled to shrink by 0.4 percent in real terms during the current biennium; if nonrecurrent activities, such as funds earmarked for the forthcoming conferences, are included, it will rise by 0.5 percent. Thus, the differences between the $1,975 million approved for 1990–1991 and the final appropriations of $1,772 for 1988–1989 is almost all due to inflation and shifting exchange rates. While budgetary comparisons over time are difficult to make—e.g., because of the many intricacies involved in accounting for inflation, exchange rate movements, and the movement of posts from budgetary to extrabudgetary status and vice-versa—it seems clear that the rapid real growth in the U.N. regular budget expenditures in the 1970s was followed in the 1980s by a remarkable stability, which is now being extended into the early 1990s. Of course, this stability does not extend to the Organization's peacekeeping operations, which are assessed separately and whose costs have been increasing rapidly because of widely supported decisions to send out new forces.

The extent to which the recent reforms have produced substantive as well as procedural improvements will be tested by the introduction of the first all-new medium-term plan in eight years (the old one having been extended for two years because of the changeover in procedures). By May 1990 the Secretariat's draft of the plan, which covers the years 1992–1997, was ready and being reviewed by the CPC. It is still a bulky document; efforts to reduce it to a more manageable length have had limited success. But there has been some simplification in the way in which activities are presented, and the number of programs and subprograms has been substantially reduced. Program objectives, so difficult to articulate clearly, have been focused on what the Secretariat's role should be, especially on what it should be asked to do, in each of the many areas in which the

Organization is active. This should make it simpler to establish the necessary linkages between plan and program budget and easier to determine afterward whether an activity has been achieving its objectives.

Procedurally more intergovernmental sectoral bodies, such as the Population Commission and the Governing Council of UNEP, have had an opportunity to review and comment on the sections of the plan that focus on their specific spheres of involvement. It also appears that on the whole they have taken this opportunity rather seriously and that their inputs have strengthened the substantive character of the planning exercise.

Furthermore, the Secretary-General and his staff have put a great deal of effort into writing an introduction to the plan that will suggest the new directions in which the United Nations should be moving in the 1990s on the economic and social fronts, as well as on the political front. In 1988 the General Assembly and the CPC reviewed a first draft of such an introduction, and this year a new text is in preparation, which will be presented to both bodies. The main challenge for the Secretary-General has been to find common ground for the differing views that member states hold with regard to which program sectors ought to receive priority for the limited resources in the years immediately ahead.

The need for establishing proper priorities, particularly in the economic and social fields, has bedeviled the Organization since it was founded in 1945. Its broad mandate in these fields allows it an unusually wide scope for action, but the many sectoral and cross-sectoral demands on the very limited funds and staff that governments are willing to make available have always necessitated the making of hard choices. Until now, these choices usually have been made indirectly through the budgetary mechanism rather than deliberately by increasing what is being done in one program sector at the expense of another.

The Secretary-General's introduction may signal some progress in addressing this delicate problem in sectoral and cross-sectoral terms. He earlier proposed certain guidelines for improving the Organization's capacity to set meaningful priorities on all levels of the programming process. For example, he suggested that the nature of the objectives should be such that multilateral action is demonstrably important to their achievement. And when the plan is revised every second year, the priority designations of subprograms within a given sector should be reviewed and adjusted in cases where this seems desirable. He also suggested that sectoral, functional, and regional intergovernmental bodies should be involved in this process of adjusting the priorities of subprograms in the areas for which they are responsible [A/44/272, p. 13].

Still another opportunity to crack the problem of priorities will arise in late 1990 when the CPC and the Fifth Committee are presented with the

Secretary-General's outline for the 1992–1993 program budget. He had not found it possible to tackle the priority question in the outline he submitted two years ago, but his analysis of the conceptual and methodological problems involved in priority setting may now have made this issue somewhat easier to deal with.

The Secretary-General will have to propose a ceiling on expenditures for that biennium. In reaching his decision on that ceiling, he will need to take into account a recent joint suggestion by the governments of Japan, the United Kingdom, the United States, and the Soviet Union that once again there should be a no-growth approach to spending. He will also have to take into account the position of the Indian and some other delegations that the United Nations should be playing an increasing role in many areas, such as assistance to developing countries, and that its budget should not continually decline in real terms but instead show a modest rate of increase. Whatever decision the Secretary-General may reach, no one can doubt the combined influence of the major contributors in determining the eventual level of the ceiling. Accordingly, despite the wishes of developing countries, continuing small reductions in the total number of posts may be unavoidable [A/C.5/44/SR.14, p. 2].

There can also be no doubt of the seriousness with which governments regard the outline and the ceiling established by it. Many Fifth Committee speakers complained of the increase in the Secretary-General's initial estimates for 1990–1991 (though it was quite small, amounting to less than 0.1 percent of the total) over the figure that the Assembly had set in 1988. Others supported what they regarded as a nominal increase. The representative of Japan spoke for many when he said that the outline was a means of letting member states know the total amount of resources that would be required and that it should "serve as a basis for dialogue between the Secretariat and Member states for the preparation of the proposed program budget and therefore describe the content of programs and set priorities, not only within a sector but also among sectors" [A/C.5/44/SR.13, p. 10].

The outline for the 1992–1993 program budget was expected to become available in August and to be reviewed by CPC at its September session before submission to the Fifth Committee.

A perennial problem of long-term planning at the United Nations is how it can adjust what it is doing to the evolving needs of the world community. By its very nature, such planning must act on imperfect forecasts of events and trends far in the future—imperfect because many such events and trends are unforeseeable and therefore cannot be planned for. There is also a much greater tendency for governments to perceive the need for new activities than to reach consensus that certain existing activities are no longer required. This means that additional funding usually has to be sought to pay for new unplanned activities that suddenly command wide support. In the 1970s requests for such new activities—called add-ons—came with increasing regularity and particularly upset the major contributors whose opposition to some of them was often overridden by Third World majorities in the voting process.

The recent reforms included a solution to this problem. It was agreed to establish a contingency fund that would provide both a ceiling for add-ons and an orderly way of dealing with requests for additional activities. It was also agreed that the contingency fund accompanying the 1990–1991 budget would be set at 0.75 percent of that budget, or $15 million, and that amounts to be withdrawn from the fund would be appropriated only after the activities for which they were to be used had been approved. At its last session the General Assembly noted that $13.1 of the $15 million remained in the fund [A/Res/44/201A, sect. IX]. However, some $7 million has now been earmarked for preparatory activities for the Conference on Environment and Development to be held in Brazil in June 1992 and about $1.5 million for additional activities combating drug abuse.

The arrangements surrounding the use of the contingency fund have systematized, and introduced a new restraint in, the introduction of new activities in midstream. Although the fund will probably be used up by the end of 1990, leaving a gap of 12 months, new activities may still be introduced provided that they are offset by the elimination of other activities that have outlived their usefulness or by the postponement of those having lower priority.

It is also generally accepted that the need for new activities should be determined not in isolation but within the framework of the ongoing plan and program budget. As a vehicle for achieving this, the Secretary-General has been asked, each time a proposal for new activities is introduced, to submit a "statement of program budget implications." Under the rules, this should include information on

> the modification of the work program necessitated should the proposed draft resolution, recommendation or decision be adopted, listing changes or deletions to programs, sub-programs and program elements [and,] in cases where it is proposed to finance such additional activities totally or partly by the redeployment of existing resources, an indication of the output, program elements or sub-programs in the current work program that would be changed, curtailed or terminated in consequence [be provided] [Rule 104.9 as quoted in A/44/234, para. 13].

In his report on this subject, the Secretary-General acknowledged that these requirements had yet to be fully honored, partly because of the inherent difficulties of integrating new activities within existing program structures and partly because the time allocated for the submission of statements is too brief (the Secretariat has suggested that it be extended from 48 hours to 72). It is also virtually impossible to reach decisions to curtail or drop existing activities within such a brief time span. Indeed, the Assembly has forbidden that activities and programs being carried out "as a result of legislative mandates" be dropped without its permission. Nonetheless, it is widely recognized that the logic of planning and programming calls for greater attention to be paid to the integration of new programs with ongoing ones and to the modification or weeding out of some of the latter on the basis of their lower priority. The mechanisms for achieving this goal, however, continue to be elusive.

One of the main prospective advantages of program planning is that it facilitates the feedback of experience gained in carrying out past activities into the planning and programming of future ones. This may be achieved in two ways: by the systematic monitoring of performance and by evaluating completed projects and outputs. For a variety of reasons, neither approach has yet had the full impact hoped for from it.

The CPC and the Assembly will have before them the Secretary-General's sixth report on U.N. program performance, this time for the biennium 1988–1989. In December 1989 the General Assembly had emphasized the importance of having a reliable methodology for such monitoring and requested improvements to facilitate "the meaningful determination of implementation rates and comparison between actual delivery of final outputs and commitments set out in the program narratives of the approved program budget." It also asked the Secretary-General to develop a methodology for harmonizing program performance and budget performance (they are now reported on separately) [A/Res/44/194, sect. III].

The Secretary-General's report compares the number of final outputs planned with the number completed, thus maintaining a quantitative rather than a qualitative approach. He acknowledges that it does not attempt to assess the quality and relevance of the outputs produced and treats outputs equally that are very different in their call on resources; he holds that such limitations are intrinsic to the exercise. The report does break down the final outputs into five main categories: meetings (15 percent of the total); reports (19 percent); technical publications (41 percent); public information outputs (12 percent); and other outputs, such as the organization of hearings, investigations, studies and consultations, ad hoc meetings, and briefings of official visitors (13 percent)).

Within these limitations the report throws a good deal of light on the effectiveness of the program planning process. For example, of 8,954 planned outputs, 6,597 (74 percent) were implemented during the 1988–1989 biennium, with 1,012 (11 percent) postponed and 1,345 (15 percent) terminated. This information is then broken down by major program and budget section and by outputs enjoying the highest and lowest priority. Of the 1,698 outputs having the highest priority, 1,358 were carried out, 117 were postponed, and 178 were terminated. Of the 546 with the lowest priority, only 291 were completed, 130 were postponed, and 93 terminated. The implementation rate was even lower for the 621 outputs carried over from earlier biennia; only 234 were completed, 177 were again postponed, and 210 were terminated. The report suggests that when outputs have been postponed for more than two biennia, their relevancy ought to be reviewed.

The reasons for the shortfalls may be of interest. For example, the cancellation of meetings (common in the political and international trade areas) meant that the outputs associated with them also had to be cancelled. There are a number of other reasons that outputs may be cancelled. According to the report, the termination of a programmed output may signal the good management of a complex and evolving program, deficiencies of the original programming, the failure to receive expected funding from voluntary contributions, or a combination of all three factors. Postponements of outputs were most common with regard to publications and reports. Often these were caused by delays in the printing and publication of completed manuscripts.

The Secretary-General sets out certain methodological issues that he hopes to solve in the near future. Partly they involve difficulties in defining outputs; for example, operational projects have had to be left out because there are no standardized citations for their related outputs. Partly they involve complications of interpretation arising from the difficulty of establishing whether an output is financed totally or in part from extra-budgetary resources [A/45/218].

The other source of feedback is program evaluation. Here a two-pronged approach is being followed. Certain program sectors are designated for an in-depth evaluation of all their activities by the CPC. But because of the work involved and the limited resources available for this purpose, only a few program sectors can be tackled at any time. For example, in 1989 the CPC had before it full-scale evaluations of the programs on development issues and policies, on human rights, and on disarmament; in 1990 it will undertake evaluations of the programs on human settlements and on science and technology. The committee also examines, two or three years later, the extent to which its recommendations have been carried out by the various program managers. Only about 28 percent of the activities have been scheduled for in-depth evaluation during the period 1985–1994.

The other prong is the system of self-evaluation of the 472 subprograms by their managers. The **U.N. Central Evaluation Unit** has established a training course for program managers to help them evaluate the activities being carried out within their respective subprograms and analyze the findings. The expectation is that these findings would then be fed back when these same managers implement their activities within ongoing plans and program budgets or are involved in preparing new ones. Even such self-evaluation cannot be done everywhere at once; during the six-year period 1986–1991, 253 of the 472 subprograms (slightly more than half of them) have had or will have had self-evaluations, and similar exercises are scheduled for the other 219.

The CPC has welcomed these efforts to refine the methodology for evaluation but has stressed the need for further improvements. In particular, it has urged the Secretariat to adopt a more qualitative approach in its evaluation analyses "wherever justified by programmatic considerations." The committee has also offered itself as a "geographically diverse sample of Member states for future questionnaires" on in-depth evaluations, beginning with the one on human settlements scheduled for 1990 [A/44/16]. In 1989 the General Assembly echoed the need for a more qualitative approach, supported the self-evaluation exercises, and urged that program performance and evaluation reports should be submitted to the intergovernmental and expert bodies that provide policy direction for the programs concerned [A/Res/44/194, sect. IV].

There are two major obstacles to comprehensive long-term program planning. One is the increasing role being played by extrabudgetary funding in U.N. economic and social activities. In 1990–1991, $2.5 billion is expected to be received in such funding, more than the total amount of the regular budget. While much of this large sum is allocated to the field projects of large entities such as the UNDP, UNICEF, and the Office of the High Commissioner for Refugees, there are also 106 little-known substantive trust funds that will spend $325 million during the biennium. Extrabudgetary funds support some 2,500 posts, many of them involved in carrying out substantive headquarters-type activities. During the recent downsizing of staff, while 1,300 posts were being dropped from the regular budget, some 600 posts were being added by means of extrabudgetary funding. While budgetary resources have remained little changed in real terms, extrabudgetary ones have tended to increase more rapidly.

This clearly complicates the task of overall program planning—not just because most extrabudgetary funds are designated for specific purposes and thus are not reallocable to meet shifting sectoral priorities but also because the activities they support are not under the same degree of administrative and financial control. Also, it is sometimes held that program sectors such as population and drug abuse that have proportionately larger extrabudgetary resources at their disposal should receive somewhat less from the regular budget. It seems logical that the activities being carried out by the

Organization in a given field should be reviewed in their totality regardless of their funding sources.

The ACABQ has been actively addressing the role being played by extrabudgetary funding in the areas of its own mandate. In 1988 it drew attention to the need to perfect the methodology used to forecast the level of extrabudgetary resources so that plans and program budgets could reflect the overall resources likely to be available. This will not be made any easier by the fact that additional resources are quite often received during a biennium and thus have an impact on the work program while it is under way and, indirectly, on the ordering of priorities. The committee added:

> In view of the magnitude of resources involved, the Advisory Committee believes that it is essential to define precisely the role of extra-budgetary financing in the over-all financial structure of the United Nations. It is also necessary to refine approval and reporting mechanisms so as to ensure that these expenditures are submitted to a greater measure of scrutiny and control [A/44/7, para. 82].

The committee noted that indications of financing through extrabudgetary resources for program elements and outputs are still given in the program budget only when such financing constitutes more than 50 percent of total requirements. It went on to urge that the overhead costs attributable to activities financed from extrabudgetary funds should be fully reimbursed by such funds. Finally, pointing out that the U.N. Fund for Drug Abuse Control (UNFDAC) plans to spend $130 million in the current biennium without its disbursement's being overseen by any intergovernmental body, the ACABQ envisaged the possibility of reviewing the attendant administrative and budgetary arrangements for UNFDAC and other similarly situated funds.

While the General Assembly did not take any action on this matter at its 1989 session, the Secretary-General is to report on all of the many aspects involved this year in time for their review by ACABQ and CPC prior to their consideration by the Fifth Committee. The former body set forth ten issues that it wanted to see covered in the Secretary-General's report.

There is a second obstacle that is almost equally disruptive to the rational planning of economic and social activities: the fact that such planning is done separately by each organization of the U.N. system without any effective centralization of the process. Yet the United Nations and its various specialized agencies carry out closely related activities in as many as 20 program sectors and cross-sectoral areas, which should be jointly planned. These include the gathering and analysis of national statistics, population, water resources and energy, industrial development, combatting drug abuse, assistance to the handicapped, the advancement of women, the environment, housing and human settlements, science and technology, education and training, public administration, the planning of economic and social development, and activities with regard to outer space and the use of the seas, to name just some of the most important ones.

In each of these program sectors and cross-sectoral areas, the United Nations and the specialized agencies are carrying out activities that under the Charter are supposed to be "coordinated," but this coordination rarely takes the form of joint planning among the units concerned. Indeed, each major specialized agency, such as the World Health Organization and UNESCO, continues to have its own program planning mechanism, which typically includes a medium-term plan and program budget. However, these are still prepared by the various organizations in separate processes, with only very limited coordination of their content. Such coordination as there is takes place mostly at periodic meetings of the program managers or in the informal contacts they often have with one another. The meetings are mainly problem oriented, dealing with cases of overlapping or duplication of ongoing activities that the program managers seek to iron out. Major issues that they cannot resolve may be passed up to the **Administrative Committee on Co-ordination (ACC)**, a high-level inter-Secretariat committee chaired by the Secretary-General. ACC's members are the executive heads of the specialized agencies (including those of the World Bank, the International Monetary Fund [IMF] and the General Agreement on Tariffs and Trade [GATT]). The ACC submits an annual overview report to the Economic and Social Council (ECOSOC), which under the Charter is responsible for coordinating the activities of the entire system. The CPC, as it name implies, also has important responsibilities in this area.

In addition to the annual overview report, ECOSOC and the Assembly have called for a series of "cross-organizational program analyses." In 1989, CPC received such analyses of system-wide activities in two program sectors: industrial development and the advancement of women. But ECOSOC has now decided to discontinue these analyses in their present form, though one on industrial development will still be submitted in 1990. They may be succeeded by thematic analyses whose precise form is still under discussion by ECOSOC.

In fact, ECOSOC and the Assembly continue to struggle with the problem of how best to approach their coordination responsibilities. CPC, in its report, articulated the goals being pursued in the following terms:

> The Committee recognized that co-ordination should be aimed at greater compatibility and mutual complementarity of the activities and programs of the UN system. In that regard co-ordination should concentrate on those issues and problems that require the attention of the international community and effective joint action on the part of the system.

> The Committee agreed that co-ordination as a policy instrument to improve the performance and enhance the quality of output of the organizations of the UN system should also aim at avoiding unnecessary duplication, eliminating overlap and improving cost-effectiveness [A/44/16, paras. 326–327].

While these goals are unexceptionable, they remain as difficult to attain as they have been for the past 45 years. The CPC continues to seek the assistance of the ACC and the Secretary-General in their attainment, partly through the annual joint meetings it has with them but mainly through seeking improvements in the quality of their reporting.

It asked the ACC to provide it with "a more forward-looking and analytical" report that would provide "alternate suggestions on policy measures for major programs" and would "improve the quality of its analysis, which would be more critical in nature." Beyond that, it invited the ACC to make its role more effective, to review its working methods, and to make its work "more visible and transparent." It also reaffirmed the role of the Secretary-General in coordinating the activities of the U.N. system. Regarding long-term planning and programming, however, it limited itself to calling for the "harmonization of planning and budget cycles," which means that the various plans and program budgets should cover identical time spans. This would facilitate the prior exchange of comments on such plans and budgets during the course of their preparation but remains far removed from the goal of joint planning in the many program sectors and cross-sectoral areas of common involvement. Even this limited goal, pursued for many years, may prove unattainable [A/44/16, paras. 358–360].

The General Assembly requested the ACC "to modify substantially the format and content of its annual overview report" in accordance with CPC's conclusions and recommendations. It also invited ECOSOC and CPC to "improve their consideration" of that report. Finally, it sought to improve the quality of the joint meetings by inviting both bodies at their 1990 meetings to "discuss, in a thorough manner, all measures for improving the efficacy of the joint meetings, including their structure and the level of participation" [A/Res/44/194, sect. V].

The General Assembly asked the Secretary-General to provide it with a "general critical assessment" of the reforms in the program planning process, some of which have been described. Below are a few extracts from this unusually frank assessment of the current situation, which will be before the Assembly at its forthcoming session:

> In the administrative and financial areas, a satisfactory process of confidence building between Member states and the Secretariat is also emerging. . . . [This] was reflected in the adoption without a vote of all resolutions in the Fifth Committee during the forty-fourth session of the

Assembly. . . . [The reforms] have resulted in an increased consciousness among Member states and within the Secretariat about the way in which the UN spends its resources and encouraged a more effective use of available resources. They have also largely allayed the concerns of the major contributors.

A practicable consensus on action required in the economic and social sectors has not yet emerged, in contrast to the progress achieved in the political, administrative and financial areas. The Secretary-General has been requested once again to submit proposals to the Assembly at its forty-fifth session, including recommendations for reforms in the inter-governmental sector. He intends to do so taking into account the results of a number of important meetings and deliberations taking place this year.

The problem of maintaining a proper balance between growing operational activities of the various entities funded through extrabudgetary sources and their mandated programs under the regular budget still remains to be addressed in full. At the Secretariat level, the interrelationships between research and policy analysis and operational activities require further study.

With respect to intergovernmental machinery, experience has shown how difficult it is to overcome certain obstacles [which] stem from the persistent basic political divergence of views among Member states over priorities [and] over the role and decision-making powers of the various UN organs. . . . The subject of reform in the economic and social sector cannot be dealt with piecemeal or in a fragmented manner. What is needed, above all, is a fresh and courageous re-examination of positions and attitudes, particularly in the light of the momentous changes taking place in the world. . . . The Secretary-General believes that opportunity exists to extend to the economic and social spheres the same spirit of co-operation that has recently been harnessed to achieve positive results in the political field. . . . The seriousness and urgency of the economic and social problems confronting the international community, and the developing countries in particular, render the role of the Secretariat in assisting Member states . . . in program formulation, in setting of priorities and in enhancing co-ordination and coherence in the UN system, even more important. . . . The UN is not only a universal organization but must also be concerned with the totality of the human condition on earth. Nowhere else can national policies, priorities and concerns come together, interact and forge a global consciousness as a foundation for comprehensive collective action for the betterment of that condition.

. . .The lengthy political process that culminated [in the various reforms] has largely achieved its purpose. The Organization received a mandate for reform to be implemented over a three-year period, which it has fulfilled to the best of its abilities. The mandate has been carried out without serious negative effects on programs, but not without pain. Retrenchment has put considerable strain on several parts of the Secretariat. . . . In a climate of renewed confidence in the capacity of the Organization, the reforms may be seen as a contributing factor in changing attitudes

> towards the UN and its ability to respond to new challenges. Today there is a greater and more effective use of the Organization's capabilities. . . . There is a noticeable improvement in public perceptions of the Organization as an institution for the resolution of conflict. On the basis of these objective criteria, it may be concluded that the ultimate purposes in the minds of the legislators . . . have been achieved [A/45/226, paras. 242–260].

3. Personnel and Staff Administration

Comprehensive Review of Conditions of Service

The U.N. family of international organizations and its **International Civil Service Commission (ICSC)** are in the final stages of their first comprehensive review of the conditions of service of their professional staff. The comprehensiveness of this review stems from the fact that what is being reexamined is not just the U.N. family's common system of salaries and allowances but also the nonfinancial factors that, together with the financial ones, make up the overall conditions of service. The ICSC's goal has been to find out whether international organizations are still able to attract and retain the gifted people and highly trained specialists that they need to carry out their challenging functions. The review has thus also had to be concerned with the motivation and productivity of staff and with the reasons that so many of them have been reluctant to move from one duty station to another or to serve in field posts away from the comforts of the various headquarters.

Of course, as in all other lines of work, the assurance of adequate remuneration is an important condition of service. Until now, this has been maintained through the common system of salaries and allowances. This system was created to ensure that all staff working for the United Nations or its specialized agencies (except for the IMF and the World Bank, which have their own quite different system) receive the same remuneration for performing similar functions, regardless of the organization or duty station with which they happen to be associated. The proper level for this remuneration has been ascertained by means of applying what is called the Noblemaire principle, which ties the remuneration of international officials to that of the highest-paying national civil service—since 1945, always that of the United States. The pay package has also long included a margin factor—now ranging between 10 and 20 percent—to compensate professional staff for, e.g., living abroad and the more limited career prospects offered by international organizations in relation to national civil services.

This system, highly regarded in the past, has been shaken in recent years by a number of adverse developments: volatile currency exchange rates, efforts to keep many exchange rates at artificially high levels, widening rates of inflation that run the gamut from virtually none to runaway, and difficulties in adjusting remuneration to the hardships and dangers associated with an increasing number of duty stations where large numbers of staff are required. Perhaps the most upsetting development has been the gradual deterioration in the purchasing power of all professional staff, averaging 11 percent since 1984, which has resulted in large part from the current gap of 28 percent between the salaries actually received by U.S. federal civil servants and those recommended under the U.S. Pay Comparability Act. As the Canadian representative in the Fifth Committee pointed out, this "left the international civil service staff in the unenviable position of being held hostage to the national civil service policies of a single Member state. Clearly, that had not been the intention of the Noblemaire principle" [A/C.5/44/SR.35, p. 3]. Some members of the commission saw in this situation a potential conflict between the Noblemaire principle as currently applied and the need for the U.N. system to attract the high-level staff it requires. It was the combined impact of these adverse developments that lay behind the General Assembly's call for the comprehensive review.

The complexity of such a review is revealed by the guidelines set for it by the General Assembly. Any alternative system must:

1. Make it possible to recruit staff having "the highest standards of efficiency, competence and integrity."
2. Have greater "transparency" and simplicity in the concepts and administration of the remuneration system.
3. Have sufficient flexibility to respond to varying requirements resulting from different types of appointment (e.g., fixed term or career) and changing circumstances.
4. Adjust the relativity of benefits at the various duty stations to promote staff mobility.
5. Equalize remuneration at these same stations through what the United Nations calls the "post adjustment system," which sounds easy but is far from being so [A/Res/42/221].

What that resolution did not point out was that any new system needed not just the support of the Organization's 159 member governments but also the acquiescence (and probably more than that) of those in the various organizations who would be responsible for administering it and of the professional staff whom it would deeply affect. The administrators of the many organizations coordinate their views through an interagency organ known as the **Consultative Committee on Administrative Questions (CCAQ)**, and the thousands of professional staff are represented through two omnibus associations—the **Federation of International Civil Servants Associations (FICSA)** and the **Co-ordinating Committee for Independent Staff Unions and Associations (CCISUA)**. These bodies are highly organized and well placed to press their views and even to torpedo proposals they dislike.

The ICSC has had the unenviable task of finding some new system that could win acceptance among governments holding very different views on many of the basic concepts of staff management and the proper level for staff costs and, at the same time, find favor among those who would have to administer it and those whose professional careers would be governed by it.

Complicating the commission's task was the General Assembly's additional injunction that the overall costs under any new system "should, as far as possible, be comparable to the costs of the current remuneration system" [A/Res/44/198]. Because this threatened to make permanent the lower levels of remuneration that had accompanied the long financial crisis, it fostered in administrators and staff alike wary attitudes toward whatever new system the commission might devise that abided by this stricture.

The commission undertook its complex task by dividing its work into a number of compartments:

1. Competitiveness of the present system in terms of its capacity to attract and retain staff.
2. Remuneration structures—whether there should be any fundamental changes in the system and, if so, what they should be.
3. Problems of determining the highest-paid civil service and of establishing the most appropriate margin between U.N. remuneration and that of the comparator civil service.
4. Technical problems of the post adjustment system designed to ensure equality of remuneration at duty stations throughout the world.
5. Mobility and hardship questions and the way in which they affect transferability of staff when they are needed at other duty stations, including unattractive ones in the field.
6. Motivation and productivity questions.
7. All kinds of allowances above and beyond basic remuneration, including not just family allowances and educational grants but other entitlements, such as service separation payments and travel standards.
8. Consequential adjustments in pension entitlements.

Competitiveness and Capacity to Recruit and Retain Professional Staff. Many executive heads of U.N. organizations—including those of UNDP, the U.N. Industrial Development Organization, and the International Atomic Energy Agency (IAEA)—informed the commission that their professional staff were dismayed by the continuing erosion in the purchasing power of their take-home pay. The commission found that this erosion had been 7.5 percent at the base city of New York and higher at other headquarters locations such as Geneva, Paris, Rome, and Vienna. It also noted that this had made it especially difficult to recruit staff to serve at hardship locations in the field; a UNDP survey detailed some 700 instances of job refusals or early departures. The situation was aggravated by the increasing tendency of staff to be lured to employment with other international organizations that are not part of the U.N. common system, such as the World Bank and the Organization for Economic Cooperation and Development (OECD). Furthermore, particular recruitment and retention problems were faced by such organizations as the IAEA and the World Health Organization, which had to hire atomic physicists or medical specialists who were extremely well paid in outside jobs. Comparisons of U.N.-U.S. expatriate compensation levels showed that the U.N. was as much as 20 to 30 percent behind at some locations. All this pointed to the need, in the words of the Administrator of UNDP, to bring about "a substantial improvement in the value of the pay package" [A/44/30, vol. 2, para. 78–79].

The commission noted that some organizations had had to resort to exceptional measures to attract and keep the staff that they needed for their operations. Such measures included recruitment of new staff at higher than entry-level steps in a given grade; the greater use of recruitment bonuses and secondment; an increasing resort to special service agreements, in effect establishing a class of nonstaff entirely outside the common system; allowing some staff to work in their own countries rather than coming to the Organization's headquarters; and hiring subcontractors. In addition, some countries, including a few of those most anxious to hold down personnel costs, have been making supplementary payments to their own nationals serving in the various secretariats. None of these devices for circumventing the rules of the common system can be regarded as desirable.

In the end, the commission recommended, not unanimously but "by a majority," to the Assembly that it immediately grant an across-the-board salary increase of 5 percent. It was apparently led to this step by what seemed to be a deteriorating situation, as well as by the fact that on January 1, 1990, the margin between U.S. and U.N. salaries would drop to 108.3—below the floor of the desirable range of 110–120.

While some government representatives in the Fifth Committee questioned the timeliness of the proposed 5 percent increase and others were opposed to any increase at all, the majority felt that it was justified. Accordingly, the General Assembly subsequently approved this recommendation without voting and authorized expenditure of the $61.2 million ($35.2 of it in the regular budget) required to carry it out but with the proviso that it take effect only on July 1, 1990 [A/Res/44/198H]. At the same time, some observers felt that this increase alone would not be sufficient to restore the competitiveness of the common system, pointing to the fact that, on May 1, 1989, the World Bank had granted an increase of 10 percent.

Remuneration Structures. *Remuneration structures* refers to the traditional division of the pay package into its two elements: base salary, which is the same everywhere in the world, and post adjustment, which corrects the base salary to conform with the specific cost of living at each duty station. The commission has been considering the possibility of subdividing post adjustment into two categories by separating out housing costs. Giving housing a category of its own would seem to be justifiable because its costs vary, depending upon duty station, over a range of 300 percent (as against only 50 or 60 percent for other cost-of-living components) and because the comparison of relative housing costs poses very special and complex problems. The commission concluded that

> the continued inclusion of housing as an element of expenditure within the post adjustment system would maintain the numerous complexities associated with inter-city comparisons of housing costs, as well as the resulting inequities among duty stations and among staff members at any given duty station. . . . A number of anomalous situations had developed that were difficult to explain to the staff affected [A/44/30, para. 184].

A number of options were brought to the commission's attention by a working group that it had created to study how a tripartite structure might best be brought into being. The commission singled out one of them as being the most viable but did not have enough data on what its effects would be to recommend it to the General Assembly. Specifically it was not clear how governmental control would be exercised over the basic elements of the pay package or how such elements could be utilized to determine the proper level for pensionable remuneration (of special importance to staff since it determines the level of their future pensions). Moreover, these two matters could be dealt with only seriatim since the first must be settled before the second could be tackled.

The commission accordingly refrained from submitting any recommendations to the General Assembly in 1989. Instead it established a working group to answer such questions as whether intercity comparisons of housing costs could be eliminated, whether housing costs could be wholly or partially removed from margin calculations, and what would be the costs of the various alternative structures under consideration.

Later in the year, the Assembly noted with concern that the commission had not come forward with a revised remuneration structure and urged the commission to present to the Assembly in 1990 its "final and complete conclusions" with regard to all issues involved in a revised remuneration structure for the U.N. common system, including its impact on margin consideration and on the housing needs of staff stationed at hardship duty stations [A/Res/44/198A].

At its March 1990 session the commission had before it the report of the working group, which had elaborated three possible structures. In the view of the organizations, only one of them constituted a viable option. It would provide for a housing allowance reflecting its market costs and largely independent of margin considerations. Yet there remained difficult problems of implementation; they did not think it appropriate for housing allowances to be paid to all staff irrespective of what they actually paid for their housing, while the reimbursement of actual housing costs at main duty stations was deemed to be administratively unworkable. The representatives of the organizations concluded that "the disadvantages and potential pitfalls" of this option outweighed its advantages. At the same time, they urged that if housing were to remain within the post adjustment system, means should be urgently sought of improving the way it was measured. The staff representatives largely concurred with these views.

The members of the commission were surprised by the substantial change in the positions now being taken by the organizations and by the staff. They noted that instead of seeking some grand design in the form of a new remuneration system as the outcome of the comprehensive review, they were now proposing only a series of modifications in the present system. Some members nonetheless welcomed this as the product of a realistic assessment of the situation; at the same time, clarifications were sought on the underlying reasons for the about-face. It appeared that margin and pension considerations had proved to be bigger obstacles than had been expected in framing any totally new remuneration structure and, more generally, that the disadvantages entailed by the new structures proposed were perceived to outweigh their advantages.

Some of the commission's members remained unconvinced that efforts to create a new system should be abandoned; they wished first to understand better the current proposals and to have clarified the detailed modalities for margin control under two of them. Accordingly it was decided to postpone final action until the commission's summer 1990 session, while establishing still another working group to analyze and report on the complex questions that had arisen during its discussion. It seems less and less likely, however, that further study will lead to agreement on some totally new structure for the common system. At the same time, the absence of any proposal in this area may be an issue at this autumn's Assembly.

Highest-Paying Civil Service and Margin Questions. Three major issues emerged under this heading: how to determine which government has the highest-paying civil service, how to establish the proper margin between its remuneration and that of the United Nations family, and how to ensure that that margin is maintained over time.

The first issue proved the easiest to resolve. No one disputed that the highest-paying national civil service is still that of the United States. But there is much less confidence than in the past that this will be the case five or ten years hence. The commission therefore concluded that the situation should be reassessed at five-year intervals on a total compensation basis, which would include such items as pension entitlements, bonuses, performance awards, and health and life insurance subsidies. The Assembly reaffirmed that the U.S. federal civil service should remain the comparator, pointing out that its size and structure facilitated the carrying out of comparisons. In addition, it endorsed the idea of conducting quinquennial checks to determine the highest-paying national service and called upon the commission to present a methodology for such checks at its 1991 session [A/Res/44/198B]. At its spring 1990 session, the commission set in motion the arrangements to produce such a methodology one year hence.

It proved much harder to agree on how the margin between national and international remuneration should be established. The main factor justifying this margin is the need to compensate professional staff for being uprooted from their home countries and gradually losing their connections there. In its report, the commission presented this problem in rather cogent terms:

> While some staff might, depending on circumstances, adjust to the local environment over time, that was certainly not the case for all less mobile staff. Indeed, as their links with their home country became more tenuous, those staff members could be considered more, not less, expatriate. Those staff were, in many cases, discouraged by the host government from integrating themselves with the local population. Thus, they were frequently confronted with a series of legal and other restrictions (relating, for example, to the employment of the spouse or children or the acquisition of property), which had the effect of making them feel that they were not "at home" and, once their employment with the international organizations was completed, they were often encouraged, or obliged, to leave the country [A/44/30, para. 150].

On the other side, it was argued that the impact of expatriation diminished with continued long service, particularly when it was at one location over an extended period of time. The possibility of reestablishing an expatriation allowance as an alternative to this part of the margin differential was considered and rejected, partly because the number of professionals serving in their own countries was quite small (only 10 percent) and the individuals involved were relocated quite often.

The major problem with respect to the margin was the nonquantifiable character of the disadvantages of long-term expatriation, as well as of the more limited promotion prospects, shorter careers, and the reduced stability and security of employment characteristic of the international as compared to the comparator civil service. Any quantification of the impact of these three factors was bound to be somewhat arbitrary.

In the end, the existing system of establishing the margin was largely retained, in particular the proviso that the margin should not be less than 10 percent or more than 20 percent. However, certain minor adjustments were made: The calendar year was used for calculations instead of the U.S. fiscal year, and average salaries at each grade level were made the basis for comparison instead of the first steps (thus greatly enlarging that basis). It was agreed that U.S. bonuses and performance awards should not be included in the calculations. The Assembly went along with these proposals.

The most controversial issue proved to be the difficulty of managing the system over time. The underlying problem here is that the United Nations adjusts automatically for cost-of-living changes, while the United States does not. As a result, in the years just prior to 1984, U.N. compensation got far out of line with that of the U.S. federal employees. But because the United Nations operates in many countries where inflation is rampant, its remuneration system can hardly avoid being tied to cost of living. Thus, the commission has been faced with the need to find a practical way of reconciling two quite different approaches.

Matters have not been helped by the sharp decline in the purchasing power of U.S. federal civil service salaries or by the steps taken to offset this by offering special inducements to attract specialists required by that service. For example, it is reported that about 15 percent of the federal white collar workforce—some 200,000 persons—are part of a special pay rates program. Also, bonuses were in some cases an important part of the pay package (for example, in the case of doctors).

The commission tried to tackle the dilemma between rigid adherence to keeping U.N. remuneration as close as possible to the midpoint of the margin scale (115) and the need for the New York duty station to remain within the post adjustment system (and thus to compensate for cost-of-living increases in New York). It suggested to the Assembly the following compromise:

> The Commission noted that, from a conceptual point of view, it was anomalous to control over-all remuneration levels through manipulation of the cost-of-living mechanism. At the same time, it did not consider it realistic to allow the system to operate completely unchecked in the future. It therefore agreed that, as a general principle, the basis for management and control of the system in the future should be an approach between the two extremes of a non-defined margin range and a narrow margin range, that is, a range within which the margin level would be allowed to float, *without being constrained to remain at or near the mid-point* [emphasis added]. That margin range would allow for a reasonable cost-of-living movement, while ensuring some overall control through the application of margin considerations at a certain point. . . . If, however, it became evident that the margin would drop below the lower limit, the Commission would make a recommendation to the General Assembly for an across-the-board salary increase. On the other hand, if it became evident that the margin would exceed the top of the range, a freeze on emoluments would be applied until such time as the margin would be brought within the approved range [A/44/30, paras. 170–171].

The commission added that the aim was not to have the margin near or at the top of range over time but rather to allow it to move freely over its entire span.

The Assembly, while supporting the idea of a flexible margin, called upon the commission to monitor the margin over the next five years to ensure that by the end of that period the average of successive annual margins will be around the desirable midpoint of 115, which would be rather difficult to achieve [A/Res/44/198C].

Reform of the Post Adjustment System. The principle of such a system is simple and unexceptionable, but its application is infinitely complex. The principle is that the purchasing power of all professional staff occupying the same position within the civil service grading hierarchy should be the same, regardless of the duty station at which they happen to be stationed. It also requires that salaries should remain constant over time unless they are deliberately modified by the General Assembly. Thus, the two components of remuneration are a *constant* salary and a post adjustment that *varies* according to location and cost of living. The United Nations is only beginning to learn how to apply this principle with reasonable accuracy, and any refinement in calculating the post adjustment component is of great interest and importance not only to international organizations but also to governments and multinational corporations and indeed to all entities whose activities require them to station personnel across the globe.

The post adjustment system aimed at achieving this goal had originally operated in a relatively benign economic environment of stable exchange rates and generally moderate inflation. In addition, it had had the advantage of being based on a strong and stable currency, the U.S. dollar. In the 1970s, however, it had been put under pressure by the replacement of fixed by floating exchange rates and by the emergence of associated high inflation affecting some hard currencies (including the U.S. dollar) more than others. Procedures had had to be found to deal with obvious inequities; eventually there were special measures for abrupt devaluation, for continuous devaluation, for higher inflation, for "floor protection," and for a host of other technically complex problems. The cumulative effect of these special measures had been to make the operation of the system harder to understand and less predictable in its operation and to burden it with an ever-lengthening number of anomalies until it had even become necessary to introduce a "remuneration correction factor" for some hard-currency duty stations.

In 1989 the commission proposed a far-reaching overhaul and simplification of the existing system, which was almost entirely accepted by the General Assembly. The changes involved both the way in which cost-of-living data were gathered and the methods by which they were employed to equalize remuneration. Perhaps the biggest changes were made in data gathering. All cost-of-living surveys require that average weights be assigned for each item of consumption—that is, for housing, food, clothing, medical care, recreation, and so forth. Under the old system, these weights had to be established by separate surveys at each duty station. In the future, there will be common "item of expenditure" weights that will be the same for all duty stations. These weights will be established by calculating the average expenditures of professional staff for each item of consumption at the eight duty stations having the largest aggregations of such staff. In addition, the process of data gathering was simplified by reducing the number of items and subitems from 900 to 250. It was also agreed that instead of all such data having to be collected by the commission's own staff, external data sources might be used with proper safeguards to ensure their accuracy and consistency.

A perennial problem, especially for staff stationed in the field, involves their out-of-area expenditures, that is, the part of their income that they spend not on local goods and services but in other parts of the world or on imported goods. In some duty stations this may amount to more than 80 percent of their actual expenditures, and everywhere it constitutes a factor that cannot be wholly disregarded. The commission decided to set up a single out-of-area index for all duty stations to improve the internal consistency of the post adjustment system. In local cost-of-living surveys, out-of-area expenditures would be weighted at between 10 percent and 85 percent of the total, depending primarily on the extent to which staff have to purchase imported goods. For such goods, expenditures would be calculated in dollars, and the dollar amount would be the same for each specific item in all duty stations.

It also makes a big difference how such data are fed into the actual process of post adjustment; that is, it affects the upward or downward adjustment of the number of dollars to which staff members would be entitled under the base salary scale. One improvement introduced by the commission was to eliminate regressivity from the post adjustment system. Formerly each cost-of-living increase of 5 percent resulted in a change in net remuneration of only 4.5 percent; that is, only 90 percent of inflation was recognized. When there was rapid inflation, this loss of remuneration was offset by the remuneration correction factor. Henceforth, the full entitlement will be allowed immediately, thereby eliminating one administrative complexity. Similarly, in cases of exchange rate variations, the percentage variation (up or down) will be fed immediately into the rate of adjustment for the duty station concerned. The old method tended to overstate the impact of currency devaluations and to understate those of revaluations.

One other proposal of the commission was accepted by the Assembly, this concerning the frequency of time-to-time adjustments with regard to local inflation. The commission posed the problem as follows:

> In situations of abrupt devaluation, an immediate reduction in take-home pay expressed in United States dollars was made in respect of the devaluation (to prevent staff from gaining a windfall), but consequential, often offsetting, increases due to local inflation were reflected only with considerable delay. Existing special measures to cope with such circumstances often worked unevenly, with resultant situations of over- or under-compensation [A/44/30, para. 248].

The commission proposed to the Assembly that increases in post adjustment allowances should be granted either after a full 5 percent upward movement in the cost of living had been measured or 12 months after the previous change (in which case, there would be only a fractional increase of less than 5 percent). This would eliminate the current four-month waiting period. Changes resulting solely from currency fluctuations should continue to be implemented monthly whenever they became due. The Assembly approved the elimination of the waiting period for full post adjustments in situations in which the cost of living increase is associated with a substantial currency devaluation. At the same time it called upon the commission to reconsider its proposal for fractional post adjustments, which would affect only duty stations where the rate of inflation has long been very low (for example, Geneva).

The foregoing are merely a sample of the many small technical changes that together constitute a far-reaching adaptation of the post adjustment system to the floating foreign exchange rates and higher levels of inflation that now characterize the world economy. It remains to be seen whether the commission has created a system that will work more equitably and effectively.

A major step in getting the readapted post adjustment system under way is to conduct the place-to-place surveys using the new simplified methodology proposed by the commission. The Assembly instructed the commission to complete this task, if possible, by the end of 1991, with major duty stations with more than 150 professional staff surveyed by the end of 1990. Executive heads and staff were urged to cooperate with the commission in carrying out this task [A/Res/44/198 D].

Staff Mobility and Assignment to Hardship Areas. The inducements to staff to move from one duty station to another have long been deemed inadequate, judging from the small numbers of transfers taking place. The situation has been especially difficult with transfers to the field, partly because staff sometimes have no concrete assurances as to the length of their stay in what are often hardship posts. Also, in terms of financial inducement, the United Nations has not been in a position to be as generous to its field staff as the United States has been to its expatriate counterparts.

This situation should in future be considerably improved. The commission has defined hardship on the basis of deficits in the following factors: security, healthfulness, climate, educational facilities, isolation, housing, and entertainment. The old regime of hardship entitlements, financial incentives, and installation grants has been transformed into a new one reduced to two basic elements: a mobility/hardship allowance and an assignment grant. The mobility/hardship allowance takes the form of a matrix with entitlements calculated as a percentage of base salary. On the horizontal axis of the matrix is listed the number of assignments and reassignments; on the vertical axis, the degree of hardship (in ascending order from A to E). No allowance is offered for transfers between headquarters duty stations, but allowances amounting to between 5 percent of base pay (at level A) and 30 percent (at level E) are offered to serving staff if they agree to move to less desirable field locations. With successive reassignments, the allowance is increased; for the fourth reassignment, for example, the range rises to 19–44 percent. Eligibility for the mobility/hardship allowance is limited to those having five years or more of continuous service.

In addition, the movement of staff to field service is facilitated by their receiving an assignment grant that includes a 30-day daily subsistence allowance and a lump-sum payment equivalent to two months of the staff member's salary. In addition, staff at hardship levels C, D, and E will be offered accelerated home leave (every year instead of the usual once every two years). The problems of younger children having to be sent abroad for primary or secondary schooling (because educational facilities at the hardship post are either unavailable or inadequate) will henceforth be taken into account through increasing the reimbursement of boarding costs for each child to $3,000 per year.

For the United Nations, the costs of this new regime are estimated at $23 million; they will be divided between the regular budgets financed by assessed contributions and the field programs financed by voluntary contributions. For example, the regular budget will sustain an increase of $7.9 million in connection with these changes. In approving them, the Assembly has asked the commission to report in 1992 on how they have operated in practice.

Motivating Staff and Increasing Their Productivity. In 1988 the General Assembly directed the commission to consider improving productivity "through the introduction of incentives for merit and rewards on promotion payable on a one-time basis, coupled with less financial reward for longevity, which should be linked to a more rigorous performance appraisal system" [A/Res/43/226].

In short, the Assembly wished to make the international bureaucracies a little less bureaucratic. The organizations supported this goal, though realistically they called for a system that was neither wholly merit based nor wholly seniority based. It was left to a staff representative to put her finger on the heart of the difficulty:

> She stressed the inadvisability of introducing a scheme for rewarding merit before a foolproof method of identifying and evaluating merit had been devised. . . . The extension of lump-sum awards for meritorious performance lent itself to abuse on all levels, ranging from the desire not to offend to outright favoritism. The larger the number of recipients of such awards, the greater the magnitude of the problem. . . . An appeals mechanism would have to be set up. The resentment of the large majority who did not receive an award would far outweigh the additional motivating effect on the minority of staff who did [A/44/30, para. 340].

The commission overrode these objections to merit-based awards, pointing out that the comparator service and other international organizations such as the World Bank did give them out. It proposed that they should be given to staff members who exceeded expectations on one or a few assignments that were "particularly critical" while performing at the expected level on the other elements of their job. It also suggested that "sustained performance exceeding expectations" might be rewarded by accelerated within-grade salary increments. These proposals were not endorsed by the General Assembly, which did, however, approve non-monetary rewards, such as service pins, plaques, and certificates of achievement, as well as so-called environmental motivators, such as health, exercise, and recreation facilities, day care centers for children, and pleasant cafeterias, which were to be introduced "to the extent possible."

The commission also felt that the current salary structure of seven grades (P-1/P-5 and D-1/D-2) and horizontal steps within each grade contributed in several ways to the poor motivation of the professional staff. One was the clustering of 75 percent of the professional staff in three of the middle-level grades (P-3/P-5), which unduly limited their career prospects. This led inevitably to the tendency for staff to bunch up at the highest step of their grade. Another was that promotion was accompanied by very little financial reward since the grade pay scales were largely overlapping, and the person promoted only received a little sooner the equivalent of the step increase that he or she was due to have received anyway.

To deal with these and other defects, the commission proposed a number of changes in the salary structure, which the General Assembly later endorsed. The value of each step increase was reduced, but more steps were added. The overlap between grades was somewhat reduced. Finally, the salary spans of the lower grades were widened to facilitate keeping staff in them longer, and the salary spans of the higher grades were correspondingly narrowed. Measures such as these addressed the problem of motivation only indirectly in the hierarchical way common to civil services.

The question of the automaticity of step increases, which comes closer to the concerns expressed by the Assembly, was also addressed, though in a gingerly way. The staff representative who had been so frank with regard to merit awards simply pointed out "that the fact that it had acquired a certain degree of automaticity did not imply that the rationale for the within-grade increment had changed, but merely its application." The commission, while recognizing the lack of any automaticity in the formal sense, said that the staff perceived the step increase as an acquired right, and the current practice was to grant within-grade increases quasi-automatically. The commission reiterated its rather sensible gloss on this practice.

> Organizations may withhold or delay the next within-grade salary increment of a staff member whose performance at the end of an appraisal period is lower than expected. For motivational purposes, delaying the within-grade increment for the first instance of poor performance, pending satisfactory performance during a specified period of time, is normally a better course of action than withholding it altogether. Withholding should normally be reserved for instances of repeated non-performance or for severe cases of poor performance [A/44/30, para. 352].

The Assembly endorsed the commission's proposal that promotion should be accompanied by an increase in salary equivalent to one step in the new grade. It also called on the commission to review again performance evaluation systems in the various organizations to ensure their objectivity and to tie within-grade step increments and promotions to merit rather than "primarily to longevity" [A/Res/44/198].

Comprehensive Review of Allowances. The third major element of remuneration, in addition to basic pay and post adjustment, is allowances. These include such things as the education grant, dependency allowances for spouse, children, and secondary dependents, payments on separation from the international service, and travel entitlements.

In 1988 the General Assembly approved as an interim measure a 50 percent increase in the education grant and in the children's allowance, while not providing for any increase for spouses or secondary dependents. In 1989 it returned to this subject on the basis of a full-scale review by the ICSC of the rationale for, and amounts being paid under, most of these allowances. While the commission's review of these matters seems to have been as thorough as in other fields, the need and rationale for most of the allowances being paid are well established and attention centered on whether the amounts being paid were adequate or justified.

Since 1946 an education grant has been paid to expatriate staff members to offset in part the clearly identifiable extra expenses they incur in providing for the education of their children. This grant is payable with respect to primary and secondary education and up to the end of the fourth year of postsecondary studies or the award of a first recognized degree, whichever comes earlier, subject to an age ceiling of 25. The commission recommended to the Assembly that the grant remain solely an expatriate benefit payable at the primary, secondary, and postsecondary levels and that the amount of the grant be reviewed every two years [A/44/30, para. 406].

As in most countries, the United Nations has always provided additional remuneration to persons with dependents—spouses, children, and secondary dependents such as parents or siblings. Since 1977 a dependent spouse (or alternatively, the first dependent child) was recognized by differentiated rates of staff assessment—that is, by reductions in the income tax paid by all U.N. staff to the Organization in lieu of national income taxes, as well as by slightly higher rates of post adjustment. The extent of this differentiation varies somewhat, with single staff at entry levels receiving 94.3 percent as much remuneration as staff with dependents and single staff at very senior levels only 90.3 percent. Despite some complaints that the system seemed biased against single staff, the commission did not propose any change in the way in which the pay of staff with and without primary dependents is differentiated. The actual amounts, of course, do not have to be fixed since they change automatically with pay scales.

There has also always been an allowance for children, and the commission proposed a new basis for calculating this allowance that would eliminate the need for constantly discussing how large it should be. If it were also fixed as a given percentage of an average professional salary, its amount would move automatically with any salary change, thereby simplifying the operation of the system. The commission suggested to the General Assembly that the allowance should henceforth be 2 percent of net remuneration at the P-4, step VI level for the children of all staff at all duty stations. The Assembly did not see fit to adopt this proposal, which would have cost $700,000, or a companion proposal that the allowance for secondary dependents should be one-half that for children. At the same time, it did endorse a further suggestion that the allowance for a disabled child should be double that of the ordinary allowance.

Finally, the commission did not propose many changes in the current system of separation payments for staff leaving the U.N. service. It did recommend that the repatriation grant for single staff retiring from the service should be somewhat liberalized by raising it to 75 percent of the rate for staff with dependents, a proposal later rejected by the Assembly. The latter did go along with the commission's other proposals, including one that authorized unused annual leave to be commuted at a somewhat higher rate to retiring staff who had been unable to take advantage of it.

The General Assembly did not seem satisfied with the outcome of this part of the comprehensive review since it asked the commission to gather further information on the practices of the organizations with regard to expatriate entitlements and on the methodology for determining dependency allowances and then "to provide an overview of the package of common allowances, including the level, rationale and procedure for review of each allowance, inter alia, by reference to the package of allowances provided by the comparator" [A/Res/44/198G]. The commission has been asked to submit all of this information to the 45th General Assembly, so that presumably this request will need to be dealt with at the commission's July 1990 session.

Comprehensive Review of Staff Pension Entitlements. Just as there have been concerns that the margin between U.S. federal civil service salaries and those of U.N. professional staff has tended to become too wide, some governments consider that the margin between the pensions offered by the two services has become excessive. Figures purporting to show that U.N. "pensionable remuneration" is more than 30 percent higher than that of the comparator service have led to calls for reforming the system for establishing such remuneration.

The ICSC does not operate alone in this area; it must work in close cooperation with the **Joint Staff Pension Board**, which is composed of representatives of governments, organizations, and serving staff. As long ago as 1986 the General Assembly called on both bodies to conduct a comprehensive review of the methodology employed for the determination of the scale of pensionable remuneration.

There are inherent conceptual difficulties involved in establishing such a scale. On the one hand, the Assembly has agreed (and equity would seem to require) that pension levels should be based on replacement of a preagreed portion of final average income. On the other hand, it is generally regarded as desirable, and even necessary, that the pensions of international officials not get too far out of line with those of the comparator service, although maintaining the necessary parallelism has been complicated by the fundamental changes the United States has made in its own tax system. The Pension Board and the ICSC have had to face the fact that the two goals are sometimes incompatible.

In 1989 these tensions were temporarily defused by the commission, which submitted proposals that had the effect of reducing the differential in pensionable remuneration between the two services. In the first place, it suggested the elimination of "a 1.22 multiplicative factor" designed to offset the progressive effect of U.N. assessments, which was justified by the fact that the comparator's income tax (unlike the U.N. assessment scheme) is no longer progressive at the upper pension levels, and it recommended that this change be made retroactive. These changes resulted in a one-time saving estimated to be about $5 million, which was readily approved by the Assembly.

At the same time, the underlying problem remains and is complicated by the fact that no decision has yet been taken with regard to whether the basic structure of the U.N. remuneration system will be changed to include a separate housing component. Should that take place, more time would almost surely be needed to adapt the calculation of pensionable remuneration to the new circumstances. In view of the General Assembly's call for the comprehensive review of pension methodology to be produced in time for the 1990 session, the commission came up with a series of recommendations in March 1990.

The commission decided that income replacement in New York "should continue to be used as the basis for the methodology for the determination of pensionable remuneration," while the relationship between pensionable remuneration amounts for U.N. and U.S. officials "would also have to be borne in mind." It decided that the scale of staff assessment rates would have to be adjusted, presumably to bring them into closer line with those of the comparator service. It went on to agree that the margin range of 110–120 applicable to net remuneration should apply with regard to pensionable remuneration. Regarding the operation of the new system, the commission proposed that it should, in cooperation with the Pension Board,

> make appropriate recommendations to the General Assembly, particularly when the pensionable remuneration margin had reached or was forecast to reach the upper or lower limit of the margin range, as long as the authority for such action rested with the Assembly [Report of the 31st Session, para. 41, (i)].

These decisions were subject to review both in the light of what happened with regard to the proposed new remuneration structures and any observations that the Pension Board might make at its June session. It would not appear, on the face of it, that the commission has found any foolproof way around the potential incompatibility of the two underlying concepts. However, with a certain flexibility in application and assuming that the purchasing power of U.S. federal civil salaries may be nearing the end of its long decline, the compromise may prove to be viable technically and politically.

The General Assembly took two steps that should please U.N. pensioners and potential pensioners. For many years, the combined contributions of staff and governments have fallen short of maintaining the actuarial balance of the fund. Now the Assembly has increased the rate of contributions from 22.5 percent to 23.7 percent of pensionable pay (two-thirds payable by governments and the remaining one-third by serving staff). At the same time, it raised the normal retirement age for new professional staff to 62 and made early retirement somewhat less attractive. As a result, the actual imbalance of the fund has been largely eliminated, and serving and retired staff are reassured that their pension entitlements will be honored.

It is hoped that the comprehensive review will be largely completed when the General Assembly meets in autumn 1990 with the ICSC's report on its two 1990 sessions before it. This summary, written in April 1990, cannot anticipate what the commission will ultimately propose for those areas still not completely addressed, but review had proceeded far enough to permit certain general conclusions. It seems highly unlikely that the existing system of staff conditions of service will be replaced or even drastically changed. What is occurring instead is a rather grudging admission that the founders of the present system built more soundly than had previously been acknowledged. The present exercise has mainly focused on how better to apply principles whose soundness has now been confirmed not only by long experience but also by the investigation of possible alternatives. The main importance of the rethinking process that has taken place rests in the fact that it has confirmed the fundamental wisdom, perhaps even the inevitability, of approaches long followed. At the same time, it has called forth the ingenuity of administrators and staff within and outside the commission to adjust and modernize the vastly complex machinery, which was beginning to creak a little, through which these principles and approaches are put into practice.

Composition of the Secretariat

Preoccupation with the comprehensive review did not prevent the General Assembly from attending to other issues of staff management. The question of the composition of the Secretariat, as always, inspired interest, particularly among delegations that felt that their countries were underrepresented in its ranks. In recent years, however, this question has been largely divorced from North-South and East-West tensions because, as table VII-1 shows, none of the main political groups stands out as being greatly overrepresented or underrepresented.

What constitutes proper representation (the word does not imply that staff members "represent" their governments but rather the entitlement of each member state to have some of its citizens in the Secretariat) is determined by three criteria: (1) a basic entitlement of each member to between 2 and 14 posts, (2) population levels, and (3) assessed rates of contribution to the U.N. budget. These criteria are applied unequally, with 40 percent of the 2,500 posts subject to geographical distribution allocated on the basis of membership, 55 percent on the basis of contribution rate, and only 5 percent on the basis of population.

As of March 31, 1990, the representation of 109 of the 159 member states (an increase of 4 over 1989) fell within the ranges allocated to them, 19 were above their range, 20 were below it, and 11 had none of their nationals in the Secretariat. The most underrepresented countries were Japan (60), Saudi Arabia (14), East Germany (7), and Italy (4). The most overrepresented countries were the Philippines (47), Chile (14), Ethiopia (13) and Thailand (11). The unrepresented countries were Albania, Bahrain, Brunei, Djibouti, Guinea-Bissau, Kuwait, Maldives, Mozambique, Sao Tome

Table VII-1
Distribution of Staff in Posts Subject to Geographical Distribution 1989

Group	*Desirable Range*	*Group Midpoint*	*Number of Staff*	*Percentage of Staff*
Afro-Asian group	689–932	810.6	824	30.0
Latin-American group	256–346	301.3	272	11.2
Western group	1098–1486	1292.1	1153	47.8
Eastern European group	252–340	295.9	252	11.0

Source: Adapted from Table C in A/44/604.

and Principe, Solomon Islands, and Vanuatu, many of them small, developing countries with very few educated people who could be spared for (and who would wish to join) the international service. The total shortfall for underrepresented and unrepresented countries was 120, with 71 percent of that attributable to the four underrepresented countries listed.

The better geographical balance within the Secretariat as a whole has increasingly switched attention to the 126 senior posts, that is, to the 41 posts for under- and assistant secretaries-general and to the 85 posts for directors. As of June 30, 1989, these were allocated as follows: Africa (22), Asia and the Pacific (19), Eastern Europe (18), Western Europe (28), Latin America (13), Middle East (5), and North America and the Caribbean (21). Only a handful of these highly prized posts become available each year, and the competition for them is probably more intense among countries within each group than among candidates from different groups. In a new initiative, the General Assembly has asked the Secretary-General to prepare proposals for new ways of grouping member states in his future reports on the composition of the staff, presumably to replace the strictly geographical approach long followed with one more attuned to various political alignments [A/Res/44/185A].

In 1989 the Assembly also asked the Secretary-General to prepare reports on the following subjects: (1) a methodology for holding national competitive examinations for posts at the P-3 level; (2) a comprehensive career development plan for all staff that would allow for "fair and transparent post bidding" throughout the Secretariat, that would ensure equitable promotion procedures, and that would include a better staff evaluation and reporting system capable of recognizing merit; and (3) a personnel policy to increase the mobility of staff [ibid.].

Women in the Secretariat

Another personnel issue continuing to have high visibility and priority is the still-too-low proportion of women in the Secretariat, particularly in posts subject to geographical distribution. In 1985 the General Assembly set a target of 30 percent that was to have been reached by the end of 1990. It now looks increasingly unlikely that that target can be met. Still, progress, though slow, continues to be made. The proportion has risen from 23.1 percent in mid-1985 to 26.9 percent in mid-1989 and 27.7 percent on March 31, 1990. If professional posts not subject to geographical distribution are included, the figure now stands at about 30 percent. Both the Assembly and the ICSC are applying pressure on the United Nations and the specialized agencies to improve upon this record.

A major obstacle seems to be the difficulties of some developing countries, particularly in Africa and the Middle East, in providing sufficient

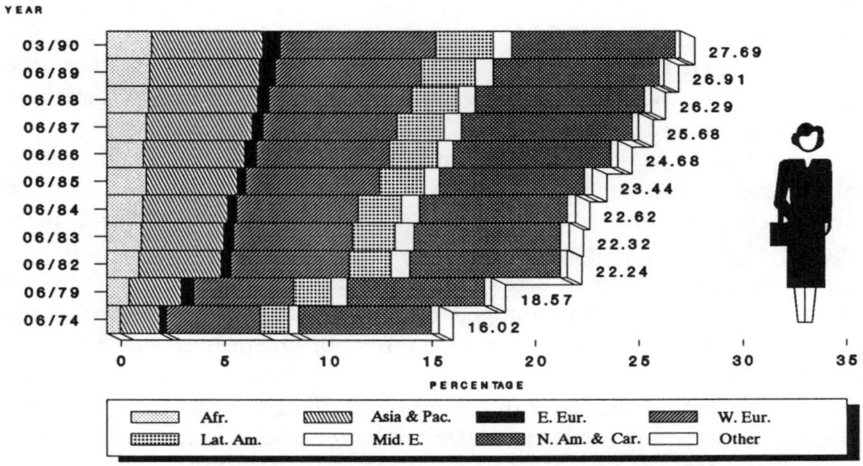

Figure VI-1
Percentage of Women in Geographic Posts by Region and Year (6/30/74–03/31/90)

numbers of qualified candidates. Only 18.7 percent of staff coming from the Middle East are women, and for Africa the figure is only 12.7 percent. At the same time, other developing regions seem to have fewer problems in meeting their quotas. The corresponding figures for Latin America and for Asia, for example, are 32.9 percent and 33.4 percent respectively, both well above the current target.

Eastern European women are the most underrepresented in the Secretariat of any other group, comprising only 7.8 percent of the staff coming from that part of the world; however, this may soon change. The representative of the Soviet Union told the Fifth Committee that his government had arranged for officials of the Human Resources Management Office to meet with a large group of Soviet women experts with regard to their future employment at the United Nations. The representative of the Byelorussian SSR also signified the readiness of his government to cooperate in this effort [A/C.5/44/SR.41,44].

The Assistant Secretary-General for Human Resources Management has asked each permanent mission in New York to authorize one of their staff to work with him to increase the proportion of women professionals in the Secretariat.

In explaining the slowness with which progress is being made in this effort, account must be taken on the lingering effects of the financial crisis and the sharp cutback in staff that accompanied it. Recruitment still continues on a much reduced level. During the year ending on June 30, 1989, only 134 persons, 36 of them women, were recruited. Recently the tempo has been increasing; 42 women were recruited in the first five months of 1990. When normal recruitment resumes, it is hoped that there will be even more rapid progress.

The effort to right the balance of women to men at the higher policy making levels of the Secretariat is also proceeding very slowly and in some respects even going into reverse. At the two highest levels of Under-Secretary-General and Assistant Secretary-General, there are now only two women, as against four in 1987. In the same time period, however, the number of woman directors jumped from two to eight. The record at the senior professional level has also been improving. The proportion of woman P-5s rose from 11.4 percent to 14.7 percent and of P-4s from 22.2 percent to 26.4 percent. This evolution at the upper middle levels of the career ladder is especially significant, for it is creating a larger pool of women who will warrant consideration for promotion to director-level posts.

A number of steps have been taken to meet the Assembly's goal of 30 percent by year-end 1990, including special emergency measures by the Office of Human Resources Management. Recruitment missions, which had been temporarily suspended, have now resumed and are instructed to emphasize the need for woman candidates. Staff traveling to supervise national competitive examinations or on other official business have been asked to inform professional women's groups of employment opportunities at the United Nations. About 45 percent of the successful candidates taking those examinations in recent years have been women. Within the Secretariat, all department heads have been urged to ensure that the target is met for their units by the deadline. Also, some women professionals have been extended beyond age 60, the statutory deadline for all staff serving currently.

Career opportunities continue to be opened up for women through the Vacancy Management and Redeployment Program. This program provides for the wide advertisement of open posts, ensuring that women have an opportunity to apply for any that they feel qualified to fill. This has facilitated the movement of women within the Secretariat. Volunteering for field missions is another way for women professionals to gain experience. Forty-five percent of the staff serving in Namibia and 42 percent of the group that supervised the recent Nicaraguan elections were women. Such field service increases women's chances of promotion when posts open up at higher levels.

In March 1990 the ICSC also addressed this issue. Most members felt that affirmative action programs favoring women would continue until targets had been attained. The representative of UNESCO suggested that the host countries of international organizations should be asked to liberalize their work permit policies for the spouses of international staff. This would help in recruiting married women who may be reluctant to come unless their husbands can find work. The commission is expected to recommend that the U.N. organizations should not only abolish rules barring the employment of spouses but, as appropriate, facilitate such employment. It will also probably encourage these organizations to increase the number of women in their policy-level posts.

The Assembly has requested the Secretary-General to report on how the action program for improving the status of women in the Secretariat is progressing and to present his recommendations for further action, including his approach to the setting of new targets for 1991–1995 [A/Res44/185C].

Staff in the Field

The problem of the safety and mistreatment of staff in the field continues to arouse deep concern. The Secretary-General's report [A/C.5/44/11] contained the following statement:

> The reporting period has been marked by one particularly disturbing development, namely the report of the brutal murder of Lieutenant-Colonel William Richard Higgins. Colonel Higgins, an officer of the United States of America, was serving as the chief of a group of military observers assigned to the United Nations Interim Force in Lebanon (UNIFIL) when he was abducted on 17 February 1988. On 31 July 1989, an announcement at Beirut by his captors stated that he had been killed. The Security Council took note with great concern of the reports from Beirut that day, saying that, if true, the murder of Colonel Higgins was "a cruel and criminal act." [S/20758] On 1 August, the Secretary-General sent Mr. Marrack Goulding, Under-Secretary-General for Special Political Affairs, to the area to ascertain, as far as was possible, what had happened to Colonel Higgins. Despite extensive conversations with various parties who may have been in a position to know the facts, Mr. Goulding could not obtain definitive proof of Colonel Higgins' fate. On 9 August, the Secretary-General, having received Mr. Goulding's report on his mission, announced that he had regretfully come to the conclusion that it was almost certain that Colonel Higgins was dead. He said he would continue to try to establish the facts and, if his fears were confirmed, to recover the body [para. 3].

In noting the Secretary-General's report, the General Assembly expressed its grave concern in connection with this case and over the very high number of new cases of arrest and detention of U.N. officials carrying out their duties, as well as "the very negative developments in respect of various previously reported cases under this category" [A/Res/44/186].

Under Article 105 of the Charter, U.N. officials are entitled to "enjoy such privileges and immunities as are necessary for the independent exercise of their functions in connection with the organization." This special legal status is needed not just for their own protection but because any organization entrusted with delicate and sometimes unpopular missions anywhere in the world requires safeguards for the security and safety of its servants.

This protection does not cover the private activities of staff in the field. In all cases of detention, determinations must be made by the organizations to which they belong whether they have been arrested or detained because of their official activities. If this is the case, their immunity is immediately asserted. If not, the Secretary-General, or the executive head concerned, still seeks to ensure that each person so involved is treated fairly, properly charged, and promptly brought to trial.

According to the Secretary-General's most recent report [A/C.5/44/11], the number of cases of arrest, detention, or disappearance of officials for which organizations have not been able to exercise their rights fully has been increasing "substantially." Most of these cases have been occurring in the Middle East. Some staff members simply disappear, but in most cases they are being held by governments, with the governments of Israel and Syria most frequently involved. Governments named in other cases include those of Afghanistan, Chad, Egypt, Ethiopia, Jordan, and Mauritania.

The organization dealing with Palestinian refugees, the United Nations Relief and Works Agency for Palestine Refugees in the Near East (UNRWA), has been particularly affected. Between mid-1988 and mid-1989, 157 UNRWA staff were arrested or detained, 9 of them twice. Ninety-three of the latter were released without charge or trial and 8 were sentenced to various terms of imprisonment. The Secretary-General reports that in no case did UNRWA receive adequate and timely information on the reasons for the arrest and detention despite requests to authorities. The organization has also experienced difficulties in moving its staff in and out of the West Bank and the Gaza Strip.

In addition to Colonel Higgins, a locally recruited UNRWA staff member, detained in Lebanon by Syrian forces, died in prison. An official in Ethiopia was sentenced to life imprisonment.

One celebrated case involved Dumitru Mazilu, a Romanian national who served as a Rapporteur of the Sub-Commission on Prevention of Discrimination and Protection of Minorities for which he prepared a report on the question of human rights and youth. The Romanian authorities refused to allow Mazilu to travel to Geneva to present his report. On May 24, 1989, ECOSOC sought an opinion from the International Court of Justice on Mr. Mazilu's status. Subsequently the Court found that Special Rapporteurs do enjoy the privileges and immunities of U.N. officials.

The General Assembly urged the Secretary-General to follow up all cases or arrest and detention promptly and to review and appraise the measures already taken to enhance the proper functioning, safety, and protection of international civil servants. A report on these matters will be before the Assembly's forthcoming session.

Index